Also by Tim Whitmarsh

*Beyond the Second Sophistic: Adventures in
Greek Postclassicism*

*Narrative and Identity in the Ancient Greek Novel:
Returning Romance*

The Second Sophistic

Ancient Greek Literature

*Greek Literature and the Roman Empire:
The Politics of Imitation*

Battling the Gods

Battling the Gods

ATHEISM IN THE ANCIENT WORLD

Tim Whitmarsh

ALFRED A. KNOPF

NEW YORK

2015

THIS IS A BORZOI BOOK
PUBLISHED BY ALFRED A. KNOPF

Copyright © 2015 by Timothy Whitmarsh

All rights reserved. Published in the United States by Alfred A. Knopf,
a division of Penguin Random House LLC, New York, and in
Canada by Random House of Canada, a division of
Penguin Random House Ltd., Toronto.

www.aaknopf.com

Knopf, Borzoi Books, and the colophon are registered trademarks of
Penguin Random House LLC.

Library of Congress Cataloging-in-Publication Data
Whitmarsh, Tim.
Battling the gods : the struggle against religion in ancient Greece /
Tim Whitmarsh.—First Edition.
pages   cm
Includes bibliographical references and index.
ISBN 978-0-307-95832-7 (hardcover)—ISBN 978-0-307-95833-4 (eBook)
1. Atheism—Greece—History.   2. Greece—Religion.
3. Christianity and atheism.   I. Title.
BL2747.3.W45 2015   200.938—dc23   2015005799

Jacket image: Marble bust of Apollo. Regent Antiques, London, UK
Jacket design by Oliver Munday

Manufactured in the United States of America
Published November 13, 2015
Second Printing, December 2015

To the people of Greece in these difficult times

Contents

PART FOUR

Rome

THE NEW WORLD ORDER

Preface

This book is about atheists in the ancient world, primarily in Greece: their ideas, their innovations, their battles, their persecution. It is a work of history, not of proselytism. It is not my aim to prove the truth (or indeed falsehood) of atheism as a philosophical position. I do, however, have a strong conviction—a conviction that has hardened in the course of the researching and writing of this book—that cultural and religious pluralism, and free debate, are indispensable to the good life.

Battling the Gods

A Dialogue

THERSANDER: The gods are dead. Their withered bodies lie immolated on the altars of science and reason. The pious are exposed for credulous fools.

DIOTIMUS: Nonsense! Belief in the gods is stronger than ever. It is true, of course, that the peacocks of the academy deceive themselves that their worldly knowledge is all. But you should get out into the streets. Leave behind your chattering dinner parties and take a walk through the city: the shrines are packed, the temples blackened with the smoke of sacrifice.

THERSANDER: Their belief is skin-deep. They act this way because they have always done so, not out of deep conviction. They do not have the time or inclination to question; they are too busy trying to survive, while their foolish leaders pitch them from one disaster to another.

DIOTIMUS: The people need their gods, in this perilous world of ours. It is their comfort and stay.

THERSANDER: Yes, of course religion offers comfort and hope. But it also makes for anxiety and fear! It plays on the emotions of the credulous. It has nothing to do with truth. Only observation, testing, and rational enquiry can lead us to proper understanding.

DIOTIMUS: You blind yourself to the truth that is not of this world. It is obvious that humans are born capable of glimpsing the divine. All people have that capacity, even if some choose not to use it. That is why there has never been, and never will be, a society without gods.

THERSANDER: Humans created gods. Primitive humans saw divinity in the sun, moon, and stars, in the cycles of the seasons.

They lacked scientific understanding of matter, the cosmos, and nature. In time, politicians and rulers realized the power of religious belief and cynically twisted it to their own ends. There are no gods overseeing social order, punishing wrongdoing; that is simply what our leaders teach us, to keep us in check.

DIOTIMUS: Atheism is a fad. Future generations will look back on it as a passing folly.

THERSANDER: Quite the opposite: it is religion that is dying. It has no answers to the questions of the modern world, only adherence to outdated dogma and ritual. I know that belief in the gods is deeply rooted, and those who profit from it will fight tooth and claw to preserve it. But as true understanding of the world grows and spreads, it will be exposed for the vanity that it is.

This dialogue, between a religious devotee and an atheist intellectual in Athens at the end of the fifth century BC, did not take place. But it could have done. All of the ideas in it are to be found in ancient Greek sources. If the terms of the debate seem arrestingly modern, that is no coincidence. We are still, in the twenty-first century, grappling with issues that are at least two and a half millennia old.

Atheism, we are so often told, is a modern invention, a product of the European Enlightenment: it would be inconceivable without the twin ideas of a secular state and of science as a rival to religious truth. This is a myth nurtured by both sides of the "new atheism" debate: adherents wish to present skepticism toward the supernatural as the result of science's progressive eclipse of religion, and the religious wish to see it as a pathological symptom of a decadent Western world consumed by capitalism. Both are guilty of modernist vanity. Disbelief in the supernatural is as old as the hills. Already in the fourth century BC, Plato imagines a believer chastising an atheist: "You and your friends are not the first to have held this view about the gods! There are always those who suffer from this illness, in greater or lesser numbers." We may balk at his disease imagery, but Plato was surely right in his general point. There have been many throughout history and across all cultures who have resisted belief in the divine.[1]

It is of course undeniable that religion has dominated human culture as far back as we can trace it. The problem lies with the *normative* claims built on that observation. Too often religious practice is imagined to be the regular state of affairs, needing no explanation, whereas any kind of deviation is seen as weird and remarkable. This view underpins the modernist mythology: the post-Enlightenment West is seen as exceptional, completely unlike anything else that has preceded it and unlike anything elsewhere in the world. This is a dangerous misprision. To the religious, it can suggest that belief is somehow universal, essential to the human condition, and that creeping secularism is an unnatural state. Atheists, on the other hand, can be seduced into delusional self-congratulation, as if twenty-first-century middle-class westerners have been the only people throughout history capable of finding problems with religion.

Religious universalism—the idea that belief in gods is the default setting for human beings—is everywhere in the modern world. There is a growing trend toward speaking of religion as "ingrained," or even "hardwired" into the human subject. So-called neurotheologists have even sought to identify a part of the brain, the so-called god spot, where religious impulses originate. Others have argued that the human propensity toward religion emerged as an evolutionary advantage. These are controversial claims, and fortunately it is not our job to evaluate them here. The crucial point is that they can all be taken to buttress the normative view of religion. They project the idea that supernatural belief is fundamental to humanity. They follow Karen Armstrong in redefining *Homo sapiens* as *Homo religiosus*. Such views have their modern roots in the ideas of European theorists of natural religion like Joseph François Lafitau, who aimed to demonstrate that all peoples have the innate potential for Christianity (and hence to legitimate the missionary project); they were, however, already seeded in the religious revolutions of late antiquity.[2]

The notion that a human is an essentially religious being, however, is no more cogent than the notion that apples are essentially red. When most of us think of an apple we imagine a rosy glow, because that is the stereotype that we have grown up with. Picture books, folk songs, Disney cartoons, and television advertising have conspired to generate this normative picture of "appleness." And indeed it is true enough that many apples are tinctured with red. But it would be ludicrous to see a

Golden Delicious as less than "appley" just because it is pure green. Yet this is in effect what we do to atheists in acquiescing to the modernist mythology: we treat them as human beings who are not somehow complete in their humanity, even though they are genetically indistinct from their peers. We connive in the etymological quirk that identifies them only by their lack (a-) of that sense of god (theos) that is assumed to be the norm.

There are atheists the world over, not just in the industrialized West. The evidence for this is unmissable, since many states (including, among others, Afghanistan, Iran, Mauritania, Malaysia, Pakistan, Saudi Arabia, and Sudan) seek them out and execute them. Anthropologists too have found plenty of evidence for skeptics in non-Western cultures. Sir Edward Evans-Pritchard, researching among the Azande of the Congo in the early twentieth century, spoke to one man who thought the witch doctors to be frauds; after probing a little further, Evans-Pritchard concluded that this was the general attitude of the people. It is not strange or exceptional to adopt a skeptical approach toward the supernatural: anyone in any culture at any time can do so. Such people do not always show up in the standard accounts of the religious culture of a given society, however, because the standard ethnographies are normative ones: they tend to project religion as not just uniform within a particular cultural group but even constitutive of it. When we want to capture the essence of a given community we typically ask about their religious systems: "Zoroastrians believe that . . . ," "Yoruba believe that . . ." This cultural flattening creates a false impression of uniformity.[3]

Just as atheism exists cross-culturally, it also (as Plato rightly says) exists throughout history. A thoughtful study by John Arnold of Birkbeck College in the University of London, for instance, has explored the position of the "unbelievers" in medieval Christian Europe, arguing that the idea of a single, unified faith community is a mirage: there was "a spectrum of faith, belief and unbelief." If we shift our attention away from ecclesiastical texts, which are specifically designed to perpetuate the idea of doctrinal unity, and toward religious life as it was actually practiced, we can find all sorts of cases of disbelief. Arnold cites, for instance, the case of one Thomas Tailour of Newbury, who was punished in 1491 for calling pilgrims fools, denying the power of prayer, and doubting the survival of the soul into the afterlife.[4]

The history of atheism matters. It matters not just for intellectual reasons—that is, because it behooves us to understand the past as fully as we can—but also on moral, indeed political grounds. History confers authority and legitimacy. This is why authoritarian states seek to deny it to those they do not favor, destroying historic sites and outlawing traditional practice. Atheist history is not embodied in buildings or rituals in quite the same way, but the principle is identical. If religious belief is treated as deep and ancient and disbelief as recent, then atheism can readily be dismissed as faddish and inconsequential. Perhaps, even, the persecution of atheists can be seen as a less serious problem than the persecution of religious minorities. The deep history of atheism is then in part a human rights issue: it is about recognizing atheists as real people deserving of respect, tolerance, and the opportunity to live their lives unmolested.

Atheism, in my opinion, is demonstrably at least as old as the monotheistic religions of Abraham, which means at least as old as the monotheism of Israel. That claim raises a separate question, since the processes whereby the temple cult in Jerusalem adopted Yahweh as their one god were complex and long-lived and are not fully understood. I am persuaded by those who see monotheism in the biblical form that we know it today as shaped by the returning Israelite exiles in the Second Temple period (in the aftermath of the conquests of the Persian king Cyrus the Great in 539 BC). This is around the time when we find in Greece the first philosophical articulations of skepticism toward traditional religion, in the writings of Xenophanes of Colophon (ca. 570–475 BC). But the exact dates do not greatly affect my point, which is rather a rhetorical one: that atheism has a tradition that is comparable in its antiquity to Judaism (and considerably older than Christianity or Islam).[5]

The difficulty in telling the story of atheism in deep antiquity, however, is that the evidence is often complex and elusive. It is very hard to locate the atheists in many ancient cultures. We do not find them in Ugaritic royal literature or in the Hebrew Bible, say; nor indeed would we expect to. In their different ways, both bodies of text are strongly normative. Their role is to present a view of the world in which the existing social order is fixed and guaranteed by divine mandate. There are, to be sure, some traces in the Bible of awareness that not everyone commits equally to belief in Yahweh. The Psalms speak of wicked men who say that "there is no God" (10:4, 14:1). Job abuses Yahweh (quite understandably, in the circumstances) for his capricious cruelty. The book of Job as a whole, perhaps, creates room for an attitude of suspicion and doubt toward the divine. But these are slender pickings. As a rule, this type of literature exists to insist on the incontrovertible truth of a divinity that favors its own acolytes.

In the Western world, it is only for ancient Greece, and later Greek-influenced Rome, that the scattered tesserae can be pieced together into a coherent mosaic. (Ancient China also had its atheists; but that would be a different story.) This is in part because vastly more material survives in Greek than in all other ancient languages (including Latin) put together. Indeed, I would wager that more words survive written by the Greek medical writer Galen alone than of the literature of ancient Sumer, Babylon, Egypt, and Israel combined. Add in the huge amount of material culture, art, stone inscription, and papyrus that Greece generated over a thousand-year period, and we can begin to get a sense of why the documentation for the inhabitants of this small peninsula and its diaspora is so much richer. But it is not simply a question of density of evidence. Greece has bequeathed a diversity of material that is so unfortunately lacking for other ancient peoples: as well as the official record, as it were, Greek historians have the outtakes and the alternative versions. Greek history tells us about eccentrics, deviants, miscreants, and skeptics.

History is, so we are often told, written by the winners. Much of the labor of social history, from the mid-twentieth century onward, has been directed toward recovering the voices of those who do not loom large in the dominant script: women, slaves, children, the infirm, minorities. The book in your hands, by contrast, deals with a relatively small segment of ancient society. Most of those named in these pages were educated males from the upper tiers of Greek and Roman life (not because atheism is an exclusively elite, male prerogative, but because that narrow demographic sliver is disproportionately represented in our sources). Yet they too have often been airbrushed out of ancient history, or their significance minimized. Accounts of Greek religion and culture have almost always been written from the point of view of the believers. The result is a misleading impression of ancient religion as a smoothly functional system, with no glitches. It is time to restore the other partners in the dialogue to life.[6]

Why has history been written in this way, so as to favor religion? The answer is not straightforward. It is true enough, certainly, that some modern scholars have allowed their own religious values to percolate into their writing about antiquity. Even today, scholarly discussions of ancient atheism can prompt undignified tirades against "populist, fundamentalist atheism" and its "zealous preachers." Classical scholars, however, are not usually known for their piety; quite the opposite, they have usually liked to see themselves as fiercely secular. The discipline of classics as we know it today, indeed, emerged in the nineteenth century as a result of a messy divorce from theological studies. Since then, historians of Greek religion have sought to define it by contrast with the monotheistic religions of the modern West, and particularly Christianity. But this itself has been part of the problem. So keen have classicists been to avoid "Christianizing" the Greeks (a cardinal offense in the academy!) that the standard textbooks have tended to describe Greek polytheism as in effect a straightforward inversion of modern Christianity (particularly in its Protestant guise): focused on collective ritual rather than individual contemplation, the public sphere rather than the private self, outward performance rather than inner belief, conformity to past practice rather than scripture. There is much in this portrait that is true, but rigid, schematic oppositions can be deeply misleading. It is demonstrably wrong to suggest that Greek religion was unproblematically "embedded" (to use the scholarly parlance) in society, fully naturalized in all of the day-to-day rhythms of the ancient city, to the extent that no ancient could imagine a world without religion.[7]

This view has been buttressed by a tendency to use official state inscriptions as the main sources for the history of Greek religion. Some of the reasons for this are perfectly sound: whereas literary texts give us the perspectives of individuals, often hypereducated and hyperprivileged, the inscriptions found all over the Greek-speaking world often record decisions made collectively. They are better evidence for what groups as a whole thought. Yet there is a downside too. Official inscriptions, naturally, give the official, ideologically sanctioned versions of events. They tend to promote the fiction that societies work smoothly and seamlessly. It is, then, hardly a surprise that ancient inscriptions barely mention heterodox views of the gods. Normative sources will only ever paint a normative picture of a society. Imagine a history of twenty-first-century British politics that relied solely on the parliamentary records in Hansard: it would tell you much about the institutional workings of Westminster government but very little of the complex diversity of attitudes and practices of real people.

Not all inscriptions, however, are of this public kind. One intriguing case tells, precisely, of a ritual "malfunction" when someone refused to believe. In around 320 BC, a number of dedications were set up to the healing god Asclepius, near his shrine at Epidaurus (a small town in the Peloponnese). Among them is the case of a man who lost the strength in his fingers. Arriving at the sanctuary, however, he mocked the other stories of miracle cures inscribed there and refused to believe in them. When he slept in the sanctuary (a common type of ritual activity, known as incubation), Asclepius appeared to him in a dream. His fingers were cured, but the god chided him: "Because you disbelieved things that are not unbelievable, your name from now on shall be Disbeliever (Apistos)." Aside from the story's wonderful self-consciousness—a miracle inscription about someone who didn't believe in miracle inscriptions—it also provides precious evidence for religious skepticism in practice, as espoused by a regular, everyday Greek. Nothing is known about his social background, but there is no reason to assume that he was wealthy. Certainly the inscription itself is of a pretty rudimentary type, the language lacking in any grand, rhetorical pretension.

Of course, because it is a temple inscription, this is a morality tale, and the disbeliever gets his comeuppance. But surely the initial reactions of "Apistos" must have been relatively common. It does not require a post-Enlightenment mentality to come up with the idea that miraculous stories of divine salvation are open to suspicion. Miracles, by their very definition, test the limits of plausibility. Greeks could see that just as well as Evans-Pritchard's Azande. There is a comparable story told of Diogenes the Cynic, Greek philosophy's most subversive wit. It is said that while another man was marveling at a series of temple dedications put up by survivors of sea storms, Diogenes retorted that there would have been many more if the nonsurvivors had also left dedications. The one-liner's subtext is that "miraculous" experiences have nothing to do with divine intervention and the power of prayer and everything to do with the normal laws of statistical probability. Like Apistos (before his dream), Diogenes disbelieves the miracle stories. Indeed, Diogenes's central point is in effect the same as mine: that officially sanctioned religious records only tell you when worship seems to work and excise all evidence to the contrary.[8]

In this book I seek to tell the story of Greek atheism over a thousand-year period, against the backdrop of huge historical changes: the emergence of Greece from its "dark ages" into a world of literate city-states; the development of citizenship and democracy; the conquests of Alexander the Great and the fragmentation of his empire; the subsuming of the Greek-speaking world into the Roman Empire; and, finally, the arrival of Christianity. The Christianization of the classical world did not happen overnight, nor was it a uniform process. There were many different varieties of Christianity, each with its own (conflicted) relationship to the Greek intellectual tradition that preceded it. Even so, despite this fluidity, the Christian Empire did change things fundamentally. Christianity marked the end of a long period during which many respectable thinkers had explored radical ideas about the nature of the gods, even to the point of dismissing them altogether. Pre-Christian atheism was certainly not uncontroversial, and there were periods of severe repression. But as a rule, polytheism—the belief in many gods—was infinitely more hospitable toward disbelievers than monotheism. Under Christianity, by contrast, there was no good way of being an atheist. Atheism was the categorical rejection of the very premise on which Christians defined themselves.

This book thus represents a kind of archaeology of religious skepticism. It is in part an attempt to excavate ancient atheism from underneath the rubble heaped on it by millennia of Christian opprobrium. But there is topsoil to dig through too, of a very different kind. In eighteenth- and nineteenth-century Europe, the formative era for modern atheism, classical learning was ubiquitous (among the educated at least). In that period, those who campaigned for a world without gods could appeal to the authority of Epicurus and Lucretius, or refer to Diagoras of Melos and Theodorus of Cyrene, in full confidence that they would be understood. Since the early twentieth century, however, classical awareness has shrunk with alarming rapidity. Much of the blame for our collective blindness to the long history of atheism lies with an educational system that fails to acknowledge the crucial role of Greco-Roman thought in the shaping of Western secular modernity. This loss of consciousness of that classical heritage is what has allowed the "modernist mythology" to take root. It is only through profound ignorance of the classical tradition that anyone ever believed that eighteenth-century Europeans were the first to battle the gods.

PART ONE

Archaic Greece

NEW HORIZONS

1

Polytheistic Greece

The territory that we today call Greece—and which the Greeks have since antiquity called Hellas—is a peninsula jutting down southward into the central Mediterranean. Sited at the point where the African tectonic plate collides with the Aegean, it is prone to seismic activity and volcanoes and possesses a fractured, jagged coastline, further shivered into thousands of islands, the largest of which (Crete) lies immediately to the south. The predominantly limestone landscape is notable for its steep, rocky mountains (about two-thirds of the peninsula is hilly or mountainous) and fertile plains fed by rivers.[1]

Greece is a country of natural borders: mountain ranges, valleys, gulfs, rivers, and seas. To travel from one part to another is often challenging. Everyone knows of Thermopylae, the narrow pass between Mount Oeta and the sea, where the invading Persian army led by Xerxes I was held for a while by a small group of Spartans and Phocians. Long-distance travel by land in Greece always involves confronting physical obstacles. It was for this reason that Greeks turned to the sea. During the middle of the second millennium BC, the Minoans (based on the island of Crete) developed overseas trading networks. Large galleys with steep sterns allowed them to navigate the open seas, exchanging their olives, grapes, wool, and timber for crafted goods from the Near East. Thanks to contact with Egypt they acquired, amongst other skills, the art of writing.

Minoan culture collapsed rapidly, perhaps thanks to ecological disaster in the form of a massive volcanic eruption on Thera (modern Santorini). In the Minoans' stead emerged a new power, based now on the mainland: the Mycenaeans. They too ran a maritime economy, trading far afield, but they also adapted their predecessors' shipping technology for new, military purposes, expanding overseas into Crete and the eastern Aegean. Records kept by the Hittites in Anatolia (modern Turkey) in the fourteenth century BC make reference to kings of "Ahhiyawa," probably a form of "Achaea," a name for the Greek mainland that appears in Homer. Indeed, if Homer's legend of the expedition to Troy has any historical basis, it would have occurred around this time. The Mycenaeans may also have been the "sea peoples" named in Egyptian inscriptions of the reign of Rameses III in the twelfth century, the marauders who caused havoc throughout the Nile delta and along the Syro-Palestinian coast. Archaeology also suggests links with the Hebrew Bible's Philistines. Like its Minoan predecessor, the Mycenaean palace culture declined suddenly, from about 1100 BC, for reasons that remain unclear. The period up until 800 is conventionally known as the "dark age," since evidence is sparse. The art of writing was lost. Monumental buildings fell into ruin. Local societies were probably dominated by warlords who gained their fragile power through charisma and force rather than in stable, dynastic succession.[2]

When civilization reemerged in the eighth century, it was again the sea that stimulated it. The emergence of long-distance marine trade in the second millennium BC had meant that the entire Mediterranean as a whole had become a game board, and Greece and Italy, with their central geographical locations, occupied the most powerful positions on it. Overseas trade, colonization, and intermarriage meant much greater interaction with neighboring peoples and the opportunities to learn new technologies. They thus powered a huge expansion in Greek wealth between the eighth and the sixth centuries BC, the era known as the archaic period. By every index, prosperity seems to have risen rapidly. Life expectancy shot up, and health and diet improved (as indicated by dental conditions and heights of surviving skeletons). Houses grew in size. The mainland Greek population seems to have doubled. During this period, Greece reacquired literacy and borrowed from its neighbors many of the distinctive cultural features for which it is known today: temples, statues, painted ceramics, and epic poetry.[3]

The most significant characteristic of all was the development of a new mode of social organization, the city-state. By the eighth century BC, we can see the first signs of the emergence of the *polis* (the root of the English "political," "policy," and "police"). The *polis* (at least the larger variety) would gradually develop a particular form, which followed wherever Greek culture went: it would typically have city walls separating the urban hub from the agricultural hinterland, an acropolis ("high *polis*") or citadel, a temple associated with a presiding deity, a water supply, and areas of shared space devoted to different kinds of communal activity (commercial, religious, political, juridical, recreational). In the course of the archaic period, the larger *polis* would come to be adorned with the stunning marble architecture that we now think of as typically Greek, with its troupes of columns, its pediments, its triglyphs, metopes, and friezes. And, most of all, acres of writing. The Greeks of the *polis* inscribed their laws, decisions, and offerings on stone, presenting the ancient viewer with the powerful impression of an ordered, civilized community—and the modern viewer an invaluable record of their values and priorities.[4]

The culture of the *polis* was financed by international trade and colonization. Greece was ideally placed to exploit the opportunities opened up by long-distance sea trade, and not just geographically. The new trading economy was powered not by large, bureaucratic imperial powers but by the enterprise of individuals and smaller communities. The absence of political centralization worked to Greece's advantage, stimulating competition between states in both technological innovation and the exploitation of overseas markets.

Competition was also stimulated during the archaic period by external rivals, chiefly the Phoenicians, who similarly benefited from a non-centralized city-state structure. The Canaanite inhabitants of Tyre and Sidon, in modern-day Lebanon, were a highly developed, skilled, literate people who spoke a Semitic language not too distant from Hebrew. By the eleventh century BC they were trading with Cyprus; in fact, it was probably they who founded Larnaca, the modern capital. By the late tenth they were in Crete too. Within one hundred years their reach had extended to Sardinia and modern Tunisia. In time, their taste for precious metals took them as far west as mineral-rich Spain and to the "tin islands" in the Atlantic (often, rather fancifully, identified with the British Isles). By the early first millennium BC, the Phoenicians had turned the entire Mediterranean into a trading network, or at least an interrelated complex of multiple networks. Silver, for example, could be mined in Spain, worked in Greece, then sold in the Levant.[5]

Archaic Greece was formed by interaction with its eastern and southern neighbors. It was the Phoenicians who inspired the Greek adoption of the script still in use today. The letter *aleph* was originally named in Phoenician and its predecessors for its resemblance to an ox, while *beth* means "house." The Greeks took over these signs as *alpha* and *beta*— and so the "alphabet" was born. This kind of mimetic adoption of others' technologies (for alphabetic writing is indeed a technology) is typical of Greek practice of the era. Greece was not "European" in the sense that we understand the word today. It found itself in a vibrant eastern Mediterranean trading bloc, with strongest cultural links to Egypt, the Levant, and Anatolia (Turkey), whose western seaboard they populated in such wealthy cities as Miletus, Ephesus, and Halicarnassus. But relationships were not always harmonious, particularly with the Phoenicians. Disadvantaged by their position on the eastern seaboard of the Mediterranean, the Phoenicians founded their own colonies in Italy and Sicily, which vied with the Greeks' own newer settlements. In particular in the late ninth century they built a capital on a northeastern coastal spur of what is now Tunisia, just across the sea from Sicily, the Greeks' primary western base. This new Phoenician capital was known as Qart ḥadašt, the "new town," translated by the Greeks as Karkhedon and by the Romans as Carthago. Had the Greeks been slower to exploit their advantage and had the dice fallen differently, Carthage might have come to dominate the Mediterranean, and the languages of medieval Europe might have been Semitic rather than Indo-European. But as it turned out, the Greek overseas expansion prevailed. Carthage remained strong but was eventually obliterated by the Romans in the Punic Wars of the third century BC.[6]

It was, however, the very diversity of archaic Greece that was its characteristic feature. There was no national hub, no capital, no single, stable core radiating Hellenism outward. Around 1,200 separate Greek *poleis* have been identified for the period between 650 and 323 BC, each with its own customs, traditions, and mode of governance. In the archaic period, power in many cities swung between bands of aristocrats (a constitution known as "oligarchy") and the rule of single men, "tyranny" (the word that at this stage lacked negative connotations). There were of course regional powers, but no single state exerted influence over the entirety.[7]

Greece was not politically unified until the time of the Roman emperor Augustus. Until that point, the idea of Greece as a totality was a hazy, imaginary ideal rather than any kind of political reality. In the *Histories* of Herodotus, the fifth-century historian, the Athenians are said to have rejected out of hand an alliance with the Persians against the other Greeks, on the grounds that "we are all Greeks: we share blood and language; we have temples and rituals in common; we practice the same kind of customs." In lieu of any national unification, Greeks were held together solely by a sense (however fictitious) of common descent, and by shared religion and culture. Formal mechanisms reconciling all of this multiplicity were few: chiefly the Olympic Games and the oracular shrine at Delphi, and the shared investment in the epic poetry of Homer and Hesiod. Delphi and Olympia began to achieve their central, Panhellenic status from the eighth century onward. It was at this time, too, that the mythological epics were being forged, the *Iliad* and the *Odyssey*. These project an image of Greek cultural solidarity, through the story of a shared expedition to go and rescue a Greek woman (Helen) abducted by a foreign power. Such shared institutions aside, however, Greek culture was but the aggregate of numerous related but distinct regional cultures.[8]

Language use provides a neat example of Greece's highly regionalized nature: there was a high level of dialectical variation in the archaic period, with no one form achieving dominance. On Lesbos, in northwest Anatolia, and in the northeastern region of the mainland a branch called Aeolic was spoken (and had its own subdivisions). In southwest Anatolia, in the northwestern part of the mainland and the Peloponnese, and on Crete, Doric was used. The remaining parts of western Anatolia and Athens employed Ionic. In Arcadia and on Cyprus a different dialect (Arcadocypriot) again was found. The poems of Homer and Hesiod were composed in Ionic, which may be expected to have given a certain prestige to that particular dialect, but in fact epic language was so different from anything actually spoken that the effects were minimal. All these dialects were recognizably the same tongue grammatically but different at the levels of morphology and local vocabulary. For an approximate parallel, imagine a nineteenth-century conversation in English between a Glaswegian, a New Yorker, and an Afro-Caribbean.[9]

Greek religion too was an expression of these multiple regional identities. Ancient polytheism—the worship of many gods—was fundamentally different in kind from the modern monotheisms (Islam, Judaism, Christianity). There was no desire or attempt to impose theological orthodoxy. The idea of a common place of pilgrimage like Jerusalem, Mecca, or Santiago de Compostela is alien to Greek polytheism. Greece simply had no political or religious hub. Delphi, Olympia, and the island of Delos, for sure, were universally acknowledged centers, and respected as such. During the quadrennial Olympic Games, a truce forbade the invasion of Olympia and the forcible prevention of travelers to the site. But most Greeks will have understood religious practice and belief as a much more local matter. There were private cults within the household, or in rural shrines and caves. There were village rituals within the countryside areas. And there were the major festivals of the cities, which happened at fixed times in the year.[10]

Place was central to Greek religion. The Greeks had innumerable gods who could come in many forms: alongside the twelve Olympians (Zeus, Hera, and the extended family), there were rustic gods such as nymphs of the woods and springs, and the half-goat Pan; there were local deities like the Muses; primeval forces like Earth and Hestia ("Hearth"); imported divinities like Thracian Bendis and Egyptian Isis; abstractions like Peitho ("Persuasion") and Nike ("Victory"); heroes, deified humans, like Ajax and Achilles (and in time historical individuals like Alexander the Great and any given Roman emperor); and an almost limitless assortment of minor beings whose roles were limited to specific ritual functions (like Aglaurus, by whom young men in the territory of Athens swore their oaths). The crucial point, however, is that in almost every case, a god was associated with a particular building in a particular location. The Olympians, whose worship was common to the Greeks, were regionalized by the addition of a surname. Apollo, for example, was called "Pythian" at Delphi, "Sminthian" at Hamaxitus, "Cynthian" on Delos, and "Acraephian" in Acraephius. "How shall I sing of you," runs one hymn to that god, "you who are sung of in so many ways?"

Sometimes these names simply described the town in question. On other occasions, the surnames were more oblique and mysterious even to the Greeks themselves: so Zeus was called Apomyios ("the Fly-Repellent") in a cult at Olympia, and Apollo Lykeios ("the Wolf-God") in one area of Athens—inadvertently lending his name to Aristotle's Lyceum, and hence to French *lycées* and Italian *licei*. Each of these manifestations of the god was different in the sense that the traditions, rituals, and clergy were wholly specific to that particular site. A priest of Apollo attached to one temple, for example, would not have been qualified to perform rituals in a different Apollonian sanctuary, even though he would have recognized the god to be in some sense the same one.[11]

The Olympian gods were the same but different throughout the Greek-speaking world. Take Artemis, for example, who at Brauron near Athens presided over a ritual involving young girls of marriageable age dressing as bears; who near Ephesus on the Anatolian coast occupied the largest temple in the region and was depicted in the guise of a pre-Greek deity with a profusion of what have been variously interpreted as breasts, eggs, or even bull's testicles; and who at Patrae was worshipped, as Artemis Laphria, with a huge fire onto which were thrown wild animals of all kinds, including the cubs of bears and wolves. She is the same deity in all cases but also fully individualized to match the local culture and environment. This combination of diversity and cohesiveness was the perfect expression in the religious sphere of the plurality that was so distinctive to Greek culture generally.

Just as there were no mechanisms for creating moral or spiritual orthodoxy across the whole of Greece, so within the individual cities themselves the power of religious institutions was curtailed. Not that religion occupied a marginal position: sacred festivities took up a large part of the city's annual calendar (a formidable 120 days in classical Athens), and temple buildings were the most visible sign of a city's splendor, the material embodiment of its very identity. The Greeks devoted an extraordinary amount of energy to keeping the gods happy. But there were close limits to the power of human clerics. The job of priests was to sacrifice, not to pronounce on ethical or spiritual issues. The idea of a Greek priest or priestess using his or her influence to sway public debates on (for example) the definition of marriage or the treatment of the poor was unthinkable. Priesthood was a role within the community, not a spiritual calling. There was no formal religious training, there were no convents or seminaries. Some positions were hereditary, others were short-term and awarded by the state. The holding of other offices was not excluded. A priesthood was simply one of a number of civic jobs that a successful (which usually meant privileged) citizen could expect to hold. The playwright Sophocles, for example, was a priest of the hero Halon, and perhaps of the healer god Asclepius too, yet he also served Athens as a military commander, a controller of the public finances, and an emergency commissioner in the aftermath of the disastrous assault on Sicily in 415–413 BC. Priests never seemed to have banded together as a unified body: there were no guilds or corporations of priesthood in Greek cities.[12]

Scholars have disagreed on this point, but it now seems pretty clear that the Greeks did distinguish categorically between the sacred and the secular realms. In democratic Athens, for example, the Council divided its items for discussion into three categories: "the sacred," "questions connected with heralds and embassies" (that is, foreign policy), and "the profane." They also distinguished between sacred and profane buildings, and between money destined for religious and for nonreligious purposes. These categories are, of course, likely to have been less distinct in practice (for example, the treasury of Athena located within the Parthenon was deemed "sacred," but its resources were on occasion used to equip the military). And equally obviously we should not assume that their sacred-secular distinction maps exactly onto our own. The important point is that they recognized that religion should have a defined place within the city and should not (ideally) transgress into other realms. This does not mean that religious activities such as prayers, libations, and sacrifices did not feature in "secular" contexts (they did). It means simply that those in charge of religious matters had no jurisdiction over secular matters. To say (along with one respected scholar) that religion was "embedded in all aspects of life, public and private" seems to misrepresent the situation.[13]

There are other areas of Greek civic life that we would define as "secular." Crucially, the gods had little to do with the law. Legal judgment was never theologized in ancient Greece: verdicts were pronounced in the name of the city rather than that of the gods. Nor was invocation of the gods by the participants required. A large body of speeches composed for performance in court survives (from democratic Athens, the source of most of our written evidence for early Greece). Dr. Gunther Martin has patiently analyzed this material for its religious content and shown that there are huge variations in practice: while there were some who fulminated in vague terms about divine intervention and pollution, others (notably the famous orator Demosthenes) put forward an essentially secular worldview. How much religion a legal orator included depended on what kind of persona he wished to project and not on the requirements of the context.[14]

Even the deities themselves were different in kind to their monotheistic cousins. The defining feature of the god of the modern monotheisms—Judaism, Christianity, and Islam—is that he is transcendent and remote. Christianity has grappled since its very inception with the question of Christ's transcendence: How can a god be born into human flesh? How can a deity be of this world? In the fifth century AD, the Christian Church found itself locked in a battle between "monophysites" (who believed that Christ's human and divine aspects were fully integrated) and "dyophysites" (who thought he had distinct human and divine natures). When in AD 451 the Council of Chalcedon attempted to pronounce definitively on the issue, many Eastern churches rejected the outcome, a schism the effects of which are still felt today. This was not a problem that presented itself in traditional Greek religion, since gods were thought (except by a few philosophers) to be entirely of this world. They may have dwelled on the most remote, elevated mountain in Greece (standing at nearly ten thousand feet, the peak of Olympus would not be scaled until the early twentieth century), they may have been capable of flight, but they nevertheless belonged to the same ecosystem as we do. As well as Olympus, they inhabited the local temples and shrines that dotted the Greek landscape: these were the homes of the gods among mortals. They could appear to humans too, usually in human form: they could fight, share food, and even mate with them.

It is tempting for those raised on a modern, monotheist conception of religion to see this polytheism as deficient. Where is the spiritual dimension? Where is the sense of an eternal, omnipotent deity? Where is the grace? Where is the idea of a spirit that survives after death? To understand Greek religion one needs to cast off such assumptions and see it on its own terms, as an articulation of local identity within the community. But even so, all of these features were in fact available to ancient Greeks, particularly from the classical period onward. If you wanted a sense of mystical communion with the divine and the promise of eternal life, for example, you could join a mystery cult and become a devotee of Diony-sus. A number of Dionysiac texts etched onto gold leaves have survived in burial sites across Greece and southern Italy, giving instructions on how to survive in the afterlife. (Typically, initiates are told to follow the path between the white cypress trees and the marsh until reaching the lake of Memory; there, they are to instruct the guards that they are children of the gods and that they need to drink.) Those who wanted to purify their bodies and cleanse their souls could follow the philosopher Pythagoras (ca. 570–500 BC) and take up a vegetarian diet and a life of seclusion. Greeks of the classical period and later had plenty of options for a contemplative life pondering the divine, whether through mystery cults, philosophical schools, or other, more personal and inventive forms of communication with the divine. It was not that the Greeks were by constitution not "spiritual"—it was just that they were not required to be by their state religions.[15]

The organized religion of the ancient Greek city-states was not designed for personal communion with the divine. For sure, many partici-pants must have felt emotionally involved in the drama of ritual sacrifice, transported even. Ritual necessarily involves immersion in the experi-ence of otherness. But there are many dimensions to religious experience, and this personal, emotional aspect is only one of them. It is, certainly, central to modern practice (particularly in Protestant Christianity), but in fact the ancient Greek sources rarely speak of it, prioritizing instead the sense of collective involvement with the community. Viewed in terms of its effects on society as a whole rather than the individual, civic cult existed to foster local identity within the *polis* and a looser sense of attachment to Greek culture as a whole. It was an articulation, in the idiom of religion, of that sameness-but-difference that characterized the kaleidoscopic culture of Greece as a whole.

The story of the ancient Greek world, from the archaic age through to late antiquity, is one of both expansion and centralization. Expansion because Greek became the dominant language and culture in the eastern Mediterranean and much of the Near East, and centralization because in the aftermath of the conquests of Alexander the Great in the fourth century BC various powers competed to absorb territories into their international empires, until finally in the late first century BC Rome became the undisputed controller of the Mediterranean. In 27 BC Greece became a single province, known by the Homeric name Achaea. The effect of incorporation into the Roman Empire was not entirely dissimilar to that of capitalist globalization in the modern era. There were markers of Romanness everywhere: inscriptions, legal institutions, Roman citizens, coins, soldiers. Most strikingly of all, Greek cities housed temples dedicated to the worship of the living emperor, whom they competed with one another to praise. Conversely, however, there were all sorts of counterassertions of traditional identity: long-dead cults were revived, antique dialects were reinvented, classical names came back into fashion. The Roman Empire was defined by the tension between the centripetal pull of Rome and the centrifugal push of the provinces. That story will be told in more detail in later chapters. The crucial point for now is that with centralization came the possibility of imposing a single religious order on the entire empire. The explanations for the rise of Christianity are many and contested, but one thing is indisputable: when Rome's rulers began to adopt it as the official cult of the empire in the fourth century AD, their aim was not just to spread spiritual succor. The challenge they faced was how to hold together a huge, diverse, multi-ethnic and multilingual territory (sometimes with multiple armies afoot) without the instruments of modern nationhood. Imposing a single, central belief system based around a single (albeit triform) god must have seemed an attractive gamble. Whatever the effects religion generates at the emotional level for those who practice, it is also at the structural level an allegory of political power. Just as in the archaic period the many gods of Greek polytheism met the needs of a complex assemblage of independent states, so the one god of Christianity reflected the aspirations of the political classes of the later Roman Empire.

Monotheism and polytheism are different in kind. Neither, for sure, exists in any pure form. In Christianity, the Trinity is a kind of polytheistic relic, and Judaism, Christianity, and Islam all have their angels, divine beings translated into a lower register. Conversely, polytheisms can often look to one particular god as supremely powerful (a phenomenon known as "henotheism"). If we accept, however, that we are talking about tendencies rather than absolute states, clear differences can be identified. The German Egyptologist Jan Assmann speaks of the "Mosaic distinction," which is to say the change wrought by Moses in Israelite memory when he revealed Yahweh's will to his chosen people. According to Assmann, the ancient polytheist view was that gods are transferable between cultures, so that religion had no external boundaries. Ancient Near Eastern cultures in the second millennium BC were already producing lists of equivalences between deities, which were essential to any kind of international diplomacy: you had to be sure that you both agreed on which gods were in charge of which pacts. Greeks too thought that the world's gods were essentially the same, even though they might be worshipped in different forms. "The Assyrians," writes Herodotus, "call Aphrodite 'Mylitta,' the Arabians 'Alilat,' and the Persians 'Mitra.'" The same goddess, just different names. Monotheism, on the other hand, puts up firm barriers between insider and outsider: the one god demands absolute loyalty. It is this absolutism and inability to include alternative perspectives that (so Assmann's theory goes) has made for monotheism's inglorious history of holy war. Polytheism, on the other hand, was by design pluralist, capacious, and flexible; no one ever fought a war in the name of Zeus, Baal, or Amun (although plenty of wars were, of course, fought in antiquity all the same).[16]

The history of atheism in antiquity suggests that Assmann was right. Certainly, atheism was not always approved of in Greek polytheism. Occasionally it was forcibly repressed. In general, however, it was tolerated by the religious because there was little interest in generating religious orthodoxy. Priests were there to manage ritual and temple finance, not to tell people what to believe, and in any case there was no orthodoxy, no revealed truth, no sacred word. There were (as in all societies) plenty of people with strong views on the nature of the gods, but all they could do was clamor to be heard above the hubbub. There were no social mechanisms whose jobs were to create consensus in the matter of religion, and in any case society as a whole invested little in defining the nature of divinity precisely. This meant that for much of Greek antiquity atheism was not treated as a heretical position, the "other" of true belief; it was seen rather as one of the many possible stances one could take on the question of the gods (albeit an extreme one). It was only in Christian late antiquity that atheism began to be constructed in systematically antithetical terms, as the inverse of proper religion, a threat to the very foundations of human civilization. Until that moment—borrowing from Assmann, we might speak of "the Christian distinction"—atheism was an integral part of the cultural life of Greece.

2

Good Books

Sacred scripture is one of the major reasons why monotheism demands orthodoxy. When gods reveal their thoughts to mortals in written form, then mortals can be held to account by reference to fixed texts. Jews, Christians, and Muslims have of course argued endlessly over the interpretation of specific passages of their scriptures, but their texts themselves are imagined as nonnegotiable contracts with the divine, inspired or authored as they are by God himself. Even as a physical artifact, the sacred book is inviolable: it should never be besmirched, let alone damaged. This conception is rooted in ancient Near Eastern traditions associating the written word with supernatural powers. In Egypt, the god Thoth was credited with the invention of literacy. Although Egyptians used writing for a variety of administrative purposes, they had one particular script (known to the Greeks as "hieratic") that was ultimately restricted to priests. Books in Egypt could be imagined to possess magical properties. The first tale of Setne Khaemwas (from the third century BC or so), for example, showcases a wise magician who understands the properties of all kinds of writing and who quests after the ultimate source of magical power: the Book of Thoth himself. The processes that led to the creation of the Hebrew Bible as divine scripture reflect the same kind of belief in the sacro-magical power of writing. Hebrew was known as "the sacred language" from early times and its alphabet invested with numinous power. From antiquity onward, Torah scrolls were treated as objects of veneration, and imagined to have (for example) health-giving properties. This Jewish idea that the book embodied the divinity of its sacred subject matter shaped the formation of the Christian Bible and the Qur'an. From antiquity onward, the idea of a material book as the ultimate source of truth has persisted. The Roman emperor Justinian passed a law in AD 530 requiring the presence of "holy scriptures" in court throughout proceedings; in the United Kingdom, as recently as 2013 the Magistrates' Association reaffirmed the need for witnesses to swear on sacred texts.[1]

Jewish, Christian, and Muslim religion is structured around the idea of holy scripture. For Greeks, by contrast, the idea of a text having magical properties was fundamentally alien. In fact, it was the Greeks who named Egyptian writing systems "hieroglyphic" and "hieratic," precisely to mark the difference from their own literature, which was not *hieros* (sacred) in this way. Some religious sects associated with Dionysus, certainly, made use of texts (inscribed bone plates have been found in a Greek colony in Olbia in the Black Sea, for example, and gold leaf tablets in Greece), and popular magical spells could be cast on papyri and metal plaques. But in general the Greeks did not associate writing with divinity, except when they were describing Egyptian or Jewish culture. Writing was not considered a highly specialized skill, as in Egypt, nor was it the preserve of scribal elites, as in Israel. Anyone could write, providing she or he had the skills and the money to afford expensive materials. Although literacy levels were low by modern standards, and Greece remained throughout antiquity a largely oral society, it is likely that there were more readers and writers here than elsewhere in the world.[2]

So the Greeks had nothing comparable to sacred scripture. What they did have were Homer's *Iliad* and *Odyssey,* and Hesiod's *Theogony.* These were their earliest poems, composed at some point in the eighth or seventh centuries BC at the dawn of Greek literacy, and the bedrock of their culture. It was unimaginable that a Greek would not know the epic tales of Troy: how the Trojan prince Paris ran off with Menelaus's wife Helen, and Menelaus and his brother Agamemnon raised a Greek expedition, sailed to Troy, and sacked it after a nine-year siege; or how Odysseus journeyed home after the war, to be reunited with his wife Penelope. These stories were central to Greek identity: they spoke of Greeks' moral and military superiority over other peoples, of the terrors of distant sea travel, and of the central importance of home, family, and community. Throughout antiquity, the Homeric poems in particular achieved a level of dissemination comparable to that of the Bible in nineteenth-century

Europe. To judge from surviving papyrus fragments, the only continuous texts that schoolchildren read in Hellenistic and Roman Egypt were by Homer, Euripides, and Menander, and they did so in the proportions 6:2:1.[3]

What the Greek epics were not, however, were theological or liturgical works. Excerpts might be performed at festivals, but there is no evidence that they were used in a specifically ritual context. The performers themselves were not priests but rhapsodes, specialist singers known for their showy dress and gesture. These might claim to be divinely inspired (as the rhapsode Ion does in Plato's dialogue of the same name), but their aim was to thrill, inspire, and instruct, not to fill their audiences with a sense of the godhead. Relative to Israel and other cultures of the ancient Near East, Greece handled its national literature in a strikingly secular way (from a monotheistic perspective).

Not that the poems themselves are free of gods. Hesiod's *Theogony* takes as its theme the arrival of the Olympian order, headed by Zeus, and the defeat of the various monsters and Titans who threaten their supremacy. In the *Iliad,* gods fight on either side of the conflict between Trojans and Greeks; Zeus, however, stands aloof and sees to it that the outcome happens in accordance with Fate. The *Odyssey* features a much reduced pantheon: Athena and Hermes help Odysseus return home, while Poseidon, angered by the blinding of his son the Cyclops, seeks to obstruct him. Zeus, meanwhile, has decreed that Odysseus will return to exact vengeance on the suitors, in the interests of justice. Epic poetry certainly endorses the power of the Olympian gods and sometimes (as in the *Odyssey*) presents Zeus as the guarantor of morality. If you asked any ancient Greek what the Olympian deities were like, and how they managed the universe, the answer would probably refer to or derive from the *Iliad,* the *Odyssey,* or Hesiod's *Theogony.* Herodotus, the historian of the fifth century BC, wrote that "Homer and Hesiod were the first to compose accounts of the origins of the gods, and give the gods their epithets, to allot them their several offices and occupations, and describe their forms." These texts were seen to be foundational in every sense, including the religious.[4]

It is, however, hard to derive a coherent or moral view of the gods from these poems, particularly from the *Iliad,* the central text. The poem opens with a description of the carnage caused by the war—bodies strewn around to be consumed by dogs and birds—and mysteriously claims that "the plan of Zeus was coming to pass." It looks as if the king of the gods has some kind of program that he is working through—but it is not at all clear what it is. Ancient readers had no more idea than we do now. One later writer claimed that the Earth was overpopulated, and so Zeus wanted to kill off some of its inhabitants. Some modern scholars have argued that Zeus's plan was to take revenge upon the Trojans for the kidnapping of Helen (but why then so much suffering on *both* sides?). There are other theories, but they all suffer from the same flaw: they assume that Zeus is, like the Judeo-Christian god, steering human history providentially. There is very little evidence for this in the rest of the *Iliad*. In general, the Iliadic gods, mathematically split as they are in their support for the Greeks and the Trojans, seem strikingly uninterested in human morality. Although they can at times show pity for their favorites, they can also express contempt for "insignificant mortals, who are as leaves are: for a while they flourish and grow warm with life . . . but then later they fade and die."[5]

What is more, the gods' own behavior can be disturbingly immoral. In the *Odyssey,* the blind bard Demodocus sings of Aphrodite's affair with Ares, and how Hephaestus (her cuckolded husband) traps the two of them for all of the gods to laugh at. Nor are they always omniscient or omnipotent. Even Zeus: in the *Iliad,* Hera borrows Aphrodite's girdle to seduce him, leaving him to sleep in postcoital bliss while the pro-Trojan gods manipulate the course of the war in his absence.[6]

The Homeric and Hesiodic poems were comparable to the Hebrew Bible in terms of their cultural significances but very different in their depiction of gods. To portray deities as by turns weak, stupid, comic, and possessed of awesome cosmic power may seem to a modern eye remarkably cavalier. But it is not; the point is rather that the epic gods are performing a very different set of cultural functions. Within Greek polytheism, gods were not expected to be just or omnipotent, or at least not all of the time. Zeus, certainly, could be invoked in his capacity as overseer of morality. In general, however, gods represented facets of human existence: the urges that drive us, the skills that enhance our lives, the problems that beset us. For example, the dying Hector prophesies that

Achilles will perish at the hands of "Paris and Apollo" (22.359–360): this means not that the two of them will effect a simultaneous assassination, but that Paris will shoot him with his bow (for Apollo is the god of archery). Similarly, Aphrodite represents the power of sexual allure, Hermes the possibility of swift movement, Ares war, Zeus kingship, and so on. This may give a rather reductive impression of these complex beings, who have different aspects at different times, and in a narrative poem like the *Iliad* or the *Odyssey* receive individual characterization too. But the central point is that we should not expect the transcendent power and morality of the gods of Judaism, Christianity, and Islam. The gods of the Greeks are grounded in the lived reality of the world.

More than that, however, judging the Greek epics by the standards of the Bible risks mistaking the different role that the Greek poems played in society. The *Iliad* and the *Odyssey* are about what it is to be a human, not a god. The *Iliad* focuses on Achilles, whose raging anger against his leader Agamemnon drives him to withdraw from the battle against the Trojans and pray for his own side's destruction. This hostility against his own people is the poem's major crisis. It is only the death of his close friend Patroclus at the hands of Trojan Hector that prompts him to rejoin the war, transferring his hatred from Agamemnon onto Hector, whom he kills and mutilates. In the course of events, Achilles gradually comes to terms with the fact that humans die and that all death causes pain to loved ones: a moving scene in the final book has him bond in sorrow with Priam, the father of his adversary Hector. The *Odyssey* is about Odysseus's reintegration into the civilized society and family life on his home island of Ithaca, after the barbarous violence of the Trojan War, and the challenges of his wanderings abroad. Both poems express that distinctively Greek idea that life is best lived in compact local communities in which individuals treat one another with respect and generosity. Not that either raging Achilles or tricky Odysseus is a straightforward paradigm of ethical behavior; the point is rather that societies should be flexible and open enough to absorb such magnificently unusual beings. The challenge addressed by these poems was, as ever in early Greek culture, how to keep together the regional community, the "city-state," within the loose structure of Greece as a whole.

It would be misleading to deny any kind of divine savor to the epic poets. Their narrator claims inspiration from the Muses, daughters of Zeus and Mnemosyne ("Memory"). The language in which they are composed is not everyday Greek: the diction is elevated and archaic and embedded in a verse form (the dactylic hexameter) that has a religious aura to it: it is sometimes used, for example, for oracles. The divinity of the Homeric poems, however, has nothing to do with the revealed word of a god. Rather, they cast themselves as huge, sweeping accounts of events that happened long ago; they are based on knowledge that would be normally inaccessible to a mere mortal, in a predominantly oral culture. The Muses are there to guarantee the factual accuracy of the singer's tale. "Tell me, Muses, dwellers in the halls of Olympus, tell me—for you are goddesses and everywhere so that you see all things, while we know nothing except by report . . ."[7]

Some ancients felt that the Homeric poems could and should be more religious than they are. One early philosopher, Xenophanes of Colophon (ca. 570–475 BC), suggested that epic depictions of the gods were the result of human beings, with all of their moral failings, projecting their own capacity for adultery and deception onto the gods. In the fourth century, Plato was even more aggressive in his condemnation: Homer, Hesiod, and the other poets, in his view (or at least that of Socrates, whom he reports), were dangerous peddlers of untruth whose misrepresentations of the gods and heroes as immoral would infect the populace, particularly the young, with dangerous ideas. Interestingly, Plato's primary anxiety is directed toward Hesiod's story of Cronus castrating his father Uranus: like so many an authoritarian, he instinctively associates social order with patriarchal phallic power. What better image for the terrifying effects of morally subversive thought than that of a son castrating a father? Plato has Socrates counsel the banishment of all such poets from the ideal city that he is imagining. In the place of the Homeric gods, he proposed (in *Timaeus*) a transcendent deity who presided over an unchanging, ideal world, separate from our own earthly one. For Plato, gods had to be perfect, remote, and untouched by the decadence of our own existence: the polar opposite of the divinities presented by Homer and Hesiod.[8]

For other ancient readers, the theological "failings" of the epic poets could be compensated for by allegorical readings. Allegorists took the apparent contradictions of the Homeric poems as invitations to read deeper into the text, which they took to be a world of codes and ciphers for alternative truths about the nature of the universe. The poems were only irreligious if you read them literally: "If Homer meant nothing allegorically, he was impious through and through, and sacrilegious fables, loaded with blasphemous folly, run riot through his epics." But of course (so this author argues) he meant *everything* allegorically. This tradition seems to have begun already in the sixth century BC with the now shadowy Theagenes of Rhegium, who was particularly troubled by the battle between the gods in book 20 of the *Iliad*. Theagenes argued that Homer was in fact speaking obliquely about the incompatibility of physical properties: dryness "fights with" wetness, heat with cold, light with heavy. Theagenes associated Apollo, Helios (the sun god), and Hephaestus with fire, water with Poseidon and the river god Scamander, Artemis with the moon, Hera with the air (the two words are anagrams in Greek: *ēra* and *aēr*). He also saw gods as oblique ways of talking about human faculties: Athena signifies the intellect, Ares folly, Aphrodite desire, Hermes reason. In the fifth century BC, Metrodorus of Lampsacus decoded Homer's text systematically into a symbolic representation of the world. The original texts of Theagenes and Metrodorus are now lost, but in 1962 an allegorical commentary on a now lost mystical poem based on Hesiod, dating to the late fifth century, was discovered near Thessaloniki: the surprise discovery of the so-called Derveni papyrus opened a window onto the ingenious practices of the early allegorists.[9]

This kind of allegorical approach in effect removes the divine element completely, treating the Homeric "gods" as concealed ways of thinking about the physical universe. But allegory could also serve to theologize the epic text, to enhance its numinous glow. In late antiquity, when Greeks wanted a sacred text of their own to set against the Jewish and Christian Bible, neoplatonists reinterpreted the poems of Homer to match their own conception of divinity. When the sleeping Odysseus is returned to his native Ithaca thanks to the magical ships of the Phaeacians, his possessions are left for him in a cave of the nymphs, which has two entrances, one for gods and one for humans. In the third century AD, Porphyry of Tyre—the author of a separate tract *Against the*

Christians—read this episode as an allegory of the physical universe, with its hidden portal toward the divine that is accessible only to philosophers. The story of Odysseus depositing his goods in the cave and taking on the role of a beggar becomes a parable for the need to offload worldly possessions, reject the superficial allure of this world, and turn toward the contemplation of the divine. So far from bundling Homer's divine system out of the way like embarrassing elderly relatives, Porphyry takes it up a level: in his hands, the *Odyssey* becomes a spiritual allegory, a cogent expression of Platonic theology and (presumably—this is unstated) a rival to Christian scripture.[10]

Allegory was, however, a niche area, the province of rarefied intellectuals. And crucially, these intellectuals had no particular authority to interpret Homer—for Homer was not scripture, and there was no priesthood dedicated to the explication of his meaning. Homer was the common property of all Greeks, and each could make of him what she or he wanted. For most of those who encountered the epic poets, these tales had nothing to do with theology, and indeed had very little to do with normative morality. Without the ingenious contortions of allegory, the only ethical "messages" that can be derived from the Homeric texts are neither abstract nor complex: treat your fellow humans with compassion, look after strangers, don't appropriate others' property, don't sleep with the wrong people. It is hard for modern westerners to imagine the centrality of the epic poets without recourse to the analogy of scripture, but that is exactly what we must do. These texts lay at the heart of the Greeks' culture not because a god had imbued them with sacral power, but because they were collectively prized for their narrative energy, because they had permeated every social membrane via a kind of narrative osmosis. When modern European scholarship on Homer began in the eighteenth century, the analogy that was drawn was with not the Bible but with folk narrative: that may well be more accurate, insofar as the dissemination of Homer in the archaic period seems to have been an entirely "bottom-up" process, driven by a popular desire to share these stories rather than any externally imposed plan. There is no evidence for any kind of centralized institution enforcing their circulation. There were certainly professional singers and (later) rhapsodes, who seem to have organized themselves into schools, but nothing suggests that they were part of a coordinated plan to indoctrinate; rather, like premodern European storytellers and folk singers, they learned their trade and then traveled to meet local demand.[11]

The absence of an institutionalized clerical structure around the epic poems also made for a certain freedom of interpretation. You could find your own truths in these texts. Most Greeks took the *Iliad,* at any rate, as basically historical: they might agree that it was poetically exaggerated in places, and embellished with supernatural grace notes, but that it described a real war featuring real people called Agamemnon, Achilles, Helen, and Paris was not seriously in doubt. The *Odyssey* was a different matter. The most troublesome episode was Odysseus's long tale of his adventures at sea, which he relates to Alcinous and his courtiers in books 9 to 12. Whereas most of the poem is relatively "realistic" (according to the standards of ancient epic), this is the part of the story that tells of his confrontation with giant Laestrygonians, the one-eyed Cyclops, Circe the witch who turned his men into pigs, the monster Scylla and the whirlpool Charybdis. Since Odysseus had by this stage lost all of his crewmen, who could validate the truth of these fantastic claims? It did not help his case that he was famed for his deceit (the wooden horse at Troy, for example, had been his idea). "Stories told to Alcinous" became proverbial for tall tales.[12]

Ultimately, Odysseus's untrustworthiness infected the perception of Homer. Later generations of Greeks would find all sorts of ways of undermining Homer's accounts, sometimes replacing them with their own, whether playfully or in earnest. Xenophanes (the critic of anthropomorphic religion) said that the mythical stories of giants and centaurs were "fictions." One tradition, reported by the historian Herodotus among others, claimed that Helen never went to Troy at all. Herodotus claims to have this story from Egyptian priests, whose predecessors had heard it from Menelaus himself. Others claimed that Homer had been bought off by Odysseus and had airbrushed his rival Palamedes out of the *Iliad.* One orator, writing under Roman occupation, claimed to have proven that Troy was never captured (a sop to the Romans, who claimed descent from the Trojans). Another writer claimed to have discovered in a Cretan cave an eyewitness diary from the time of the Trojan War, which he had had translated; this gave a very different version of events. None of these claims was blasphemous: there was nothing heretical about undermining the Homeric text, since it was not sacred scripture. To call Homer a liar might be seen as foolish, unpersuasive, silly, or sophistic—but it was not a religious crime.[13]

In fact, the nonscriptural nature of Greek epic had a significant effect on the development of logical thought. As a sophisticated, literate culture emerged, Greek thinkers became skeptical toward the more fantastical constructions of the epic poets and, stimulated by the desire to find new ways of talking about the world, built around the idea of naturalistic plausibility. This could not have happened had they been constrained by a belief in the god-given truth of scripture. Take, for example, Hecataeus of Miletus (ca. 550–476 BC). Only fragments survive now, but in antiquity he was held to be an early historian, a precursor of Herodotus. We can get a sense of how revolutionary he was from the preface to his work *The Genealogies:* "I write things as they seem to me to be true," he asserted, "for the stories of the Greeks are many and ridiculous." *The Genealogies* seems to have been a retelling of the mythical Greek past, with the divergent traditions harmonized and the supernatural elements surgically removed. The emphasis on Hecataeus's own good judgment perhaps suggests that he cast himself as a voice of commonsensical sanity in a world of storytellers and gullible audiences. In another snippet that has been preserved, he writes that "Hesiod says that Aegyptus had fifty children; I think he had fewer than twenty." Setting himself against the authority of inherited tradition and the great poets, Hecataeus attacked mythology by insisting on the same standards of plausibility that we observe in the world around us. No one in early fifth-century Miletus had fifty children; why should a mythological king of Egypt have been any different?[14]

We can get a flavor of how Hecataeus and his like proceeded from a curious surviving text that followed him down this rationalizing path, written perhaps some 150 years later. We know next to nothing about Palaephatus, its author; the assumption that he was an Athenian writing in the late fourth century BC is little more than a guess, based on various bits of evidence in a medieval encyclopedia.[15] But scholarly difficulties aside, the text is a wonderful example of the filtration of myth through a rational system. Here he is, for example, on centaurs:

What is said about the Centaurs is that they were beasts with the overall shape of a horse—except for the head, which was human. But even if there are some people who believe that such a beast once existed, it is impossible. Horse and human natures are not compatible, nor are their foods the same; what a horse eats could not pass through the mouth and throat of a man. And if there ever had been such a shape, it would also exist today.[16]

Palaephatus interprets the mythological stories about centaurs instead as a mangled memory of the first horse riders, adding the detail that they were so named because they had taken to horseback to kill bulls (an etymological pun: bulls are *tauroi*). This delightful inventiveness is typical of the author. The passage also reveals a lot about how the relationship between past and present could be imagined. At one level, nature is conceived of as unchanging throughout the ages (a reasonable pre-Darwinian assumption): a horse would at no point in the past have been able to digest human food. But human beings have (in Palaephatus's mind) clearly developed intellectually over time. In the past, humans expressed themselves symbolically through myth; nowadays, however, we respect the physical laws of the world and grasp the impossibility of breaking them.

There is a kind of schizophrenia to this attitude. Although he rejects myth as a narrative form that can admit supernatural elements, Palaephatus still thinks that myths must have, as the English cliché goes, a "kernel of truth" to them that can be rescued. This is not so far from the modern practice of taking (for example) the biblical story of the parting of the Red Sea to reflect a folk memory of a real tsunami, or the story of Atlantis as a recollection of the Santorini volcanic eruption. Although he casts himself as a skeptical modern, Palaephatus is not ready to let go of the past. His standard method is to report the familiar version of a myth and then to counter "the truth is as follows . . ." There is *always* a truth hidden in mythology somewhere, no matter how deeply.[17]

Epic myth was the Greeks' collective memory. It was unthinkable to reject it entirely: not because it was sacred, but because the past defined who the Greeks were. But figures like Palaephatus also thought of themselves as separated by a huge intellectual gulf from the more naïve world that produced such stories. That separation was marked by different attitudes toward the divine. Palaephatus was not quite a disbeliever, but gods play an extremely minimal role in his worldview. There are only eight references in the forty-five chapters, six of which are banal, incidental, and insignificant. Only in two cases does he seem, at least on first sight, to express some kind of belief. In myth, the hunter Actaeon glimpses Artemis bathing, and she exacts revenge by turning him into a deer, whereupon his own hounds maul him to death. To prove the implausibility of this story, Palaephatus comments that "it seems to me that Artemis can do whatever she wants; but it is not true that a man can turn into a deer or *vice versa*." Again, the Europa of myth was abducted by Zeus, who had turned himself into a bull; he swam from Tyre to Crete, where they consummated their union. Palaephatus's response is similar: it is not possible for a bull to swim that far, and Zeus could have found a better way to get her to Crete. We can take these cases as evidence that he thought omnipotent deities to be real—but that is not the only way of reading them. His real point is that the myth does not make sense *on its own terms*. If you believe in an omnipotent Zeus, it falls to you to explain why he had to turn himself into a bull in order to transport a young woman to Crete. Omnipotent gods are part of the problem of myth, but not part of the solution. The rewritten "true" versions he proposes do not contain deities. For Palaephatus at any rate, rejection of epic ideas about the gods had become a definitive way of being modern.[18]

The Greeks' lack of sacred scripture was not in fact a lack at all. It facilitated the great cultural revolutions of the classical period, which saw theological explanations for the way of the world displaced and new, naturalistic explanations coming in. To have a shared cultural reference point that could be debated, explored, or rewritten without fear of blasphemy was a huge cultural stimulus, without which the Greek intellectual tradition would, conceivably, have been hobbled from the start.

3

Battling the Gods

The Greeks did not have sacred scripture, but they did have myth. Huge amounts of it. Greece teemed with stories. These myths could have religious elements, but they had no intrinsic connection with religious practice. Greek religion was an expression of the community through shared sacrifice and feasting on the sacrificial meat. A myth was something completely different: a story told about people, gods, or demigods from long ago, which put its finger on an issue of collective importance.

What was myth for? First of all, it created a shared set of stories that encapsulated the values of an entire people. Knowing the stories of Achilles, Heracles, Medea, and so forth was a central part of what it meant to be Greek. On a smaller scale, there were also myths that were specific to a particular region, like the Athenian story of Aglaurus, who jumped to her death from the Acropolis when she saw Erichthonius, a primal being with a serpent's tail: this kind of local myth was important for binding together members of a *polis* community but was probably not widely known outside. Not that "Greek mythology"—the English phrase gives the false impression of a system—was fixed and unalterable. Given the regional diversity of the Greek world, and the absence of sacred texts or strong centralizing institutions, myths naturally circulated orally in multiple forms. Like religion in general, myth reflected the plural nature of Greek culture: a figure like Heracles would have been known by all Greeks, but specific details will have varied from locale to locale.[1]

Secondly, myth could explain why things are the way they are. The past was the key to the present. Prometheus once tried to trick Zeus at a feast by wrapping bones in fat, dressing the inedible parts so as to look edible. That is why mortals now sacrifice those indigestible bits to the gods, keeping the rest (conveniently!) for themselves to consume. Why are there different ethnic groups within Greece, each speaking a different dialect? Because Hellen, the original Hellene (Greek), had three sons, Dorus (founder of the tribe called the Dorians), Xuthus (whose sons Ion and Achaeus give their names to the Ionian and Achaean lines), and Aeolus (founder of the Aeolians). This type of myth—"etiological" is the technical term—represents a strong, normative statement about the way the world should be. We do what we do for a reason![2]

Finally, in the absence (in the earliest phase of Greek culture) of systematic philosophy, myth was used to explore issues of contemporary relevance. Some myths, in some tellings, could be relatively conservative, embodying the dos and don'ts of popular morality. The Oedipus story, for example, can be taken at its simplest level to express the principle that prophecies always come true. Oedipus believes himself to be the child of Polybus and Merope, the Corinthian royal household. On hearing the oracle that he is destined to marry his mother and kill his father, he leaves home never to return. He ends up at Thebes, unbeknownst to him the city of his biological parents, whom he duly proceeds to dispatch and bed. Thus we can deduce that no one can escape the plans the gods have laid for us. Sophocles's play *Oedipus the King* is a literary masterpiece of huge complexity, crammed with allusions to other literature and contemporary philosophy. But in its most stripped down form, the myth makes a simple point that can be grasped by anyone.

Stories are good for articulating ethical truths because they show causal links between actions and their results. In Homer's *Odyssey*, the suitors' outrageous behavior provokes Zeus to punish them with a brutal death at Odysseus's hands. Appropriating others' property, therefore, is bad and frowned upon by the gods: don't do it! Complex narratives can offer richer and more ambivalent explorations of moral issues, by multiplying the different actors and their motivations, introducing subplots, and blurring the relationship between cause and effect. In the full version of the *Odyssey*, for example, we learn that Odysseus himself is a far from straightforward character: acquisitive, self-indulgent, and mendacious. The story becomes a way of working through the question of what kinds of self-interested behavior are to be rewarded and what kinds punished. Myth becomes a prompt for ethical reflection.

Amongst other things, myth offered the chance to explore human-ity's relationship with the gods, in all its varieties. Many of the best known and most enduring stories were of this kind. We have mentioned Prometheus. In Hesiod's telling, Zeus exacts punishment for the meat trick by withholding fire from mortals. Prometheus goes on to steal it back (in a fennel stalk), for which Zeus punishes him by chaining him to a rock and having an eagle peck at his liver. Hesiod was a peasant farmer, who scraped a subsistence out of the soil near a small Boeotian village: the story expresses the precariousness of human livelihood and our dependence upon the gods' favor. A later Athenian tragedy, *Prometheus Bound,* offers a very different analysis. Here, fire is a symbol of human technology: this divine spark, once prized from Zeus's jealous grasp, raised us from cave-dwelling troglodytes to our current position between the beasts and the gods.

Stories like this portray, if not open warfare, then at least skirmishing between the divine and the human orders. Mortals are vulnerable and weak, their ephemeral existence under constant threat. Gods are immor-tal and unaging and live a life of luxurious abundance without toil. But this difference is not imagined as stable and permanent. The gods' power is constantly challenged. In Hesiod's creation myth the *Theogony,* Mount Olympus is assailed by monsters and Titans, who yearn to over-throw Zeus's rule. The battle is close, but the Olympians triumph. There are also numerous smaller skirmishes. Take the fate of another Titan: "Far-seeing Zeus cast the aggressor Menoetius down to Erebos, smiting him with his smoky thunderbolt, because of his arrogance and over-weening vigour." Zeus's power is repeatedly threatened by opponents of one kind or another.[3]

In myth, the gods seem ever embattled. They face crisis after crisis, war after war. Myth dramatizes not just the gods' power, but also oth-ers' aspirations to it. The privileges of dominion and immortality are the objects of constant craving and envy. Such stories capture—through narrative rather than philosophical exposition—an essential theologi-cal aspect of the Greek gods. They are not omnipotent in the way that Yahweh, Allah, and the Christian God are. They could in principle be defeated. In fact, the Prometheus of Athenian drama claims to be in possession of a prophecy predicting precisely that: Zeus will one day bear a son who will overthrow his father. In other words, atheism was a narrative possibility within Greek myth. A world without gods could be imagined. The possibility that the Olympian gods might cease to exist (or at least to hold power over the cosmos, which amounts to the same thing) was built into the Greeks' story-world.[4]

It is worth pausing to reflect on the nature of divine power in Greek antiquity. For those brought up in monotheistic traditions, the ingrained assumption is that "power" means omnipotence and eternal rule: as the Christian hymn has it, "Immortal, invincible, God only wise." These are the attributes of the transcendent deity of monotheism. Now in fact the idea of an all-powerful deity is a far from straightforward concept. The critique of omnipotence is usually traced back to the twelfth-century Arab philosopher Averroës, but in fact a version of it is already found in the Roman writer Pliny the Elder: "Not even a god can do anything: for he cannot, even if he wanted to, kill himself . . ." (Pliny goes on to list a number of things that it is impossible for a god to do, e.g., make humans immortal, change the past, or make twice ten equal something other than twenty.) But this is rarefied argumentation. The gods of Greece were in general beset by no such problems. The ancient polytheist god, even the king of the gods, has power of a different kind. Zeus's authority consists in his monopolization of violence (*bia*) and force (*kratos*). On the Athenian stage, Bia and Kratos appear personified as two thugs who serve as Zeus's enforcers. From a Greek point of view, divine power means brute force, the ability to battle down your foes. Not for nothing is Zeus the wielder of the thunderbolt, the ancient equivalent of the atom bomb: if the power of the Olympian order is in dispute, the thunderbolt settles matters definitively and irrevocably. For the Greeks, divine authority was defined, ultimately, by firepower.[5]

The god of Judaism, Christianity, and Islam holds power in the absolute. The power of Greek gods, by contrast, is relative to others: it consists in the ability to beat down rivals (whether mortal or immortal), to quell dissent, to emerge victorious in battle. For example, the *Iliad* contains an episode telling of grumbling on Olympus. Hera picks a public fight with her husband Zeus, whom she accuses of favoring another goddess. Zeus's response, however, is uncompromising: "Sit down in silence, and obey my word," he tells her, "otherwise all the gods on

Olympus will not help you as I draw close and lay my invincible hands upon you." Hera "was seized with fear and sat down in silence, curbing her heart." It is this kind of power that makes Zeus the king of the gods: the power to impose his will on others, even his awesome wife.[6]

There is a reason for this difference. Greece was, fundamentally, an honor-based society, and honor was generated—for humans and gods alike—through success in competition with others. It is no accident that sport is one of the Greeks' most enduring legacies, for competitiveness lay at the very heart of the Greek concept of (particularly male) honor. Individuals can increase their own standing in the public's eyes only by decreasing that of another. If I want to move up a notch on the honor board, I need to move you down: this is a form of what game theorists call a "zero-sum game." Hera's challenge to Zeus in the *Iliad* follows this logic: it is an attempt to enhance her own standing by diminishing his. (Being a goddess, Hera is not constrained by the normal protocols of female decorum.) In the event, her submission ensures the opposite outcome. Zeus wins, at her expense. This kind of vigorous striving between peers was not a sign of social breakdown; quite the contrary, it was absolutely central to the normal functioning of Greek society. To be powerful, one needs to display power, and to display power one needs to defeat rivals.[7]

So, myths of cosmic war were a means by which Greeks could explore the possibility of a world without gods. They had a special word for "battling the gods": *theomakhia*, which is anglicized as "theomachy." It could be used to describe a brawl between gods: toward the end of the *Iliad*, for example, the gods supporting the Trojans and those supporting the Greeks come to blows. But for the Greeks it more commonly described a nondeity taking on a deity. Euripides's *Bacchae*, one of the best known examples of the tragic drama that blossomed in fifth-century BC Athens, tells of one such *theomakhos*, a young Theban ruler called Pentheus ("Sorrowful") who will not accept the divinity of Dionysus, a god from Lydia (in western Turkey) who has just arrived in his city. The god's cult involves women indulging in orgiastic frenzies in the wild mountains beyond the habitable space of the city. (Or, at least, this is how the cult is stylized through the distorting lens of drama: there is scant evidence for any such behavior in reality.) In the play, Pentheus seems to see the god as a rival to his own power within the city and strives to oppose his worship wherever possible. He also pours scorn on the religious activity itself, which he sees as a cover for lewd behavior. His opposition to the new cult is both metaphysical and ritual. Yet he gets his comeuppance. Lured by the disguised Dionysus to go and spy on the women, he finds them turning all of their deranged, ecstatic violence onto him. The final scene shows Pentheus's own mother, Agave, rejoicing that she has killed a lion with her bare hands—until the Dionysiac illusion wears off and she sees her own son's head in her hands, probably represented dramaturgically by the mask worn by the actor. Revenge upon the young *theomakhos* is exacted in the grisliest way possible.

Like all myths, those of theomachy can be taken, at the simplest level, as morality tales. The point is a fairly straightforward one: you should not vie with the gods. Pentheus should know how the zero-sum game operates, and that gods' maintenance of their power depends on exemplary punishment of those who challenge them. But theomachy myths are not just about duty and devotion. This was not a Protestant culture demanding absolute obedience. There is something subtler and more interesting going on underneath the mythic surface. The widespread nature of these myths suggests that Greeks thought that it was in the nature of humans to envy divine prerogative. Rebelling against the gods seems to be expected of us. What the stories tell us about, as well as the gods' jealous guarding of their privileges, is humans' deeply ingrained desire to shrug off the shackles of mortality, to approach godliness.

Let us be clear on this point. In ancient Greece, the idea of humans encroaching on the gods' territory was not inherently blasphemous. It was expected that certain charismatic individuals came closer than most of us to divinity. Homer's *Iliad* regularly describes the effulgent heroes in their prime as "godlike." The Phaeacians who help Odysseus return in the *Odyssey* are *agkhitheoi*, "close to the gods." Many of the heroes of myth, indeed, received real cult honors, as Helen and Menelaus did in the Menelaion at Sparta from the seventh century onward. Hero worship was more than a metaphor in ancient Greece. Nor was this honor limited to mythical figures. The real-life, contemporary athletes praised by Pindar for their success in the Olympics and other games borrow the godlike luster of the Homeric poems. Humans could be accorded religious rites if they performed some distinguished athletic or military act. In later times, great leaders like Alexander the Great would be worshipped. Once again, the lesson is that we should not be misled by monotheist models of a god who is impossibly remote from the human realm. Greeks saw immortality as a sliding scale, not as an absolute point. Take a figure like Heracles or the healer Asclepius: god, hero, or human? The Greeks themselves were undecided in the matter.[8]

In ritual too, humans could play the role of deities. In the Athenian spring "flower festival" (Anthesteria), participants dressed as satyrs, half human and half goat. There was also a mysterious "sacred marriage," a sexual union between the wife of the city's senior magistrate and Dionysus; this may have involved the magistrate himself masquerading as the god. Herodotus has a story about the former tyrant of Athens, Pisistratus, who engineered his own return by appearing on a chariot with a tall woman called Phye, who played the role of Athena granting her blessing to his reinstatement. Herodotus is visibly contemptuous of the Athenians for falling for the trick ("They're supposed to be the cleverest of the Greeks!" he sniffs), but it has been plausibly argued that he misreads the scene. Greek role-playing rituals like this—and as a royal procession into the city, Pisistratus's entry was indeed a form of ritual—rested not on anything so crude as outright deception, but rather on a collective acquiescence in the masquerade. It is an odd feature of ritual that it allows people to believe they are experiencing divinity even as they know full well that the mechanics are conjured entirely by humans. (This is not just a premodern phenomenon: modern consumers happily succumb to the numinous aura of branded products in full awareness that they are being guided by nothing more than advertising.)[9]

There were, then, manifold ways in which humanity could achieve a kind of divinity. This is the context in which we should locate the phenomenon of theomachy, of humans battling against the gods. Jealousy of divine privilege was not "sinful": early Greece had only a weak idea of what was "sinful" because there were no god-sent commandments to break. (The Greek translators of the Bible had to adapt a rare word, *alitērios*, to express this fundamentally alien idea.) Rather, stories of theomachy explored the perfectly natural tendency of humans to yearn to better themselves, to procure for themselves a happier life, a life that they associated with divinity. If theomachy was "wrong," that was not because it contravened any heaven-sent rule book but because it was (at least in myth) a horrible misjudgment of the odds.

But battling the gods did have more profound, metaphysical implications too. According to the logic of the zero-sum game of honor, any competition puts status at risk. Were humans to defeat gods in any way, this would raise all sorts of questions about the nature of divinity. In the *Iliad,* intriguingly, there are moments where that golden generation of heroic warriors confronts and comes close to overmastering their divine counterparts. The Greek warrior Diomedes, mid-rampage, wounds first Aphrodite, goddess of love, and then—even more impressively—Ares, god of war, himself. Later, Achilles (who is half divine, through his mother Thetis) confronts the river god Scamander, although he comes swiftly to regret it when faced by the surging power of the torrent. Neither Diomedes nor Achilles suffers any serious consequences as a result of his actions. The point of these episodes is to dramatize the near godlikeness of the individuals in question, to show that they come as close as a mortal possibly could to crossing the boundary into the divine. But elevating humans in this way also threatens to demote the god. Aphrodite and Ares in particular are left nursing their resentment.[10]

In its most extreme form, theomachy expresses a kind of atheism, through the narrative medium of myth. To confront the gods was to deny their potency, what made them gods. For stories along these lines we must turn to an epic poem called the *Catalogue of Women,* written in the sixth century BC. It does not survive in its entirety: what we know of it is pieced together from fragments of papyri found in Egypt. Luckily, these are extensive: it must have been a best seller in the Roman period. At first sight, its contents do not look particularly riveting: it is in effect a family tree for the Greeks, dividing them ethnically between various descendants of Hellen, the first Greek. It is called the "*Catalogue of Women*" because it is structured around a list of women who have been impregnated by gods. But despite these unpromising signs, it seems to have been in fact a whirligig compendium of baroque myths, by turns gruesome and erotic—which no doubt explains why later readers were so keen to get their hands on it.

One particular family catches the eye, the house of Aeolus. With their heartlands in Thessaly, a notoriously wild place toward the north of Greece, the Aeolians were always easy to associate with uncivilized behavior. A surviving fragment of the *Catalogue* introduces Aeolus's sons grandly as "kings, ministers of justice," but this billing is at best ironic in view of what follows: "Cretheus, Athamas and Sisyphus with his shimmering wiles, and lawless Salmoneus, and arrogant Perieres . . ." "Shimmering" is *aiolos,* an obvious pun on their progenitor's name. So far as we can judge, Cretheus and Athamas did not do much wrong, by the permissive standards of myth, but the rest were a reprobate lot who carried wrongdoing in their very DNA. And what is interesting for our purposes is that their crimes were of a piece: they all, in their different ways, engaged in theomachy.

In the first generation of descendants of Aeolus we meet Sisyphus, he of the "shimmering wiles." The founder of the city of Corinth, Sisyphus is best known now (thanks to Albert Camus) for his punishment in the underworld: he was condemned to roll a rock up a hill, a rock that would tumble down each time he had almost reached the peak. There are different traditions relating to the crime that prompted this punishment; it is impossible now to tell for sure which version the now-fragmentary *Catalogue* contained, but the following is the likeliest. Zeus abducts Aegina, the daughter of Asopus; Sisyphus then angers Zeus by telling Asopus where she is. When Zeus sends Death to punish him, Sisyphus captures Death in chains, with the result that humans can no longer die. In time the god Ares releases Death and hands Sisyphus over to him, but once in the underworld he tricks his way out and lives until old age catches up with him. The fantasy of tricking death is a motif found in folklores across the world. What is distinctive about the Sisyphus myth, however, is that the wily king actually succeeds, not once but twice. He is punished in the end, of course, but here is a human who has come close to erasing the line between mortals and immortals, by defeating mortality itself.[11]

Then there was Alcyone, another of Aeolus's offspring. A scrappy papyrus fragment summarizes the *Catalogue*'s version of the story: "Ceyx the son of the star Phosphorus ["Bringer of Light"] married Alcyone the daughter of Aeolus. The two of them were arrogant. They loved each other; she [. . .] called him Zeus, he named her Hera. Zeus was angered at this and metamorphosed them into birds." Their names, indeed, reflect their birdiness: *kēux* means "tern," and *alkuonē* "kingfisher." The crucial point for us, however, is that they attempt to make themselves into gods. A later encyclopedia adds the detail that Ceyx "wanted to be worshipped as a god." This husband and wife team seem to have offended the gods by replacing them as the objects of religious worship. Their particular type of theomachy consisted in denying the gods by setting themselves up as substitutes.[12]

Salmoneus, the brother of Sisyphus and Alcyone, was perhaps the most intriguing of them all. In this case we have a fuller papyrus fragment detailing the *Catalogue*'s account of his misdeed, which can be filled out with later accounts. Here is how one late version summarizes the story (enough details correspond to confirm that it is the same version as in the *Catalogue*):

And being arrogant and wishing to put himself on an equality with Zeus, he was punished for his impiety; for he said that he was himself Zeus, and he took away the sacrifices of the god and ordered them to be offered to himself; and by dragging dried hides, with bronze kettles, behind his chariot, he said that he was making thunder, and by flinging lighted torches at the sky he said that he was making lightning. But Zeus struck him with a thunderbolt, and wiped out the city he had founded with all its inhabitants.[13]

This marvelous story has comic features: the idea of using kitchen utensils to compete with Zeus the Thunderer looks more like a jokey parody than a worked-up statement of philosophical atheism. Yet the story does also have a theoretical dimension. Divinity, from this perspective, is reduced to a list of easily imitable signs: a name, a noise, a flash in the sky. The implication of Salmoneus's performance is that there is nothing more to the gods than these, and if humans can replicate them, humans can achieve everything that the gods can. There is something that verges on the postmodern in Salmoneus's replication of "brand Zeus," in much the same way as a forger would the logo of a clothes designer. Indeed, other ancient authors who tell the story of Salmoneus emphasize that his crime was, precisely, to *imitate* Zeus: the Greek concept of *mimēsis* carries hints of fabrication and deception. It is possible, then, that the original version of the Salmoneus myth was a parable about the dangers that lurked in humans' capacity to fabricate gods through ritual, drama, and statuary (which was spreading through Greece at exactly this time, in the sixth century). If gods can be fashioned by mortal imitation, how real can they be?[14]

We can push the argument further. Two ingenious scholars have made the observation that the way in which Salmoneus's kettles and hides are described is almost identical to later accounts of the *bronteion,* the theatrical device for replicating the sound of thunder (*brontē*) when plays called for it. Now, when the *Catalogue* was composed, theaters probably did not exist in any significant sense in Greece; the earliest evidence we have is from a little later, at the turn of the sixth and fifth centuries. But dramatic forms certainly preexisted the theater proper, and surely these early forms of drama will have involved imitation of the gods. The *bronteion* will have been used for ritual purposes prior to the spread of theater, and this is probably how the poet of the *Catalogue* knew the device. We might add that there is evidence also that the theater had a device called a *keraunoskopeion,* which generated the effect of lightning; again, this may have its roots in older, ritual action. In other words, the Salmoneus story was not just a joke: it was a meditation on the metaphysical implications of a culture that was beginning to manufacture divinity in the human realm, through sculpture, painting, and theater. If gods can be constructed, the story wonders, do they really exist at all?[15]

The answer that the *Catalogue* gives is a (literally) resounding "yes." Zeus's booming thunderbolt reasserts his power against the upstart *theomakhos.* It is significant that Zeus punishes Salmoneus with a thunderbolt, the very object that the mortal thought he could replicate: this action is not only a punishment, it is also a reenactment of metaphysical differentiation, a dramatization of the fact that lightning is substantively different from a burning stick thrown into the air. As so often in myth, the question posed is answered in the most conservative way possible, by re-establishing the truth of tradition. But a conservative answer does not make the question a conservative one. In acknowledging that Salmoneus needs punishment, the poem in effect also signals, in narrative form, that the human manufacture of "fake" gods was the source of major cultural anxiety in the sixth century.

The conservative narrative shape of theomachic myth should not surprise us. Part of the role of myth, after all, was to lay down the law about the way in which Greek culture should operate. But it is important to underline the point that the myth presents battles against the gods as crises of power, not manifestations of sinfulness. Salmoneus and his siblings were "arrogant" (*hubristai,* hence the English "hubris"), not evil. *Theomakhoi* were imagined as fools for taking on a losing battle against the gods, for thinking that humans can aspire to divinity—but nothing more. Atheism is not inherently evil, the antithesis of religiosity, but a human urge to usurp the gods' power.

Greek myth was folk wisdom, the narrative glue that bonded communities together, not the hectoring of a priest seeking to dictate how, what, and why you should believe in gods. It was often moralistic, certainly, but it could also be playful, funny, and experimental. Myths, after all, were first and foremost stories, not homilies. Yet there was too, or so I have argued, a philosophical dimension to such stories. Although they end up reaffirming the power of the gods by showing them beating down the upstart humans who challenge them, theomachies also explore (albeit temporarily and provisionally) the possibility that the divine order might be overthrown and that humans could live self-sufficiently, without the gods. That tells us that such atheistic ideas were current enough in contemporary culture to be worth exploring, and countering, in myth. How these ideas were expressed in wider culture we can only guess. It is impossible to tell whether there were many Ceyxes, Alcyones, and Salmoneuses in sixth-century BC Greece or whether such views were confined to elite groups. But the fact that these figures appear in popular myth suggests at least that the atheistic type was understood by enough people to give the stories appeal and purchase.

4

The Material Cosmos

As a rule, Greek religion had very little to say about morality and the nature of the world. Certainly, there was a sense that it was the job of the gods to oversee the governance of the universe: Apollo's task was to steer his solar chariot across the heavens, Aphrodite ensured that the natural world kept on reproducing, and Zeus oversaw the punishment of wrongdoing. But although Greek religion carried with it an implicit sense of cosmic order (which is why cultic activities needed to be performed in set ways at set times), it was not ultimately there to encourage speculation on the nature of the universe, and still less to enforce belief in a specific way imagining it. Collective ritual practice, centered on sacrifice, was all about doing rather than speaking. The priest's job was to look after the provision of animals, the ritual procedure itself, and the preparation and distribution of meat. Sacrifice was not a spiritual experience but a sensory drama: onlookers went for the songs, the spectacular open-air procession leading the beast to the altar, the shriek of the dying animal, the savor of the roasting flesh.

When Greeks pondered the nature of the world, they did so through the medium of philosophy, not organized religion. This gulf between metaphysical speculation and the priesthood had profound implications. Greek philosophy was never state sponsored or regulated. In time, schools were created, and these had their own institutional structures. Some, indeed, became dogmatic, and almost religious in their preoccupation with the tenets of their founders. But they always kept their distance from official hierarchies and indeed often found themselves fiercely critical of mainstream beliefs and practices.

Early Greek philosophy survives now, insofar as it survives at all, in snippets and summaries preserved by later writers. What this fragmentary mosaic, laboriously reconstructed by modern scholars, indicates is a surprising set of concerns, for anyone brought up to believe that philosophy is all about logic and subtle argumentation. The pre-Socratics, as they are often called, were not a unified movement of thinkers but an assorted group drawn from all over the Greek-speaking world, over a period of over 150 years, from the sixth to the fifth centuries BC. But they did share a range of concerns. A striking number of them were centrally interested in explaining the material nature of the world around us, in replacing the traditional, epic conceptions of a cosmos dominated by anthropoid deities with newer, "scientific" models based on the properties of material substances. "Scientific" should keep its scare quotes, for although there were methodological and observational dimensions to pre-Socratic reasoning, there was also a lot of wild guesswork too—unsurprisingly, given the absence of microscopes and telescopes. Thales, for example, said that the Earth does not fall through space because it rests on a sea: this, we might say, is an unscientific answer to a genuinely scientific question (why does the Earth appear to us not to move?). The story of the pre-Socratics is not one of the orderly victory of rationalism over myth, of the steady march toward objective truth about the world. What it does tell us, however, is that ways of conceptualizing reality and its relationship with the divine were shifting, and new types of question were being asked. Paradigms were shifting, in the full sense of that phrase intended by its coiner, Thomas Kuhn: ways of understanding the world were becoming possible that had not been conceivable before.[1]

The rise of philosophy signaled nothing so simple as the rejection of divinity. Yes, Homeric and Hesiodic ideas about the gods were attacked and often rejected. The epic poets were increasingly seen as representatives of an archaism against which the philosophers defined themselves. Crucially, what is more, the pre-Socratics developed ideas about the material nature of the world around us: rejecting explanations for natural phenomena that invoked the gods of myth, they substituted ones based on the properties of physical stuff. Most pre-Socratics, however, retained some kind of role for the divine in their models of the world, but in a radically transfigured sense: gone were the anthropoid gods of myth and cult, replaced by abstract embodiments of nature and celestial order. Early Greek philosophy, one scholar has argued, was largely based on a kind of theory of intelligent design: the ordered circuits of the heavenly bodies, the procession of the seasons and the symbiotic relationships between different organisms were taken as evidence for the coherence of existence, which must point to the existence of a god. A god of this kind, however, was unlike anything known to the Greeks. When the pre-Socratics speak of divinity, we can often substitute "nature." "God" often seems to be a metaphorical way of referring to the interconnected-ness of all life. There is certainly no sense that these cosmic beings are divinities one can worship, or even interact with: the sources never speak of prayer, sacrifice, temples, or ritual.

The idea that the universe was made out of matter was a powerful and contagious one and did ultimately pave the way for a conception of a god-free reality. Only a few of these early philosophers went this far, but their example has been hugely significant for the development of atheism. The pre-Socratics mark the beginning of a journey leading ultimately to what modern atheists call "naturalism": the belief that the physical world is the sum total of reality, that nature rather than divinity structures our existence.[2]

The pre-Socratics have another role to play in the making of modern atheism and secularism in that philosophy celebrates the critical spirit, the willingness to question received values. The idea that progress is made by breaking with the past, by rejecting and questioning, is not a self-evident one, and it calls for some explanation. The historian of science Geoffrey Lloyd has argued that this sense of a critical displacement of existing models was intrinsic to the very functioning of philosophy as a social institution. The emergence of Greek speculation on the world was driven, he argues, by the competitive structure of Greek society in the archaic era: from the earliest times we hear of public contests between wise men, competing for the acclamation of audiences. You had to appeal to a broad audience, but you also had to offer something new. In Lloyd's view—and it is a plausible one—early Greek intellectual culture was fundamentally a response to the public-competitive nature of its surrounding society, which generated a continually self-renewing need for ideas that were at once innovative and accessible.[3]

For Lloyd, the explanation for this flourishing of ideas is political. Even the most repressive of Greek city-states, he claims, stimulated free expression and the diversity of opinion in a way that the societies of Egypt, Iraq, Persia, and India (for example) did not. Such political explanations have begun to look more problematic in recent years, as we have come more and more to recognize the Western-centered ideology that is often smuggled in with the idea of "freedom." The idea of an essential difference between Greek culture and those of the Ancient Near East is not as widely accepted as it once was, and the idea that any such difference should be defined in terms of "freedom" looks uncomfortably close to Western propagandizing. Greek cities in the archaic era had many different types of constitution, few if any of them resembling a liberal democracy. Assassinations, coups, and other forms of political instability were far from unusual. Environments of this kind were unlikely in themselves to produce intellectual competition.[4]

What facilitated the emergence in Greece of philosophical speculation about the natural world was not a political system that resembled a modern Western state but a combination of factors. One was certainly the absence of state regulation of ideas and (relatedly) the absence of any sense of sacred revelation or sacred text. Neither the politicians nor the priests controlled ideas or writing. The massive economic boom that began in the eighth century was powered instead by a sudden trade surge; as a result, it was the innovators and creators who held all the cards, not the priests. There was certainly a kind of freedom (with a small "f") in the absence of clerical control over the cultural sphere, but this had little to do with political apparatuses.

Another major driver, however, was contact with the cultures of the Near East, with their own ancient traditions of cosmological speculation. The initial pre-Socratic phase began in the sixth century not in mainland Greece but on the western coast of Turkey, a territory that the Greeks called Ionia, where Greeks had first settled as much as five hundred years earlier. These cities were multicultural environments, where different influences met and blended. In the late Bronze Age, much of the Ionian coast had been settled by Carians, a people originally from south-central Anatolia (roughly western Turkey). Ionia was under the control of the Hittite Empire until its collapse in the twelfth century BC; it was only afterward that Greek settlement began in earnest. Despite the passing of centuries, such ancient identities retained their vigor. The fifth-century historian Herodotus (from Halicarnassus, modern Bodrum), for example, was half Carian. The diversity of Ionia would have been amplified after King Cyrus the Great annexed the region for the Persian empire in the 540s BC. Empire always encourages migration from place to place and the traffic in ideas.[5]

According to popular tradition, the first Greek philosopher was Thales, a wealthy trader who was active in the port city of Miletus at the turn of the seventh and sixth centuries. Anecdotal traditions testify to a deep interest in the material cosmos. The original absentminded professor, he is said to have fallen down a well while looking up at the stars. A more flattering story has him predict a solar eclipse. He was also believed to have introduced geometry to the Greek-speaking world. These insights almost certainly came as a result of contact with Babylonian science, mathematics, and astronomy. The Babylonians had been recording the movements of celestial bodies for at least half a millennium beforehand, and this practice had been systematized in the eighth century under Nabonassar, whose reign saw the introduction of intercalated dating (such as we still use today on February 29) and the identification of eighteen-year cycles of lunar eclipse. Miletus in Thales's time was not yet under Persian control (that came in the aftermath of Cyrus the Great's defeat of Croesus, in 546 BC), but its position on the edge of Asia made it an ideal mediator between Greek and Near Eastern thought. As a trader, Thales would have had a wide network of cultural contacts, particularly since his family had Phoenician roots. Everything suggests that pre-Socratic speculation on the cosmos, in its Ionian phase, originated in the Greeks' discovery of Near Eastern science.[6]

The Ionian philosophers were a disparate bunch, but they shared the desire to explain natural phenomena in terms of a single material "origin" (arkhē) of the world. For this reason they are called "monists," from the Greek monos (single). Thales focused on water as the primal matter (it may not be coincidence that his name seems to derive from the Phoenician thal, "moisture": perhaps "Wetty" was his nickname?). He was followed in the mid-sixth century by two more Milesians. Anaximander had a more complex theory that everything derived from "infinity" (on which more soon), but he also gave a special role to wind. His student and near-namesake Anaximenes spoke of "air." It is striking that each of them focuses on nonsupernatural explanations: the origins of existence, they taught, lie not in divine creation but in physical matter. Because the views of these earliest philosophers survive only in the summaries of later writers, who are never systematic and often distort them for their own purposes, it is hard to gauge what "matter" actually meant to them. Did they see matter as supreme and self-sufficient? Or did they distinguish it from "god"? Or did they imagine that the material world was itself animated by a kind of pantheistic presence, to the extent that matter was itself divine? It is impossible to be certain given the state of the evidence, but it is possible at least to reconstruct a kind of radical materialism that is compatible with modern atheistic naturalism.[7]

The argument would go like this: Thales probably did imagine a rational god who created and designed the universe. For Anaximander and Anaximenes, by contrast, the later reports suggest a thoroughgoing concern with material explanation. Particularly striking is the desire to explain thunder by natural means, given that this was traditionally thought to be the symbol of Zeus's power. Anaximander thought this was the result of wind colliding with clouds, and Anaximenes had a similar explanation. Such matter-based accounts of natural marvels are a recurrent feature of the sources: Anaximenes in particular explains changes in the seasons by reference to the position of the sun in the sky, rainbows in terms of the effects of sunlight on cloud, and earthquakes as the result of the drying of the land after rainfall. Each of these explanations is also an implicit denial of divine activity: no need for the Horae ("the Seasons"), Iris (the goddess of the rainbow), or Poseidon, "the Earth-Shaker." Cosmology could be explained naturally too. The heavenly bodies are, for both thinkers, nonsupernatural. Anaximander thought that the Earth is surrounded by a ring of fire that is largely veiled from our sight; what we see as stars are the gaps in the veil. Anaximenes thought that the stars were pieces of Earth that had been borne aloft on evaporated moisture and had subsequently caught fire. Even the creation of human life had a nonsupernatural cause. In an eerie presentiment of modern evolutionary biology, Anaximander claimed that primeval life originated from water; the original aquatic animals emerged onto land from the sea, containing other kinds of creatures (rather mysteriously) within them. Humans are thus latecomers to the animal kingdom. These theories are of course fanciful when judged by modern standards: if they occasionally approximate to what we know from science this is a matter of luck rather than intuition. But modern standards are the wrong standards to apply: in sixth-century terms, what Anaximander and Anaximenes were doing was trying to account for the world in new terms, using explanations drawn from the world around them rather than mythological deities. Everyone knows what fire, rock, air, clouds, and water are like, and we know that strange things happen when various combinations of them occur. These two thinkers tried to explain the sum of existence by extrapolating from tangible, observable reality. Geoffrey Lloyd's idea that early Greek science was fundamentally competitive seems to be borne out: to win acclaim, these thinkers needed both to reject existing accounts in powerfully assertive ways and to appeal to a kind of truth that was plausible and accessible to their audiences.[8]

Both Anaximander and Anaximenes, certainly, spoke of gods. Anaximander associated the divine with infinity, which he saw as the ultimate principle of existence; Anaximenes equated air with god. These claims are, as ever, hard to judge without the authors' own words. They are usually taken at face value, to mean that there is a real divinity in the world. There is however a rather more subversive interpretation: what is conventionally called "god," they may have been saying, is in fact no more than a property of the material world itself. You say "god," I say air, wind, or some other material principle. If this is right, then the point is precisely the opposite of what we would now see as a theistic one: that things that seem to call for a supernatural explanation do not need one. In the case of Anaximenes this seems a distinct possibility, for "air" is undeniably a physical feature. But Anaximander's concept of infinity at first sight looks to be something more mystical and less physical. But even here there is perhaps a nonsupernatural explanation. Anaximander may have meant merely to distinguish between individual things that exist, which are perishable, and existence itself, which is not. "The infinite is the source (*arkhē*) of things that exist," one ancient commentator on him explains, "for it is from this that all things come to be and into this all things perish." In other words, the claim may be not that "the infinite" is a creator being on the conventional model of a deity, but that to understand reality we need to take a "god's-eye" view of it. We should not contemplate it from the perspective of an individual, since individual beings, species, and worlds come and go; what we need to grasp is the interconnected whole of the cosmos, which continues to exist irrespective of the fate of individual elements. Since this existence is defined precisely by its immortality, it can be called "divine," but this is a metaphorical extension of the traditional language of divinity rather than an affirmation of the existence of gods as conventionally understood.[9]

These issues are rather subtle and unprovable either way given the current state of the evidence. But thinking through these possibilities is a useful exercise, because it shows just what a vague and flexible concept a god is. Are we speaking of an intelligent, sentient being? That is, what we might call a "deity-max," with the capacity to design, to choose, to create? Or, at the other extreme, are we to think of god in the looser, more metaphorical way I suggested in the previous paragraph, as a way of describing nature itself? This is a vital distinction for modern readers, since it runs along one of the major fault lines of religious identity: the "deity-max" option essentially points to a theist position, the second an atheist/naturalist one. (Atheists might not be happy using the label "god" to describe nature, but the underlying model is compatible with naturalist beliefs.) These questions were probably less obviously contentious among the early Greeks, since they had no theologically canonical sense of what a god had to be like: there was no scripture to prove that one person's definition of divinity was better than another's. Even if the Milesians did present divinity in the radical way I have suggested, ancient readers are likely to have seen them as adjusting what was already a flexible concept, rather than as engaging in acts of blasphemous detonation. Certainly no ancient source accuses them of atheism. Greek religion was, perhaps, capacious enough to accommodate ideas that we would now associate with atheism. Even so, the Milesians' ideas were revolutionary in terms of the development of accounts of the world based on physical laws (or at least what were thought to be such at the time).

The first of the Ionians whom we can read in his own words is Xenophanes of Colophon, resident of another old city on the Anatolian coast, some way to the north of Miletus. Xenophanes was an approximate contemporary of Anaximenes, active in the middle of the sixth century. We have already met him tipping scorn onto Homer's and Hesiod's anthropomorphic representations of the gods. "Homer and Hesiod," he opines, "have attributed to the gods all things that are shameful and reproachable among humans: stealing, adultery and deceit." This misconception of divinity comes from a kind of projection: we assume that gods should be just like us. "Mortals think gods are born," he writes, "and have clothing, voice and body just like them." In another fragment, this naïveté comes in for some scorching satire: "Now if cows, horses or lions had hands, and were able to draw with those hands and create things as humans do, horses would draw gods in the form of horses, and cows in the form of cows, and create bodies just like they had." Then again: "Africans say that their gods are snub-nosed and black, Thracians blue-eyed and red-haired." These claims form a cumulative case against the anthropomorphic ideas of the gods enshrined in Homer and Hesiod. Xenophanes thus preempts by two and half millennia the claims of modern cognitive theorists who explain the origins of religion in terms of a human desire to explain the inexplicable in terms of the intentions of a human-like figure.[10]

Xenophanes speaks with the confidence of a new cultural era. References to Thracians and Africans present him as a well-traveled cosmopolitan with a sophisticated understanding of the world around him. Epic myths to him, meanwhile, were outdated nonsense, "the fictions of our predecessors." He also expressed disbelief in prophecy, the traditional means of communication between the gods and human beings. Like the Milesians, he based his understanding of the world instead on the observation of physical reality. The fragments of his works that survive tell repeatedly of his captivation with natural phenomena: he speaks of the heating of the Earth, of caves, rain, of multiple solar systems, of the saltiness of the sea, of the fossilization of marine life, and much more. He explains meteorological phenomena through physical causes and had a particular fascination with clouds: the sun and the moon are burning clouds; lightning comes from the flash of clouds as they move; rainbows too are made of clouds; even comets, shooting stars, and the nautical phenomenon known as Saint Elmo's fire can be elucidated in this way. As with the Milesians, the important point is not how scientifically accurate he was (the only tools at his disposal being the naked eye, an enquiring mind, and a cloud fixation), but how he positioned himself against the prevailing wisdom of the day. Once again, the desire to account for lightning and rainbows seems calculated to undermine mythological stories about Zeus and Iris.[11]

Xenophanes was in part a naturalist who rejected traditional ways of explaining the way things are in terms of the gods of mythology. He believed that the world is composed of physical matter and that its many wonders are physical rather than supernatural in original. Like Anaximander and Anaximenes, however, he also speaks of gods, or rather of "one god, greatest among gods and mortals, not at all like mortals in body or thought." This one god was the most important element in his system. He remains unmoving and unchanging in one place, quite remote from the world as we know it; he is uncreated and undying; and he causes motion in other bodies through the force of his mind. In other words, the one god is the principle that animates the cosmos, causing growth and decay and the cycles of the stars. The one god is, in our terms, nature itself. But this god is more than a metaphor: he can *think*. He has intention and will. Deity-max has made a comeback (if, indeed, he ever went away).[12]

Xenophanes, then, was not an atheist in any straightforward sense. He was not denying the existence of a deity but radically redefining it: shifting it away from anthropomorphic projections, so that it became instead the explanation for life and motion, what Dylan Thomas called "the force that through the green fuse drives the flower." Even the one god's "mind" seems entirely nonanthropomorphic: when he claims that the god moves things with his mind, he makes it clear that this is an entirely different type of mind from the human. Xenophanes shifted gods from Olympus into every living being, into science and matter. From another point of view, however, this was the most devastating assault on traditional Greek religion, a religion built around the cultic worship of temples (gods' houses) and statues. How could one *worship* the one god? What rituals would one use? The "one god" is like a conventional deity in that he is undying and possessed of immense power, but given that he cannot be known and is not of our world, the word "god" is more of a conceptual placeholder in the absence of any secure definition of this entity. Would anything be lost in Xenophanes's account of the world if we substituted "nature" for "the one god"?

In the early fifth century BC, the center of philosophical thought shifted westward, to southern Italy and to Elea, a relatively recent colony in what is now Cilento. Here Parmenides taught that the evidence of the senses is not to be trusted; the way of truth was open only to reason. Among his successors (and, according to tradition, lovers) was Zeno, who came up with paradoxes designed to deny the possibility of motion. If I wish to get from a to b, I must first travel half of the distance between the two, to a point that we might call c. But before that I must travel half of the distance between a and the midpoint between a and c, which we can call d. But before I get to d, I must travel half of the distance in between, to e . . . This process of division leads to an infinite regress, which Zeno took to indicate that the idea of any movement at all was logically impossible. What we experience as movement, then, must be the mere semblance of it; reality must, however, be constant and unchanging. The Eleatic school was in part a response to the Ionians' insistence on explaining the sum of existence by observing the nature of the physical world around us and extrapolating from there. For the Eleatics, observation was misleading; only rational reflection could lead to the truth. This distinction between the material cosmos and the abstract world of reason (*logos*) was to have a profound influence on the development of philosophy, allowing for the re-emergence of strong forms of theism. The material world and the senses were downgraded; reason was deified. Parmenides imagines his discovery of the truth about reality as a mystical journey "onto the many-voiced path of the deity, who leads the knowing mortal straight through all things." A hierarchy was thus created between mind and body, the rational and the sensory, divine truth and mortal experience. This hierarchy was later borrowed by Plato and would ultimately shape the development of early Christianity. The evangelist John has the best known opening of any of the gospels: "In the beginning was the Word, and the Word was with God, and the Word was God." "Word" is *logos,* which could also be translated "reason." The evangelist is very Parmenidean in spirit.[13]

Materialism, however, was not dead. In the course of the fifth century, the philosophical hub shifted once again, this time to Athens. By the middle of the century, Athens had become the largest and wealthiest city in the Mediterranean, thanks to its control of the sea. It was also a city obsessed with words. Thanks to its democratic political system, a recent innovation, the ability to persuade others and to reason was highly prized. As a result, it became a magnet for intellectuals from all over the Greek-speaking world, who were attracted both by the promise of financial rewards for teaching wealthy Athenians and their sons and by the prospect of living in a place that prided itself on being (at least in principle) receptive to new ideas.

One such figure was Hippo of Samos. Samos is an island just off the Ionian coast, and Hippo was very much an heir to the sixth-century tradition of Thales, Anaximander, and Anaximenes, who had flourished in nearby Miletus. Like Thales, he argued that moisture was the single material origin (*arkhē*) from which all reality was derived. Hippo, however, took the further step of arguing that the soul is entirely corporeal and that it is nothing more than the brain. This was a radical step. The belief that a living being might have a soul was relatively recent in Greece (there is no such concept in Homer or Hesiod). It seems to have arisen with cults associated with Orpheus promising existence in the afterlife. From the sixth century these spread down from Thrace. The god Dionysus in particular was increasingly associated with the idea of a part of us that survives death. From these cults the idea seems to have percolated into philosophy. The followers of Pythagoras (who originated, like Hippo, from Samos) believed not only that the soul does not die but also that it is reincarnated into other humans or animals; hence their strict vegetarianism. Pythagoras himself claimed to recall having fought in the Trojan War in a previous life as the Trojan Euphorbus. For Hippo to associate the soul with the brain, then, was a direct assault on this position. He may well have denied the existence of gods too. As so often with the pre-Socratics the evidence is sketchy, and Hippo is even less well represented than most. What we do know is that he was known as an atheist (*atheos*); he may even be the first person in Greek history to have gained this reputation.[14]

Two pieces of evidence suggest that Hippo was an atheist in the modern sense. The first is the fact that Aristotle, writing some one hundred years later, criticizes him as an excessive materialist; apparently he could not see any role in the world for anything other than matter. This certainly suggests that he did not believe in gods. The second testimony is subtler. We happen to have Hippo's epitaph, which he himself composed:

> This is the grave of Hippo, whom Fate made
> equal in death to the immortal gods.

I have given the traditional translation, which implies nothing more than a grandiose claim that Hippo's achievements have given him immortal fame after death. But there is an alternative one. Michael Hendry argues that Hippo also wanted to hint that the gods themselves are no more. In depriving Hippo of life, Fate has made him "equal to the immortal gods"—in the sense that both are now dead. The adjective "immortal" would have to be taken as heavily ironic in the context. Perhaps Hippo is even claiming to have slain the gods himself, with his materialist arguments. That would make him the *theomakhos par excellence:* the mortal who battled the gods and won.[15]

Another radically innovative Ionian was Anaxagoras, from Clazomenae (near the modern Turkish town of Izmir); he arrived in Athens in the 430s. Anaxagoras's achievement was to reconcile Ionian materialism with Parmenides's distinction between the physical world of the senses and the rational world of the intellect. Reality, he held, is composed of physical ingredients blended in different ways to produce different substances. All life is physical in origin and generated from primordial seeds. Like his Milesian predecessors, he paid great attention to natural wonders: he explained thunder, earthquakes, comets, floods, and hail in physical terms. But he also proposed something called "mind" (*nous*), which is entirely different in kind from the material world: pure, unchanging, infinite. Mind is behind the revolutions of the stars. Every animate being has some share in this cosmic mind. In this way, Anaxagoras managed to accommodate Parmenides's idea of an abstract rationality in the universe without denying the reality of the material world.[16]

Was Anaxagoras an atheist? There is nothing anachronistic about this question. In the late 430s, he was put on trial for "impiety," on the grounds that he denied the divinity of the heavenly bodies (which he undoubtedly did). This may have been the first time in history that an individual was prosecuted for heretical religious beliefs. Although he escaped, he retained a reputation for impious thought. Socrates, at his own trial, had to remind his jurors not to confuse him with Anaxagoras. On the one hand, his views were clearly reconcilable with a form of theism. The cosmic "mind" at one level resembles closely Xenophanes's "one god": it is remote, self-sufficient, all-powerful, different in kind to the stuff of matter. Elsewhere we learn that it is mind that is behind the orderly rotation of the stars and all of the celestial elements and mind that gives life to organic beings. It looks, to all purposes, like the designing will of a creator god. Yet Anaxagoras never, to our knowledge, identified it with divinity. This is a significant silence: surely if he had wanted to equate "mind" with "god" he would have done so explicitly. Indeed, he seems evasive—deliberately so?—on the question of what "mind" actually is. Plato criticized him on precisely that point: for all his talk of cosmic intelligence, he protested, he always offers materialist explanations for the way the universe is. Ultimately, as with Xenophanes, the central question is how literally or metaphorically we are to take these metaphysical perambulations. Are we to think that mind is a real cosmic property, which has godlike powers of design and creation? Certainly Anaxagoras sometimes speaks of it as acting in time, for example at the origins of existence when it separated out the elements by setting things in motion. Here, mind seems to act like the Yahweh of Genesis or the Allah of the Qur'an. But maybe in its original context (which is now lost) that reference to creation was just a figurative way of saying that the universe *as it is now* is structured and ordered. Perhaps what he meant was nothing more than that there is a coherent, unified explanation for the way that the material universe is and that this explanation can be disclosed by the inquiring human mind.[17]

For the pre-Socratics (apart from the Eleatics) "god" typically meant not a deity of popular religion but the nexus of invisible forces that holds the material world together, the sum of all that cannot be explained by observation and perception alone. Modern theologians refer to the principle of "the god of the gaps," according to which belief in the divine is thought to be confirmed by the failure of science to explain everything. Although there are some superficial resemblances, the pre-Socratic deity is in fact something completely different. It does not pick up where science leaves off; rather—this is the important point—it is an *intrinsically scientific concept.* It joins together all of our isolated experiences of the physical world into a coherent, rational, predictable structure. This is why the pre-Socratic god seems so often, from a modern perspective, to slope into the metaphorical: it is not really a god at all. This, perhaps, explains Anaxagoras's choice of "mind" instead of "god": it is a better way of expressing the idea of the intellectual coherence, and, indeed, intelligibility, of the world.

One group of pre-Socratic materialists, however, chose to go down a different path altogether. Democritus was born in around 460 BC in Abdera, a town in Thrace that had, by a nice coincidence, been founded by colonists from Anaxagoras's hometown, Clazomenae. Unlike most of his contemporaries, he spent little time in Athens ("I went to Athens and no one knew me," he reportedly said). He and his teacher Leucippus were credited with the development of the doctrine of atomism, the theory that the smallest elements of reality are tiny, indestructible, indivisible (the Greek adjective is *atomos*) particles of matter. According to Democritus, the universe is composed, essentially, of nothing more than atoms and void. Everything that we sense in the world around us is formed of clusters of atoms; all substantial changes in nature (such as the decay of a corpse or the transformation of water into steam) are simply rearrangements in the atomic structure of such clusters.[18]

Atoms have certain properties: they vibrate, impacting on other atoms, causing motion. They come in different sizes and shapes, and these qualities determine the ways in which they move through the void. This atomic habit of moving in predictable ways is a partial explanation for the orderliness of the universe: the celestial bodies, for example, will move in the predictable way that they do because it is the property of a body with their atomic structure to do so. But how, without appealing to an intelligent design behind the cosmos, do we account for the fact that everything seems so well set up for organic life? Democritus met this challenge by positing an infinite number of worlds. Some of these will not sustain life; others will, with varying degrees of success. In other words, the fact that our world is as it is is the result not of an integrated design in the universe but of luck. Democritus is the first philosopher to have given a central role to *tykhē,* "chance."

It may seem at first sight implausible to claim that our complex, symbiotic, life-supporting ecosystem is the result of mere chance. Modern theists who appeal to design-based arguments about the nature of the universe, for example, are fond of pointing out that the odds of the big bang occurring in just the right way to produce a life-sustaining universe are infinitesimal: "If the initiation explosion of the big bang had differed in strength as little as 1 part in 10^{60}, the universe would have either quickly collapsed back in on itself, or expanded too quickly for stars to have formed." Yet such arguments can be answered using Democritus's theories as a basis. Firstly, Democritus's infinite numbers of "worlds" could be taken to refer to planets, and on present evidence no other one supports life. Why would a god who created existence with the primary purpose of allowing life have designed such a vast expanse of space that could not do so? Alternatively, we might imagine multiple alternative versions of the universe as we know it. In that case, the question is whether ours is the *best possible* one for sustaining life. Could not an omnipotent designer god have created one that offered, for example, a larger Earth to avoid overcrowding, or a neighboring planet that could be colonized? Indeed, if there are, as Democritus proposed, an infinite number of universes, it follows that there are ones that are necessarily better adapted to sustaining life (and perhaps other forms of life that might be superior to our carbon-based version). Both of these Democritean objections expose a serious flaw in design-based theism, which invariably assumes that the cosmos designed by a perfect god must itself be perfect. We simply cannot test whether our world is the best possible one: we cannot rerun the formation of the universe using different variables to see whether alternative, and possibly better life-generating scenarios might have arisen.[19]

Democritus's materialist universe has no obvious room for any supernatural forces, but he does nevertheless speak of both souls and gods. The soul, he thought, was the same as the mind and composed of atoms. Soul, in other words, is what we would call consciousness, and presumably he thought it was dispersed after death (as his followers, the Epicureans, did). His views on deities are more complicated. On the one hand, he thought that the gods of conventional religion arose in former times when people naïvely mistook natural phenomena like thunder and eclipses for manifestations of divine power. Yet he also believed that it was possible for us to see gods in our sleep, because there are demonic images (*eidōla*, "idols") that exist in the air and penetrate our bodies. He clearly felt a need to explain, in physical-materialist terms, why some people claim to encounter gods in their dreams. They are, however, entirely incidental to his system: atoms and void are sufficient to explain the functioning of the world. In Democritus's material world, gods have become parasites rather than hosts.[20]

PART TWO

Classical Athens

ATHEISM AND OPPRESSION

The period of Greek history between the fifth and the fourth centuries BC is known as the "classical" period, thanks to the mesmerizing image of democratic Athens. During this time Athens became the largest city in the Mediterranean, adorned itself with the finest architecture anywhere in the world, and achieved unrivaled cultural preeminence thanks to its drama, oratory, history, and philosophy.

Although all Greek city-states depended on the idea of inclusive citizenship, democracy itself was a relatively late innovation. In the late sixth century, the city of Athens disposed of its last tyrant, Hippias. Unsurprisingly, the vacuum created a power struggle among the Athenian elite. One of these contentious aristocrats, Cleisthenes, won out by mobilizing popular support. In the aftermath, he radically reorganized Athenian society, dividing the citizen body (that is, the free male Athenian adults) into ten tribes and 139 "demes" or regional units, each self-governing at the local level. The democratic system, designed to prevent the domination of one group or another, represented each unit proportionally. He drew up a new council of five hundred men, fifty from each tribe, to set the agenda for policy and law for the city as a whole. By 501 BC, the signature feature of Athenian democracy was also in place: a popular assembly with sovereign power, open to all citizens, each of whom had an equal right to speak. Judicial decisions too would be made by the people, with huge juries of up to 1,500 members.[1]

The fifth century was the Athenian century. Under the guidance of Pericles (495–429 BC), inspirational and controversial in equal measures, the iconic temple of Athena Parthenos—the Parthenon—was completed in 438 BC. What we now call the Parthenon marbles (the relief sculptures that ran along the outside of the building) were added by 432. Pheidias, the most famous sculptor of the day, added a colossal sculpture of the goddess, wrought in gold and ivory. Intellectual life was flourishing too. Athens was coming to attract the finest talents of the day: philosophers and sophists such as Anaxagoras, Protagoras, and Gorgias, as well as other kinds of writers like the historian Herodotus. Dramatic festivals had taken place in Athens since the time of the sixth-century tyrants, but it was under the democracy that they peaked, with the famous tragedians Aeschylus, Sophocles, and Euripides, and the comedians Cratinus, Eupolis, and Aristophanes.

This cultural revolution was bankrolled by what was in effect an Athenian empire, which exacted tribute from other Greek states, particularly the islands we now call the Cyclades. This "Delian League" was named after the island of Delos, around which the other Cyclades wheel (hence their name). The league was formed in the aftermath of the Persian invasions of Greece, firstly by Great King Darius I in 492–490 BC and secondly by his son and successor Xerxes I in 480–479 BC. Athens's role in the resistance was decisive, particularly in the famous victories at Marathon in 490 BC, Salamis at 480 BC, and Plataea in 479 BC. The united Greek opposition to Persia—although in reality far from all the Greek states resisted—became part of Greece's collective mythology, particularly filtered through Athens's self-serving lens. The defeat of the Persians passed immediately into propagandistic folklore, like Agincourt, Yorktown, or Stalingrad. The names of Marathon and Thermopylae still resonate and still carry ideological heft: they conjure images of brave, hardy, resistant freedom fighters beating back innumerable hordes of despotically governed Persians. The historical reality of events is now barely perceptible behind this mythical veneer. We have no idea, for example, what the Persians' perspective was on these events. Even Herodotus's *Histories,* our fullest source and probably accurate in outline, glazes his account with triumphalism.[2]

In the aftermath of the invasions, hostilities with Persia rumbled on inconsequentially until around 450 BC, during which time Athens began to style itself as Greece's primary protector against the barbarian threat and consolidated its naval supremacy in the eastern Aegean. The Delian League was established in principle as a bulwark against further invasion, but in reality it was an extortion operation. Vast amounts of tribute were exacted from the member states. Already in 454 BC the league's treasury had been moved to Athens, a clear sign of where the real priorities lay. The Parthenon itself was the treasury's ultimate destination; it had, in fact, been constructed for this purpose, not (or not solely) as a regular cult temple.[3]

War defined much of Greek history, and that between the Greeks and the Persians was not the last major conflict of the fifth century. In 431 BC, the Spartans, seemingly aggrieved at Athenian expansionism, declared war on Athens and began ravaging Attica, the wider territory incorporating the city. Pericles's strategy in response was to avoid direct engagement with the fearsome hoplite warriors of Sparta and rely on their fleet instead. Walling up the citizenry within the city, however, encouraged a terrible plague that decimated the population. After Pericles himself died, more aggressive Athenian generals took the war to Sparta and won decisive victories. A short-lived truce was declared in 421 BC. In 415 BC, the Athenians attacked the city of Syracuse on Sicily, which had ethnic links to Sparta; the entire Sicilian expedition was, however, a disaster and cost Athens a sizeable proportion of its army. Sparta renewed war and built fortifications in Attica, thus turning the screw on a populace dependent on its ability to import grain. Athens finally capitulated in 404 BC. At Spartan insistence, the democratic system was abandoned, and a short-lived junta was instituted, the reign of the "Thirty Tyrants," which saw mass executions. The thirty were toppled and democracy was restored. The victory of Philip II of Macedon over a combined Theban and Athenian force at the battle of Chaeronea in 336 BC, however, marked the end of the city's classical period.[4]

Athens was a city of paradox. It is easy to admire its political idealism, its promotion of freedom of speech and equality before the law, and its cultural vibrancy. Yet it could also be repressive and brutal. Women had no role in political life and little public recognition, outside of religion. Slave owning was widespread among the populace; absolute numbers are hard to estimate, but the unfree were certainly more numerous than the free. Life was harsh for them, most notoriously for the workers in the silver mines at Laurion: "Neither weak nor maimed nor elderly nor a feeble woman meets with sympathy or relief; all are forced by blows to endure their labour until they die horribly in the midst of this compulsion." It must have been nigh intolerable for prostitutes, rowers in the navy, and field workers. As an imperial power, too, Athens was harsh and unforgiving toward her allies. Noncompliance was treated with the utmost severity; secession from the "alliance" could be punished by mass execution and collective enslavement.[5]

These moral contradictions permeated every aspect of Athenian life, including its handling of religion. On the one hand, building on the findings of the pre-Socratics, intellectuals explored atheism with new levels of philosophical sophistication. For the first time it became possible to explain the travails of human existence—war and disease—without reference to the gods. On the other hand, Athens went through repressive phases in which atheists were persecuted. These phases were without parallel in the history of Greece, a civilization that was generally unconcerned with enforcing religious orthodoxy.

5

Cause and Effect

Pre-Socratic philosophy posed fundamental questions about the nature of the world and the cosmos. Drawing on Near Eastern expertise in astronomy, calendars, and mathematics, the earliest Greek cosmologists explained celestial phenomena like thunder and rainbows not as extraordinary manifestations of divine intention but as the products of material causes, events that are explicable in terms of the laws of nature. In this conception of things, "god" was redefined as the sum of all the hidden motors of the physical world, rather than the anthropoid deity of myth and cult.

Pre-Socratic materialism was revolutionary. It was contagious too. By the fifth century BC, the role of the gods had been radically diminished in a number of fields. Homer's *Iliad,* that founding text of Greek culture, begins with a preface telling of the quarrel between Achilles and Agamemnon and then proposes a question: "Which of the gods was it who set these to strive in battle with each other?" The answer is instantaneous: "The son of Leto and Zeus," which is to say Apollo. In Homer's poem, where the Muse-inspired narrator can range freely from the Trojan plain to Mount Olympus and beyond, to posit a god—and a specific, identifiable god—as the cause of a momentous human event is uncontroversial. Big events demand big explanations. Athens of the late fifth century BC, however, brimming with intellectual inventiveness and thrumming with a sense of its own modernity, could no longer straightforwardly accept divine causality in this way.

Blaming gods for human actions had begun to look like evasion of responsibility. At some point in the 420s, for example, the Sicilian sophist Gorgias wrote *Encomium to Helen.* This was a self-consciously and playfully paradoxical defense, legalistic in form, of the actions of Helen

in leaving her husband Menelaus, eloping with Paris to Troy, and cata-
lyzing the Trojan War. Helen was at the time viewed in almost entirely
negative terms, constructed misogynistically as an adulterous Jezebel.
Gorgias's counterargument was that she must have gone to Troy with
her lover involuntarily: (a) if she was abducted, it was not her fault; (b)
if some god made her go, that too was a form of coercion; (c) if she fell
in love, that too was involuntary, since Eros is a god; (d) if she was persuaded by Paris, even that excuses her, for persuasive language is itself a
mighty power. The speech is a "little game," he confesses at the end. The
joke is that if you start diminishing the significance of personal responsibility by invoking external forces like gods, then the door is opened for
all sorts of moral exculpations. If you have been persuaded to commit a
crime—well, you are not responsible then, are you? Is not Peitho ("Persuasion") herself not a goddess?

Euripides, the most sophisticated of the Athenian playwrights, picks
up the baton in his *Trojan Women*, which was performed in 415 BC. The
play is set in the smoking aftermath of the sack of Troy and centers on
the attempts of the female survivors to come to terms with their losses.
One powerful episode has Hecuba, the mother of Paris and widow of
King Priam, let fly at Helen for causing the war. The scene is structured
like a legal trial, with Helen offering a defense speech before Hecuba
speaks for the prosecution. Helen's attempt to argue her innocence in
effect borrows from Gorgias: it was not my fault, she argues, since Aphrodite promised me to Paris, and who can fight the will of the gods?
Hecuba's scathing reply is that she speaks of Aphrodite when she should
be speaking of her own *aphrosynē*, her folly—a nice play on words. In
this mythical law court, blaming the gods is easily exposed as a rhetorical tactic designed to shift responsibility.[1]

The law courts, indeed, were a crucial place for testing such questions
of personal culpability. Greek courts existed well before the foundation
of Athenian democracy in 508 BC, even if they were fitted out with new
democratic purpose in the fifth century. In Athens at any rate, it seems
to have been the tyrants of the sixth century who set up courts, as a
way of restricting the power of aristocrats and building popular support. But whatever the local circumstances, Athens was also responding
to a trend that had swept across most of Greece in the sixth century:

law courts were part of the tide of reforms promoting collective citizenship that swept through archaic Greece. Courts were an essential way of arming citizens against abuse and of ensuring that power was disseminated through the state rather than concentrated in the hands of wealthy individuals.[2]

Inevitably, the Athenian legal system ended up being highly normative. There is a large surviving body of Athenian legal speeches, mostly from the fourth century BC; they survive because later Greeks, who prized rhetoric highly, canonized figures like Lysias, Aeschines, and Demosthenes. Scholars of social history have mined these texts for evidence of Athenian views on everything from gender and sexuality through the family to economics and political theory. No one speaks with such confidence about collective values as a lawyer, which is precisely why these texts are so revealing. But crucially religion plays a very small role in this. Of course, some crimes are religious in nature. Lysias, for example, defends one of his clients against the charge that he has removed one of the sacred olive trees that dotted the Athenian landscape (these were supposed to be offshoots of the original olive planted by Athena). And there are times when these orators strive to present their clients as pious types and their opponents as contemptuous of religion (although this is actually a rather rare strategy: much more emphasis is placed on responsible citizenship and on the treatment of fellow human beings). But there is never any sense that the court is itself an instrument of the gods' will, or indeed that the gods' intentions were under scrutiny at all. Athenian law was not theological. It existed solely to determine human responsibility for human action; those who tried to shift the blame onto the gods were mocked.[3]

The muting of divine explanations in law courts was part of a wider trend in Athens. The search was on for nonsupernatural causes for pretty much everything: the movement of the stars, the functions of the body, individual moral agency, political history. There was an extraordinary synergy afoot; this was one of those thrilling phases in history when humans working in different areas of culture all begin to speak the same intellectual language. And the law court, this iconic feature of the new political landscape, became the most immediately identifiable symbol of a new way of thinking. Vast fields of inquiry, in nature and human society alike, had opened themselves up to empirical testing, rational theorization, and debate between specialists.[4]

Although Athens is by some distance the best-documented ancient city for this period, we can see the effects of this process across the entire Greek-speaking world. The medical writings associated with Hippocrates of Cos (although in fact few if any of the texts linked to him are likely to have issued from his pen) offer a valuable non-Athenian parallel. Like the Athenian lawyers, the Hippocratic writers treated religion as a normal part of everyday life, but nevertheless they roundly rejected divine explanations for illness. Medical practitioners were not likely to be outright atheists—many of them were attached to temples of Asclepius—but they did reject explanations of illness based on divine intervention. The whole premise of Hippocratic medicine is that health is determined by our own distinctive physiological natures, modulated by the choices we make about our "diet" (the Greek *diaitē* refers not just to eating but to the entire bodily regimen, including sleep, exercise, and sexual practice).[5]

Take the treatise *On the Sacred Disease*. The disease in question is epilepsy, but it swiftly becomes clear that it is "sacred" only in the popular imagination. The English word derives from the Greek *epilēpsis*, which means quite literally a "seizure" or "possession," as if by a malevolent supernatural force. *On the Sacred Disease*, however, argues that the illness can be explained by factors that are entirely internal to the human organism. "It appears to me," writes the author in the introduction, "to be in no way more divine or sacred than other diseases; it has a natural cause, from which it originates, like other illnesses. People consider its nature and its cause as divine out of ignorance and wonder." The origin of this misattribution, he continues, lies with religious charlatans: "mages, purifiers, conjurors, and self-promoters, who pretend to be pious and to have some special insight." "The god," he opines on two occasions, "is not responsible"; the use of the language of legal culpability is striking. It is as if he is standing before a court and arguing the case against those who would explain epilepsy in terms of divine seizure.[6]

It would, to be sure, be anachronistic to understand the Hippocratic agenda in terms of a battle between (atheistic) science and religion. For a start, the explanation offered is not straightforwardly scientific. The claim that in cases of epilepsy veins transmit phlegm from the liver to the brain is based not on empirical observation or testing but on a priori assumptions (which are, as it happens, entirely wrong) about the way the body works. Hippocratic doctors did not dissect human bodies. What is more, this is an argument not for the nonexistence of the gods but more narrowly for their limited explanatory role in human pathology. The writer of this tract does not dispute that there is divine presence in the world; in fact, part of his argument is that those who attribute epilepsy to divine causes are actually being offensive to the gods, by blaming such seizures on them. The argument is, rather, that the human body operates according to regular physical laws. Like Xenophanes explaining rainbows or lightning, the Hippocratic writer takes an apparently mysterious phenomenon—in this case, epileptic seizures—and posits intelligible natural causes, while at the same time deriding the naïveté of those who invoke gods. Medicine is, we might say, locally rather than globally atheistic: it seeks to disprove not the existence of gods but their influence in this particular domain.[7]

The most visible and influential sign of this new "forensic" approach to the world came in the shape of the writing of history. The desire to record the past is a feature of all literate societies, but what distinguished fifth-century history from other ancient narrative traditions—those found, say, in the Iraqi epic *Gilgamesh,* in the poems of Homer, or the Hebrew Torah—were the excision of any mention of direct divine involvement in human affairs and the idea that the truth about the past needs careful sifting from competing reports. Like so many of the great intellectual developments of the period, the writing of history began in western Anatolia. Herodotus (ca. 480–420 BC) came from the southern town of Halicarnassus, present-day Bodrum. Like the Ionian pre-Socratics whom he resembles intellectually in many ways, he benefited from the confluence of traditions. Of mixed Greek and Carian ancestry, he lived in a city that had been under Persian occupation till the beginning of the fifth century BC; he also traveled far and wide in the eastern Mediterranean. His *Histories,* a huge nine-book account of hostilities between Greece and the Near East (culminating in the fifth-century invasions by the Persians Darius and Xerxes), testifies to this huge cultural and geographical sweep, ranging from the Mediterranean to Egypt,

Ethiopia, Mesopotamia, Iran, and Scythia (the area to the north of the Caspian Sea).[8]

Herodotus seems to have written his great work in Athens in the 420s or so; he certainly mentions Athens and Athenian sources more than one would otherwise expect. In many places he exhales the distinctive intellectual air of the late fifth century, and nowhere more noticeably than in his preoccupation with "causes," *aitiai,* the word that is also central to the Hippocratic view of the body. Herodotus aims, he tells us in his prologue, to memorialize not just the wondrous events of the Greco-Persian Wars but also "the cause [*aitiē*] of their fighting with one other." Like a Hippocratic doctor, he knows that amazing phenomena (like the Persian Wars) can be traced back to intelligible origins. In Herodotus's case that means picking one's way back through time. The ultimate cause of the hostilities lay in the actions of one sixth-century Anatolian monarch. "I know who it was who first initiated the injustices perpetrated against the Greeks . . . Croesus was a Lydian by birth, the son of Alyattes, and ruler of all the nations this side of the river Halys." There is no Homeric-style attempt to blame hostilities on gods. History, for Herodotus, means the study of human events, "the great, wondrous deeds wrought by Greeks and barbarians."[9]

The *Histories* are a magnificent experiment in genre bending, an amazingly adventurous attempt to underpin the writing of political and military narrative with pre-Socratic principles. Time and again, he derides implausible or non-natural explanations. The Athenians are "foolish" for falling for the schemes of the former tyrant Pisistratus, who put a tall woman in a chariot to pose as Athena and acclaim his own impending return to the city. How did king Croesus cross the river Halys with his army? "The common story among the Greeks," we are told, goes that the philosopher Thales rechanneled the river from in front to behind the army. This, however, is nonsense, since it would give them no route back on the return journey. No, he concludes, they must have used bridges. It is not plausible to claim that the Nile floods are caused by snow melting, since the river flows from hotter climates in the south. Every explanation must be "plausible" (*oikos*), which is to say in keeping with what we know about the way the world works.[10]

Herodotus's conception of divinity is also pre-Socratic. Scholars have argued fiercely over whether his references to the gods are just window dressing for what is basically a rational historiography or whether they are expressions of a traditional piety undislodged by his modernist commitment to naturalistic explanation. Both positions are wrong; each rests too heavily on an anachronistic science/religion distinction. The point is rather that like Anaximander, Anaximenes, and Xenophanes, Herodotus typically uses "god" not as a religious category—as an anthropoid being or as an object of cult—but as an extension of his rationalistic system, as a figurative way of expressing the hidden coherence of things. Certainly, he is captivated by religion in all its forms: his kaleidoscopic portrait of cultural differences reveals the huge variety of types of cult practice and conceptions of the divine, from Babylonian sacred prostitution through Egyptian worship of the Apis bull to Scythian horse sacrifice. He does suggest that individual gods are capable of acting in the world: on a number of occasions, violations of the sanctity of a temple are swiftly followed by punishment. When Herodotus reflects in his own voice about the forces that steer human fortune, however, he refers to the supernatural primarily in abstract terms as "the god" or "the divine" (*to theion*). This divine principle exists in order to regulate the moral symmetry of the world: to make sure that there is retribution for wrongdoing (sometimes several generations later) and that the fortunes of individuals and communities both wax and wane. Communicating only through ambiguous oracles that humans struggle to decode, the divinity oversees what Herodotus calls *tisis* (payback), the reciprocity that underlies everything. Herodotus sees history writing as an exercise in exposing the moral patterning of political history by setting out over a long chronology the pendulum swings of human fortune (for "human prosperity never holds still in the same place," as he says). As in the pre-Socratic cosmologies, then, "god" in this sense means not the god of religion but an abstract, underlying system that the author claims to disclose thanks to his painstaking research. God is the moral logic that holds the historical cosmos together.[11]

If Herodotus is the historical equivalent of an Anaximander or Xenophanes, equating divinity with the rational ordering of his world, then his great successor Thucydides's counterpart would be the god-free Hippo of Samos. Thucydides was a wealthy Athenian who recorded the turbulent, protracted war between Athens and Sparta that engulfed most of Greece from 431 BC until the final Spartan victory in 404 BC. Unlike his predecessor, Thucydides witnessed the war he described at first hand, having served as a general (albeit not a particularly successful one). If Herodotus describes a world full of wonders, then Thucydides exhibits a cynical verisimilitude. There is no room in his system for divine intervention or moral patterning in human fortunes. Great swings in fortune do occur, as when Athens lurches from a period of great prosperity under Pericles to a disastrous plague that decimates the population (in 430 BC). But there is no rationalization of this change in terms of cosmic principles, no Herodotean reflection that "the god gives a taste of the sweet life but then proves himself jealous in this matter." For Thucydides, there is no explanation at all: it is just cruelly ironic.[12]

According to his ancient biographer, Thucydides studied philosophy with the pre-Socratic materialist Anaxagoras and "as a result was whispered to be an atheist." Some modern scholars have agreed with the latter assessment. We will of course never know about the personal beliefs of the historical Thucydides who wrote the words, but his *History of the Peloponnesian War* certainly testifies to a striking vision of human action that is entirely free from divine intervention. This is a significant moment in intellectual history: the gods are no longer the motors of human action, even metaphorically.[13]

Religious beliefs and practices, certainly, are attributed to all parties, but never with any meaningful issue. Contrariwise, there are a number of points where they are associated with delusion or manipulation. This is most obvious in his handling of oracles (which had been so central to Herodotus's sense of the divine). In the aftermath of the plague, the Athenians call to mind an oracle predicting "Doric [i.e., Spartan] war and plague [*loimos*]," which the older citizens alleged to have been sung of old. (Thucydides's use of the word "allege," *phaskein,* suggests that he is doubtful that there was any oracle at all—but that is beside our current point.) The problem, however, is that the word *loimos* sounds very much like *limos* (famine), and a dispute arises as to what the oracle had actually foretold. On this occasion, Thucydides says, *loimos* won out: since a plague is what had actually occurred, "they adjusted their memory accordingly." But, he speculates, if another Doric war arises and this time famine (*limos*) occurs, "they will probably recite the verses in the other way." Oracles in Thucydides reveal not the gods' plan for the world but humanity's capacity to fool itself that the arbitrary processes of fortune are somehow predestined.[14]

Thucydides's story of the disastrous unfurling of the Peloponnesian War centers not on divine laws governing the cosmos but on "human nature," *to anthrōpinon*. And this nature, in his construction, is dark and brutal. One of his most engagingly repellent characters is Cleon, the popular leader; the Greek word is *dēmagōgos* (the modern idea of the demagogue is largely rooted in Thucydides's portrayal of him). Cleon began his rise to power in the 420s, after the death of Pericles and during the first phase of the war with Sparta. At this point, the financial contribution of the Athenian allies was indispensable to the war effort. So when, in 428 BC, the city of Mytilene on the island of Lesbos attempted to revolt from the league and side with Sparta, there was much consternation at Athens. Cleon fulminated that an example must be made of the Mytileneans, for "a human being naturally treats with contempt one who treats him well, and admires him who is unyielding." This is a bully's charter in the guise of a statement about human nature. In any event, Cleon is narrowly overruled and the Mytileneans are spared, but the whole event has the air of a grim farce: the Athenians have already sent one ship with orders to slaughter the entire population of Mytilene, and the ship carrying the revised orders arrives only just in time. If there is a message here about human nature, it is that it is weak, indecisive, violent, and corruptible.[15]

Thucydides's history is full of such moments of bleak irony. In a replay of the Mytilene debacle, the Athenians found themselves in 416–415 BC debating whether to slaughter the adult male population of the neutral island of Melos, which lies off the southeastern coast of Greece. Thucydides states a set-piece debate between Melian and Athenian representatives. The Melians invoke divine justice: we know you are more powerful, they say, but "we have every confidence that the gods will arrange an outcome that will not see us defeated, since we are innocent and we stand against unjust men." The Athenians have no time for this pietistic argumentation. Divine favor will in fact be on their side, they reckon, since "we follow the belief that divinity and humanity alike are subject in all things to one law of nature: where you have the power to do so, you dominate." This "law" is not a regular feature of Greek religious thought: the Athenians have simply given a religious coloring to a principle that supports their own position. They proceed to massacre the menfolk of Melos and enslave the women and children.[16]

The *History* culminates with the grandest folly of all. Thucydides never reaches the end of the war, which came in 404 BC: he may have died first. At any rate, his work finishes—famously, midsentence, as if he died at his desk, pen in hand—in 411 BC. Whether the ending is of Thucydides's design or not, however, the story of an Athenian expedition to Sicily that occupies books 6 and 7 (out of 8) makes a fitting climax. In the 410s the Athenians were desperately straitened by the war effort, and badly needed new resources. Between 415 and 413 BC they mounted a campaign against the legendarily wealthy island of Sicily, long home to Greek-speaking colonies. Despite early successes, it ended in disaster. Thucydides gives a heartrending account of the bedraggled retreat of the Athenian forces, their subsequent massacre by better equipped and fed forces from the Sicilian city of Syracuse, and their enslavement. Some seven thousand survivors, he estimates, ended up working the stone quarries of Syracuse. "There were many of them, crowded together in a narrow pit where, since there was no roof over their heads, they suffered first from the heat of the sun and the closeness of the air—and then, when the cold autumn nights drew in, the change in temperature brought disease among them . . . There were bodies piled on top of each other of those who had died from their wounds or from the change of temperature or other such causes, so that the smell was intolerable. At the same time they suffered from hunger and thirst: for eight months, the allowance for each man was half a pint of water per day, and a pint of corn." How far the mighty Athenians had fallen into shame and indignity: the Sicilian expedition was "the greatest action that we know of in Greek history: to the victors the most brilliant of victories, to the vanquished the most disastrous of defeats."[17]

When in 415 BC the Athenians debated whether or not to go to Sicily, there were two main protagonists. On the one side was the charismatic, exuberant young Alcibiades, who saw an opportunity for brilliant military success and fancied himself as the general who could deliver it. On the other side was the cautious Nicias, whose instincts were generally pacific (he had in fact already negotiated a short-term peace settlement with the Spartans in 421 BC). Alcibiades won the debate by promising the Athenians the earth, but—another grim irony—the reluctant Nicias was mandated to lead the troops; Alcibiades accompanied him but once in Sicily was swiftly recalled. In Thucydides's portrait, Nicias is a judicious, moral, and well-meaning man—"least of the Greeks of my time did he deserve to come to so miserable an end" as he did, executed by the Syracusans—but also vacillating and superstitious.[18]

In particular, Nicias prevaricated at a crucial moment because of religious scruples. In 413 BC the Spartans came to the aid of the Syracusans, and that tipped the balance against Athens. The Athenian forces, beset by sickness, decided to sail away from the camp secretly. On the decisive evening, however, there was a lunar eclipse. Nicias, who was (Thucydides tells us) "overly susceptible to religiosity [*theiasmos*] and that kind of thing," delayed the escape by twenty-seven days. The Syracusans had no such scruples and turned the screw on the ailing Athenian force. Eclipses, of course, were exactly the sort of natural phenomena that Greek intellectuals had been busily explaining in accordance with physical laws for the past 150 years. Nicias's piety is seriously misdirected—and disastrous.[19]

Questions of religion overshadow Thucydides's entire account of the Sicilian Expedition. Athenian houses and temples had outside them herms, statues made from rectangular blocks of stone with a head at the top, sometimes adorned with male genitals. One night before the expedition, most of these had their faces mysteriously damaged—by whom, no one knew. "The whole business," Thucydides writes, "was taken very seriously, as it was regarded as an omen for the expedition." This looks at first sight like a Herodotean divine sign, and indeed in terms of the unfurling of his story it does serve as a cautionary note. But Thucydides is in fact completely uninterested in this popular tittle-tattle. His attention is focused upon the political use made of the scandal. Some, he writes, took the mutilation "as evidence of a revolutionary plot to overthrow the democracy." A witch hunt began, and it was alleged that Alcibiades, who was supposed to be leading the Sicilian expedition, had been one of a number of young men who had drunkenly defaced herms at an earlier stage and had parodied the Eleusinian Mysteries. (That is why he was later recalled from Sicily and stripped of his command.) Thucydides notes wryly that Alcibiades's shrillest accusers were those who most envied his influence with the people, and those who most desired to replace him. The contrast with Herodotus could not be stronger: mysterious omens are treated not as signs of divine prognostication but as opportunities for cynical human manipulation.[20]

Thucydides's *History of the Peloponnesian War* is the culmination of the fifth-century tendency toward the exclusion of divine explanation. Not only does he refuse to admit non-naturalistic causality, but he cynically skewers any attempts on the part of the actors in his story to invoke the gods. Whatever his own personal beliefs were, the *History* can reasonably be claimed to be the earliest surviving atheist narrative of human history.

6

"Concerning the Gods, I Cannot Know"

C oncerning the gods, I cannot know whether they exist or whether they do not, or what form they have, for there are many impediments to knowledge, including obscurity and the brevity of human life." Such was the explosive start to Protagoras's *On the Gods*. The second part of the claim—the idea that the form of the gods might be unknowable to humans—was uncontroversial. Even in Homer, the gods adopt human shape and voice to appear among mortals; what they are like on Olympus is unknown. Protagoras, however, said that he could not be sure that the gods existed at all. That was an extraordinary claim.

Protagoras was the star intellectual of his day. Born in the early fifth century BC in Thracian Abdera, he won the admiration of Pericles, who entrusted him with creating a legal code for Thurii in southern Italy, a newly founded colony (whose founding members included a young Herodotus). He visited Athens for a period in the 430s and became the elder statesman of the sophists (*sophistai,* "specialists in wisdom"), the experimental intellectuals gathering around Pericles in Athens. The sophists made their money teaching the children of rich young Athenians. They placed a heavy emphasis on rhetoric, for in a democratic city the only way that the elite could exert direct political influence was by being more persuasive. But they also expounded on a wide range of issues, from morality through the interpretation of Homer and linguistic theory to the origins of human civilization. The sophistic movement was, ultimately, responsible for expanding the compass of philosophical enquiry, so that it now included not just cosmology and theology but also the more human spheres of ethics, logic, epistemology, and aesthetics.[1]

Plato's dialogue *Protagoras,* although written some forty years after the death of its subject, paints a vivid picture of the febrile excitement surrounding one of his return visits to Athens in the late 420s:[2]

> Last night, or rather very early this morning, Hippocrates, the son of Apollodorus and the brother of Phason, gave a tremendous thump with his staff at my door; someone opened to him, and he came rushing in and cried out: "Socrates, are you awake or asleep?" I knew his voice, and said: "Hippocrates, is that you? And do you bring any news?" "Good news," he said, "nothing but good." "Delightful," I said, "but what is the news? And why have you come here at this unearthly hour?" He drew nearer to me and said: "Protagoras has come!" "Yes," I replied, "he came two days ago: have you only just heard of his arrival?" "Yes, by the gods," he said, "only yesterday evening."[3]

This passage captures the knuckle-whitening anticipation of a superstar's arrival in town, the swiftness of the news grapevine, the competition between fans to be more in the know. Protagoras is, it turns out, lodging at the house of Callias, one of the wealthiest men in Athens. With some difficulty, Socrates and Hippocrates gain admission to Callias's house, where the cream of Athenian intellectual life is assembled: among them Pericles's son Xanthippus and the sophist Hippias of Elis. Prodicus of Ceos is snoozing in a pile of sheepskins. Also present are the physician Eryximachus, the tragic poet Agathon, and the impossibly charismatic (but also impossibly fickle) politician Alcibiades, three figures who also feature in Plato's *Symposium*. Even Critias is there, at this stage a young poet and intellectual and not yet the vicious leader of the Thirty Tyrants who grabbed power after the Spartan defeat of Athens. A more stellar cast could hardly be imagined. When Protagoras came to town, all of the gilded youth wanted to know.

"Concerning the gods, I cannot know whether they exist or whether they do not, or what form they have . . ." We only have the opening sentence of *On the Gods,* but there are hints elsewhere that may help us to reconstruct Protagoras's argument. This cannot have been a simple statement of agnosticism. According to his philosophical principles, if the gods cannot be known, they have no real existence. "When things are real," he said elsewhere, "their being is equivalent to their appearance." This sounds rather mystifying in English, but in Greek it is clearer. If something "appears," it appears *to someone*: it is perceived by her. In other words, things can only exist when they are perceived to exist. Trees that fall in deserted forests make no sound. It follows, then, that gods that cannot be perceived do not exist.[4]

Protagoras's claim that being is equivalent to appearance is part of a wider argument about relativism. Relativism is the theory that there are no universal truths: every society, every community, indeed every individual has a different conception of what is the case. A brief digression on Protagoras's theory of relativism will help us fill out his ideas about the gods. In the passage immediately following the claim that being is equivalent to appearing, Protagoras proceeds to discuss a series of cases where the truth of the matter is, as he puts it, "nonevident" (*adēlon*). The first is a simple one. If I am sitting down, you can only determine that that is the case if you are in the same room as I am. It is only "evident" for those who can witness it. The second case is that of the moon: it is only evident when you can actually see it. This is a more complex issue, since in a world before telescopes (and without awareness of different hemispheres) it was not self-evident that the moon exists when it cannot be seen. Protagoras was quite right to caution his contemporaries against the automatic assumption that things that are not visible continue to exist. His final example is of a different kind. Honey, he says, may taste sweet to one person but bitter to another (if that person has a fever, for example). The sweetness, then, is not an intrinsic property of the honey itself; rather, it is the judgment of the person tasting it. This is a different kind of "appearing": the "nonevident" issue here is not whether the honey exists, but what properties it has. Each of the three cases, however, is alike in that it puts the emphasis upon the subjectivity of truth. The fact that Protagoras is sitting down, the existence of the moon, and the sweetness of honey are true only for the individuals to whom these things appear to be the case.

What does this have to do with *On the Gods*? The one surviving sentence suggests that what Protagoras was centrally interested in were the questions "How can you know whether the gods exist?" and "How can you know what form they have?" The first of these corresponds to the sitting Protagoras and the moon. If you cannot see the moon (or the sitting Protagoras) you have no evidence that it exists. It is "nonevident." Similarly, if you cannot see the gods, they are "nonevident" to you. The second question of On the Gods, concerning what they look like, corresponds to the sweetness of honey. If we agree (for the sake of argument) that gods exist, then the next problem we are faced with is the fact that different cultures imagine them in different ways. Xenophanes had already observed that "Africans say that their gods are snub-nosed and black, Thracians blue-eyed and red-haired." If Protagoras knew Herodotus, either from their days in Thurii or from Athens, he may well have heard also of Egyptian animal gods, and of the multifarious deities of the Babylonians, Syrians, Iranians, and Scythians. The gods are perceived differently by different peoples—just as the taste of honey varies depending on the taster. It is likely, I think, that On the Gods argued on the basis of the variety of religions across the known world that there is no universal truth about the nature of the gods. Their nature is "nonevident": there is no stronger reason to believe, like the Thracians, that they have red hair than to agree with the Ethiopians that they are black-skinned.[5]

This is a powerful argument, and a radical one. Later generations would claim that the Athenians exiled him for On the Gods and publicly burned his books. If this report is true, it underlines Athens's schizophrenic attitude toward its intellectuals. If it is not true, it is even so evidence that he gained a reputation for atheism in later years. Modern scholars, with their penchant for painting the Greeks as pious, have sometimes claimed that Protagoras's real aim was not to deny the existence of gods but to shift the focus onto the celebration of religion as a human social practice: "His agnostic sentence at the opening of On the Gods," one critic has written, "created the space for an anthropocentric, humanistic religion that knows—not the gods but the good things the gods bring." But the evidence for this is slim, and the unwarranted language of divine beneficence ("the good things the gods bring") reveals the author's own theistic agenda. It is true that Plato's Protagoras portrays its subject speculating about early human civilizations in a way that suggests that gods do exist: "Man, having a share of the divine attributes, was at first the only one of the animals who had any gods, because he alone was of their kind; and he used to raise altars and images of them." If this is genuine Protagoras, then not only could he talk about gods as really existing but he also thought that humans worship them because they have a natural, built-in propensity to do so. But in fact there is no reason to assume that Plato—who was about five years old at the time that the visit of Protagoras he is describing took place—is recording the myth verbatim. The reference to the gods is a fleeting one and irrelevant to the main point being argued (which is that virtue can be taught). It is highly likely to be a Platonic curlicue rather than part of any authentically Protagorean doctrine. *On the Gods* was almost certainly (as its opening sentence suggests) a discourse attacking the assumption that gods have an objective existence, as opposed to a celebration of humans' subjective experience of them.[6]

There were, however, those who took an interest in the anthropology of religion—and did so to devastating effect. Among the Athenian intelligentsia awaiting Protagoras's lecture in Plato's vignette, curled up in the sheepskins, was Prodicus of Ceos. Prodicus was another sophist with a reputation in antiquity for atheism. Until the 1970s it had been hard to explain what had won him this fame, but then came a re-edited version of a book called *On Piety* by the first-century BC philosopher Philodemus. *On Piety* was not transmitted via the conventional route for classical texts, namely manual recopying in the Middle Ages: it was among the ancient books recovered from the so-called Villa of the Papyri in the town of Herculaneum in the Bay of Naples. Like all 1,800 or so of the Herculaneum scrolls, it had been carbonized and buried by the pyroclastic flow from the eruption of Vesuvius in AD 79. Further damage had been done by early attempts to unroll the scrolls: the outer layers had been destroyed in order to access the inner parts of the sheet. In the case of the first book of *On Piety*, the scroll had also been cut in two, and the halves had been catalogued separately, and later generations had been unaware that the two belonged together. To make matters worse, several fragments, and all the early drawings, had been spirited away from Italy to Oxford. The reunited and reconstructed text, which was published in 1996 by Dirk Obbink, is one of the great achievements of modern classical scholarship.[7]

It is, however, book 2 of *On Piety,* which is still not fully published, that shows there were at least two fifth-century thinkers who attacked religion as a construct of human society. One was Democritus (ca. 460–380 BC), the pre-Socratic philosopher of atoms and void. His interests, however, were extraordinarily broad and extended into the anthropology of religion. Democritus, we can now be sure, argued that humans originally lived like animals; they then formed communities to prevent attacks from other beasts; that led to communication and language; then clothing and agriculture; then shelter and fire. Civilization, this theory proposes, developed as a result of human ingenuity in response to dire need. What is more, religion was (Democritus argued) part of this civilizing process. Early humans noted the turning of the seasons; "Quite reasonably, therefore," says Philodemus (paraphrasing Democritus), "they also posited an agent behind these occurrences, and worshipped it." The logical conclusion to draw from these observations is that conventional religion is based on error: early humans simply misunderstood phenomena that should be explained through scientific materialism. What is more, since civilization has now moved on, we no longer need these primitive modes of explanation.[8]

The second person who saw religion as a product of human culture was Prodicus himself (ca. 460–390 BC). Like Democritus, he wrote on a huge range of subjects, including linguistics, ethics, and cosmology (this is an appropriate moment to recall that the distinction between pre-Socratic philosophers and sophists was not hard and fast). Again as with Democritus, none of his original texts survive, so we depend on reconstructions from other sources. The Philodemus papyrus is indispensable. The relevant passage (which, unfortunately, is fragmentary) reads:

[. . .] says that the gods of popular belief do not exist, nor do they have knowledge, and that the ancients in admiration [. . .] the fruits of the earth, and absolutely everything that is useful for life.[9]

Prodicus is not named in the gappy papyrus, but it must be him: there are plenty of other indications that he was associated with the belief that early humans attributed divinity to aspects of nature that benefited humanity (whereas Democritus included harmful aspects too). Prodicus's book on the subject was probably called *The Seasons* and seems to have tied the emergence of religion closely to the development of farming (perhaps with a nod to Hesiod, the poet-farmer who was so instrumental in the creation of Greek theology). What is significant about the Philodemus passage is that it couples this "anthropological" reading of early religion with a strongly atheist argument: "The gods of popular belief do not exist, nor do they have knowledge." It looks, indeed, as if he imagined a two-stage process. First, these primitives deified the four elements (earth, fire, water, air) and the sun and the moon. A second stage of deification came with the working of the land: they treated as gods those who discovered certain nourishing foodstuffs, so that the inventor of wine was worshipped as Dionysus, that of bread as Demeter, those of shipping as Castor and Pollux. One additional point to emphasize is that Prodicus was (we know from other sources) interested in the creative use of etymology, the study of the origins of words. In a separate part of Philodemus, Prodicus is included among those who "change the letters of" (*paragrammizousi*) the names of the gods. It is likely, I think, that among these letter changes was the derivation of "Hera" (in Greek Ēra) from "air" (*aēr*), which is attested in later sources. Prodicus's pantheon, therefore, may have looked something like this:[10]

Zeus = ? the heavens?
Hera = air
Poseidon = water
Hephaestus = fire
Gaia = earth
Demeter = the inventor of crops, agriculture, bread
Dionysus = the inventor of wine
Castor and Pollux = the inventors of shipping

Whether he completed the list, and how far down the Greeks' long list of divinities he proceeded, we shall probably never know. The important point is that, like Democritus, he saw religion as the invention of early humanity as it emerged from a state of nature, and therefore not as integral to humanity but as a cultural invention. Now, the Philodemus passage specifies that "the gods *of popular belief* do not exist," which might be taken to mean that Prodicus thought that there were indeed true gods—just not those of myth and cult. Yet the choice of translation matters greatly: an alternative would be "all those considered as gods by humans," i.e., in effect, "the so-called gods do not exist." On balance, it seems to me likely that Prodicus was an out-and-out atheist, denying the existence of any gods, given that he was always associated in antiquity with the complete denial of divinity.[11]

How far such heretical ideas percolated beyond a narrow circle of wealthy intellectuals into popular culture is hard to tell, but there is some indication that they found their way into the popular theater. In Athens, drama was mass entertainment. Plays were composed in huge numbers throughout the fifth and fourth centuries BC and performed onstage before thousands of people. By chance, one dramatic speech—again it is, frustratingly, now a fragment without its wider context—survives that shows how a full version of the kind of argument made by Democritus of Prodicus might have played out, and how it might have been received in popular culture. It was rescued from oblivion by later philosophers interested in the development of atheist thought. Its authorship is unclear: one ancient source says it is by the tragedian Euripides, while others give it to Critias. Critias is probably the better candidate, since it is likelier that a dramatic fragment should have been wrongly attributed to a famous dramatist than to someone who is not otherwise known to have written plays. Critias was famous for two things: being the ringleader of the Thirty Tyrants in the bloodthirsty coup that followed Sparta's victory over Athens in 404 BC, and being Plato's uncle. The latter is more important for the purposes of this text. He was one of those who (in Plato's description) gathered at Callias's house to greet Protagoras, a member of the hyperintellectual inner circle, and well placed to transmit cutting-edge ideas.

The speaker is the mythological character Sisyphus. That in itself is very interesting. Sisyphus was one of the sons of Aeolus and so belonged to the second generation of that mythical family (including Salmoneus, Alcyone, and Bellerophon) that seemed to have theomachy running through its veins. In the Hesiodic *Catalogue,* Aeolus's family seem always to be trying to deny the privilege of the gods or claim it for humans. In this fragment, however, Sisyphus's atheism takes the form of a sophistic account of the origins of religion:[12]

There was a time when humans' life was unordered,
Bestial and subservient to violence;

When there was no reward for the noble
Or chastisement for the base.
And then, it seems to me, humans set up
Laws, so that justice should be tyrant
And hold aggression enslaved.
Anyone who erred was punished.
Then, when laws prevented them
From performing *open* acts of force,
They started performing them in secret; and then, it seems to me,
Some shrewd man, wise in his counsel,
Discovered for mortals fear of the gods, so that
The base should have fear, if even in secret
They should do or say or think anything.
So he thereupon introduced religion,
Namely the idea that there is a deity flourishing with immortal
    life,
Hearing in his mind, seeing, thinking,
Attending to these things and having a divine nature,
Who will hear everything said among mortals,
And will be able to see everything that is done.
If you plan some base act in silence,
The gods will not fail to notice.

If anything, in fact, this is a more radical critique than those of Democritus and Prodicus. Those two saw religion as a bottom-up process, driven by early humanity's desire to master a natural world that they barely understood. For them, religion begins as a cognitive process and only then becomes institutionalized. To Critias's Sisyphus, however, it is from the very start a process of social control. There is no romanticization of the primitive here. Religion is the creation of a "shrewd man," who sought nothing more than the imposition of order on a naïve people. Sisyphus describes a two-stage process to curtail wrongdoing: first law is introduced, and then when that fails to prevent secret criminality, religion. The French philosopher Michel Foucault argues in *Discipline and Punish,* his history of the modern penal system, that eighteenth-century Europe saw a shift from the chastisement of criminal acts to a new focus on controlling the person. He takes as paradigmatic of this shift Jeremy

Bentham's design for a prison called the Panopticon, in which prisoners are visible to guards at all times but never know whether or not they are being observed. On Sisyphus's account, a similar shift occurred with the invention of religion: the wise man concocts "the idea that there is a deity . . . / Who will hear everything said among mortals, / And will be able to see everything that is done." After the invention of religion, Sisyphus says, society is no longer restricted to punishing public manifestations of disorder; it can now convince its citizens that their innermost thoughts are subject to moral evaluation. The world has become a kind of religious Panopticon.[13]

After the passage quoted above, Sisyphus goes on to play with Democritus's ideas about primitive humanity's fear of the natural elements. The shrewd inventor of religion, Sisyphus proclaims, "said that the gods dwell in that place where / They would most terrify humans, / From whence he knew mortals' terrors come, / And the benefits for their miserable lives." He located the gods in the heavens, in other words. Democritus had claimed that primitive people spontaneously associated the gods with the natural features of the cosmos that are most terrifying or beneficial; Sisyphus by contrast thinks this belief was imposed on them from above. Religion is a fiction enforced from above in an attempt to secure social order.

What happened next in the play? Given that all that survives is this fragment, we can only guess, but the guess is an educated one. Whenever he appears in myth, Sisyphus is associated with crimes against the gods. Every visitor to the ancient theater would have known, moreover, that when Homer's Odysseus visits the underworld, he sees Sisyphus heaving that famous rock up the hill. However the story was tweaked, his destiny was surely to be punished horribly. This certainly puts a different complexion on his theory of religion: in Critias's play, it is highly likely that it was precisely for his intellectual theomachy that he was chastised. But at the same time as viewers were encouraged to revel in the defeat of the atheist, they were surely encouraged to applaud this spectacular display of intellectual showmanship, deliciously marinated in the rich flavors of contemporary sophistry. Sisyphus may have been the villain of the piece, but like Milton's Satan he surely got the best lines.[14]

7

Playing the Gods

Imagine the theater of Dionysus in Athens, during the springtime festival of the Great Dionysia. Imagine not the warm, hushed gloom of an evening inside, alongside five hundred middle-class peers in frocks and suits, but a noisy, rambunctious crowd of more than ten thousand making merry under the harsh, unforgiving sun of Athens. The audience is seated not in serried rows, their gaze funneled toward the only source of light; they are spread out on wooden benches across an immense horseshoe-like arc on the slopes of the Acropolis, their gaze drawn as much to the city in front of them and to their fellow audience members as to the stage. Sometimes they are chatting, snacking, laughing; at other times they are deathly silent, riveted by the action. The audience is here not because they have chosen to spend their leisure time at the theater—the idea of "leisure time" does not really exist in a world without nine-to-fives and weekends—but because the entire city is summoned to annual festivals. This is not a celebration of elite privilege, a time for chiffon and tuxedos, but an event in popular culture. There are exclusions, for sure. If women are present, their numbers are small. Of the city's 100,000 or so slaves (around 40 percent of the total population), few are likely to be present. Even free men without citizenship—the so-called metics—may not have had an automatic right to attend. But despite these restrictions, Athenian drama is an inclusive, diverse experience, with a carnival-like atmosphere.

The Great Dionysia, Athens's major theatrical festival, lasted five days. Three of these days were each given over to four plays by a single poet: three tragedies, followed by a satyr play (a jokey drama featuring actors dressed as satyrs). One more was probably devoted to poetic performances known as dithyrambs and one to various comedies. For tragedy and comedy there was a competition, judged by individuals randomly chosen from the tribes of Athens. The results were inscribed on stone; in a number of cases, these inscriptions survive.

The origins of ancient theater are uncertain. Corinthian pottery from 630 BC onward shows padded dancers, which may suggest some kind of early ritual performance in costume in honor of Dionysus. All that can be said for sure, however, is that dramatic festivals began to appear in the late sixth century BC in Athens and elsewhere, and that the Athenian variety came to be an iconic expression of democratic identity in the fifth. The interplay between the chorus, an anonymous collective body, and the named actors neatly encapsulated the dynamics of a society that was constantly anxious about the relationship between individual and community, and between elite and mass. Tragedies, moreover, typically focused on mythological characters from the heroic past and afforded the Athenians an opportunity to think about the continuities and discontinuities between the age of aristocratic dominance and the democratic present. Comedy, meanwhile, was all about the contemporary world and explored the spectators' immediate concerns in a playful idiom. A vibrant, successful, cosmopolitan city like Athens needed mass media to hold it together, to supply a shared narrative for its diverse population. Theater gave this imagined community a sense of cohesion and solidarity.[1]

There is another major difference between ancient and modern theater. The Great Dionysia was above all a religious event, a public holiday devoted to the god Dionysus that was formally marked on the civic calendar. The theater complex was also dedicated to Dionysus, who had a temple nearby. The festivities were inaugurated with blood sacrifices. But if the context was religious, the plays themselves were not liturgical. They were written for the occasion by playwrights who had no special religious role. Their primary purpose in putting on these plays was competitive: they sought to win the first prize in the most prestigious literary festival in Greece. There is no mention in the ancient inscriptions of plays redounding to the glory of Dionysus; what counted in the competition was skill in composition.

Nevertheless, many modern commentators continue to insist that Greek drama was fundamentally religious. The fault lies in part with

Aristotle, and his claim in the *Poetics* that tragedy derived from dithy-ramb (a type of hymn sung to Dionysus) and poetry connected with satyrs, and comedy from songs accompanying phallic processions. The phrasing is a bit obscure, but it can be taken to suggest that the earliest forms of what we would now call tragedy and comedy were in fact ritual in nature, cult songs to Dionysus. In the nineteenth and early twenti-eth centuries, elaborate structures were built around this claim: follow-ing the prevailing romantic view of Greek culture at the time, scholars sought to derive tragedy and comedy from some kind of primal moment when Greek literature and religion were tightly interwoven. The Greek word for "tragedy" is *tragōidia*, which seems to suggest a song (*oidē*) for a goat (*tragos*). In fact it is entirely unclear what tragedy had to do with goats, but the romantic-influenced scholars of the nineteenth and early twentieth centuries assumed that tragedy had been originally connected either to goat sacrifice or to dancing choruses of people dressed ritually as goats. This is all fantasy. Even Aristotle's talk of satyr plays and phal-lic songs is likely to have been guesswork: he probably had no historical sources to draw on. Aristotle knew no more than we do about the real origins. And in any case, even if tragedy was *originally* connected to ritual in this way, that tells us nothing about its social role in the fifth century BC.[2]

Tragedy in particular has been assumed to be essentially religious also on the basis of its content. Many of the plays have religious themes or feature gods. Many of the plays are of a formulaic "transgression and punishment" type: mortals overreach themselves and are knocked down by jealous deities, who are keen to assert their position of authority. So—goes this line of thinking—the plays project a religiously conservative ethos, encouraging viewers to accept their authority. (This is less true of comedy, which can satirize not just religion but even the gods: in Aris-tophanes's *Frogs*, for example, Dionysus, the god of the theater itself, is portrayed as a bumbling, timorous fool.) In tragedy, going against the gods is always a bad thing to do and inevitably leads to disaster, whether we think of Oedipus's believing that he has dodged Apollo's prophecy, Hippolytus's offending of Aphrodite by renouncing sex, or Pentheus's refusing to accept the cult of the new god Dionysus. Yet even these cases cannot prove that tragic drama was primarily a religious form. For a start, the gods of tragedy are not straightforwardly the gods worshipped in the city of Athens. In Greek polytheism, religious ritual is always localized: you pray not to Athena as an abstract deity but as her specific manifestation in your local sanctuary. The gods of tragedy are not the cult deities of Athens but the literary figures portrayed in the mythological poems of Homer and Hesiod. Even more troubling is the fact that, despite all the talk of divine justice, the gods of tragedy seem cruel, vindictive, and petty. Near the start of Euripides's *Trojan Women,* for example, Athena announces that now that Troy has been sacked brutally she will no longer support the Greeks; instead she wants to ruin their voyages home. "Why do you leap from mood to mood in this way?" asks her fellow god Poseidon. "Whether you hate or love someone, you hate or love too forcefully." In the same poet's *Hippolytus,* Aphrodite's decision to kill off the play's central figure simply for choosing to avoid sex seems selfish and severe, as does Artemis's promise at the end to take revenge for Hippolytus's death by killing one of Aphrodite's favorites. The gods of tragedy rarely embody the kind of benevolent justice that a pious moralist would want to attribute to them.[3]

Athenian drama could indeed be said to be "religious," but only in the sense that it was profoundly interested in questions about gods of the most contemporary, indeed challenging kinds. It was not just Critias, the author of the Sisyphus fragment, who reacted to the atheist revolution. Already, in the 420s, in the glow of the sophistic movement, tragedies and comedies began to explore the question of whether gods exist. The ideas canvassed by Protagoras, Democritus, and Prodicus reached a broad audience thanks to the theater.

Aristophanes's comedy *Knights,* his fourth play (produced in 424 BC) is a complex, allegorical satire on Aristophanes's nemesis, the politician Cleon, who is played as one of the slaves in the household of Demos ("People," or "State"). The play opens with two other slaves complaining about the new slave and engaging in some banter about how to evade him:

> SECOND SLAVE: The best option open to us is to go to some god's statue [*bretas*] and prostrate ourselves before it.
> FIRST SLAVE: What do you mean, statatatue [*bretetetas:* the

slave acts as if he cannot even pronounce the word]? Do you really believe in gods?

SECOND SLAVE: Of course.

FIRST SLAVE: What's your proof?

SECOND SLAVE: The fact that I'm cursed by them. Won't that do?

FIRST SLAVE: Well, it's good enough for me.[4]

It's a nice joke: being godforsaken is offered as evidence that the gods must exist. But it is more than a joke; it is also a comment on intellectual fashions. The second slave suggests that believing in gods is old-fashioned ("Do you really believe in gods?") and demands instead a *tekmērion,* "proof." The use of this particular word, which has a specialist ring to it, suggests that Aristophanes is having fun by giving a slave a bit of contemporary philosophical jargon.

Aristophanes certainly associated fashionable thinkers with disbelief in the gods. In 423 BC he unveiled *Clouds,* a satire on contemporary intellectuals. The title alluded at once to pre-Socratic speculation about the nature of the heavens and to the fluffiness (as he saw it) of their ideas. The play was unsuccessful, so he revised it; the version that survives was produced at some point between 420 and 417 BC. A satire on the new intellectual culture of Athens, it centers on a figure called Strepsiades ("Twister") who wants an easy way out of paying for the gambling debts racked up by his horse-mad son Phidippides ("Easy-on-the-Horses"). Hearing of a school of rhetoric run by Socrates that can teach pupils to make any argument seem overpowering, he signs up for it. In the course of the play he learns how to make the weaker argument seem stronger before defiantly rejecting all this nonsense and putting the school to the torch. Socrates—a distorted parody of the real philosopher—is portrayed as pretentious, vain, self-serving, and ethically dangerous. His disciples reject all forms of traditional morality, including belief in the Olympian gods ("You swear by Olympian Zeus! What idiocy; to think that someone of your age should still think that Zeus exists!"). The Clouds of the play's title are represented by the chorus: they are the goddesses worshipped by Socrates and his coterie. "They are the only true deities," proclaims Socrates, "all the rest are nonsense." "What?" replies Strepsiades. "By Earth! You don't count Olympian Zeus as a god?" "What do you mean, Zeus? Stop babbling: Zeus doesn't even exist!" Socrates goes on to argue his case using "evidence" (*sēmeia*)—presumably these are the kind of "proofs" for the existence of a god that the first slave in *Knights* was craving.[5]

Tragedy responded to the sophists in subtler ways, projecting the issues onto a mythical canvas, so that the connections with contemporary culture become suggestive rather than explicit. One of the greatest examples of Greek tragedy, Sophocles's *Oedipus the King,* is a case in point. The date is not certain, but 428 BC or so seems likely; this would place it precisely in the eye of the sophistic storm. Sophocles has often been thought to be the most religiously minded of the three major tragedians, but *Oedipus the King* paints a more complex, challenging picture than this. *Oedipus* is centrally about divine prophecy and humans' attempts to assert control over lives that have already been predestined. The young Oedipus was given a prophecy by the Delphic oracle that he would marry his mother and kill his father. He has left his hometown of Corinth to avoid fulfilling the oracle and resettled in Thebes, where he has become king and married Jocasta, the wife of the old king Laius. In the course of the play he discovers the truth: that he was actually born in Thebes to Jocasta and Laius; that they exposed him to die on the slopes of Mount Cithaeron, on hearing the same prophecy about his future; and that he was rescued and brought up in Corinth. He had killed his biological father Laius in a fight on the way into Thebes. So unbeknownst to everyone, Apollo's prediction has already come true: despite his best attempts to do otherwise he ended up both killing his father and marrying his mother. In his grief, he puts out his own eyes and totters off into exile.[6]

An Athenian spectator would have seen all sorts of parallels between the play and contemporary life. When the play opens, Thebes is being ravaged by plague (Apollo's vengeance for Oedipus's unwitting murder of his father). Athens too suffered terribly from a ghastly plague in the years between 430 and 426 BC, the result of Pericles's policy of confining the citizens behind the city walls while the Spartans, during these opening years of the war between the two states, laid waste to the fields outside. Viewers are likely to have seen an immediate, if indirect, connection between the two situations. And then Oedipus himself, who is

characterized as a rational intellectual, will surely have reminded viewers of Pericles, the general and unofficial leader of Athens, who died from
the same plague in 429 BC. Oedipus's claim to intellectual distinction
rests on his having freed Thebes from the curse of the Sphinx, having
solved her riddle using his intelligence alone. The hints seem unmissable:
in the myth, Thebes has a much-loved leader who prides himself on his
rational abilities, but whose overconfidence leads to his ruin; in Athens
too, the much-feted leader Pericles, proud of his links to contemporary
intellectuals but ultimately the cause of a terrible plague.

Pericles was also one of a circle of intellectuals who were linked in the
public imagination with atheism. Among these was Anaxagoras, who
had been impeached at some point in the 430s on the charge of "not
believing in the gods." The architect of the impeachment had been a seer
called Diopeithes. He, we are told, "brought in a bill providing for the
public impeachment of such as did not cultivate the gods, or who taught
doctrines regarding the heavens, directing suspicion at Pericles by means
of Anaxagoras." This lends a contemporary complexion to the scene in
Oedipus the King where Oedipus confronts the blind Tiresias, a seer who
uses the flight of birds to tell the future. It is Tiresias who first claims
that Oedipus himself is the murderer of Laius and the source of the pollution that is afflicting the land. Oedipus responds furiously, setting his
own intellectual achievement in solving the Sphinx's riddle against the
prophet's insights. "Tell me now," he sneers, "what makes you the lucid
prophet? Why, when the dog-bard [i.e., the Sphinx] was here, did you not
come up with some utterance that would deliver the citizens from their
fate? After all, the riddle was not a common-or-garden one: it called for
prophecy. But you came forth with no revelation derived from birds or
gods. I was the one who came along, 'know-nothing Oedipus': I stopped
her, using my native intelligence, not bird-lore." In other words, Oedipus
opposes rational human intelligence to divine mumbo-jumbo. Jocasta's
brother Creon, he thunders, must be aspiring to the throne and must
have paid this "mage, weaver of tricks, fraudulent vagabond priest" to
come up with prophecies against him. All of these insults involve exactly
the kind of charges that Sophocles's contemporaries would level at religious cranks. Calling him a "mage" (*magos*) associates him with the Persian magi; "fraudulent vagabond priest" links him to the priests of new

cults that were being introduced into Athens from abroad, worshipping the Phrygian Great Mother, Sabazios, and Bendis. Beyond this general assimilation of Tiresias with some of the outlandish religious practices current in Athens at the time, he also looks—from certain angles—oddly like Diopeithes himself. Both, notably, are seers associated with Apollo. And around the time that Sophocles's play was performed, Diopeithes was being pilloried by comic poets for his eccentric religious behavior, mocked as a "madman" and envisaged as performing undignified, ecstatic dances to drumbeats. Aristophanes sarcastically calls him "the great Diopeithes" and implies (just as Oedipus does for Tiresias) that he invented oracles to suit his own needs. The fit between Tiresias and Diopeithes is not exact, nor is that between Oedipus and Pericles/Anaxagoras, but ancient audiences would surely have seen enough common ground to realize that issues of contemporary import were being addressed in the play.[7]

Oedipus's attempts to evade the oracle have profound theological significance. To doubt the efficacy of prophecy is to doubt the gods' ability to predetermine the future. Later in the play, Oedipus's wife (and, it will transpire, mother) Jocasta believes that she and Oedipus have proven Apollo wrong by escaping the implications of the oracle. She comments, "As a result, I wouldn't look this way or that as far as prophecy is concerned, in the future." To be sure, she is not denying the existence of the gods as such. But there is no minimizing the force of her words: prophecy, she says, does not work. It should be ignored. This is a powerfully heretical position, in ancient terms.[8]

The antireligious theme reaches a climax in a song that the chorus subsequently sings, concluding with what must have seemed an even more shocking claim:

> No more shall I go in reverence to the untouchable
> Belly-button of the world,
> Nor to the temple at Abae,
> Nor to Olympia,
> If prophecies shall no longer be manifestly
> Fitting for all mortals.
> But, O Zeus the mighty, if you are properly so called,

Ruler of all, let not this pass you by,
You and that eternally immortal rule of yours.
The old prophecies concerning Laius are fading
And now men give them no value.
Nowhere is Apollo glorified with honours;
Religion is no more.[9]

This is extraordinary stuff. The major prophetic centers of Delphi, Abae, and Olympia are, the chorus say, to be avoided. This neglect will have consequences for the very authority of the king of the gods, who is addressed as "Zeus the mighty, *if you are properly so called,* ruler of all." Now, it is quite right to say, as commentators on this passage usually do, that there are parallels in regular prayers for expressions of uncertainty about the proper form of address to a deity. It is imperative, in Greek religion, to get the god's ritual name right. But the words of Sophocles's chorus are anything but formulaically banal. The ode poses a logical problem, in a precise and focused way: How can Zeus truly be called "mighty" if the gods have lost control of foreknowledge? Mistrust in oracles affects belief in the gods' power in general, not just in the prophetic centers. So the chorus concludes: religion—*ta theia*, "god stuff"—is no more. There is surely a sophistic argument lying behind this reasoning: If divine predictions do not come true, then the gods are not in control of the universe and what need is there to worship them? The very phrase *"ta theia"* would have sounded jarringly modern to an Athenian audience of the later fifth century BC: it is a word drawn from contemporary intellectual life, not from poetry. And we know from other sources that there were those who denied the truth of prophecy, from the pre-Socratic Xenophanes onward. A character in Euripides's *Helen* opines (in terms that recall Oedipus's attack on Tiresias) that "the words of the prophets are base and full of lies . . . naked intelligence and good advice are the best prophet." Sophocles's chorus is declaring itself convinced by such arguments, on the basis of what they have seen before their eyes.[10]

Oedipus the King is a play that seriously explores the idea of a world without divine determination. It pushes as hard as one could, within the confines of a religious festival, the idea that the will of the gods does not dictate our lives. Later on, Oedipus—still deceived by events—refers to himself as a "child of Fortune," meaning that he is illegitimate. But the word *tukhē*, "fortune," is another term that drips with materialist, anti-determinist, nondivine philosophy; it is associated particularly with the philosopher Democritus, who believed in a world governed by chance. Oedipus revels in this world of indeterminacy. When he discovers himself to be deliciously free from divine determination—indeed, as he thinks, a bastard child with no parental obligation at all—he is *thrilled*. It is one of the most moving parts of the play.[11]

But, of course, Oedipus is proven wrong and his joy revealed to be delusional. His attempts to explore alternative theologies are crushed without compunction by the traditional divine order. "I am *atheos*!" he cries: it will have taken the ancient spectators a few seconds to work out that he means it in the older sense, "abandoned by the gods," rather than the current "atheist." He still sees himself as disconnected from the divine sphere, but he now recognizes its power. The plot arc of most ancient tragedy is fundamentally conservative: it tends to reaffirm the status quo, to restore an ideology that was threatened, and in particular to put a divine seal on events at the end. It is, in that sense, geared up to validate the divine orthodoxy. But it would be a rather unadventurous reading of *Oedipus the King* that took it as a straightforward, pietistic validation of the power of the gods. In any work of literature, the jour-ney matters as much as the destination, and Oedipus's tour of a world without divine providence resonates deeply against the intellectual back-drop of the time. It would be better to see the conservative shape of the plot line as creating a safe space in which dangerous religious ideas can be experimented with without causing offense.[12]

It was, however, Sophocles's younger contemporary Euripides who was most closely associated with exploring the nature of atheism. In one of Aristophanes's comedies, in which he appears as a character, an old ribbon seller protests that she has been put out of business by his plays: "He has persuaded all the men that there aren't any gods." Two hundred years or so after his death, an Egyptian called Satyrus wrote a biography of him, which stated that he was prosecuted for impiety (*asebeia*) by the demagogue Cleon—"impiety" being the charge concocted by Diopeithes to attack Anaxagoras and subsequently used against Diagoras of Melos and Socrates. These claims count for little in historical terms: Aristophanes, obviously, was a satirist and given to two-dimensional caricatures, while Satyrus was probably going on scurrilous reports derived from his own plays rather than hard biographical facts. Unfortunately, these two pieces of evidence have prompted a rather sclerotic reaction from certain modern scholars, who have lined up with folded arms to assure their readers that Euripides was not really an atheist. Fundamentally, their argument rests on a very simple critical move. Just because he has his characters say things that seem to deny the power of the gods, they observe, does not mean that he himself believes these things. We should, they caution, look to see what ultimately happens to the people in his plays who deny the gods: this being tragedy, they usually end up dying horribly. Now, as a general point this is undeniable. But the attack is aimed at the wrong target. No scholar in the twenty-first century should be claiming anything as simplistic as "Euripides was an atheist." The age of biographical criticism is over: we cannot divine the author's views solely on the basis of what his characters say. Nor should we be thinking of these complex, provocative, but ultimately open-ended plays as vehicles for a single, simple message (whether that is "I believe in gods" or "I don't"). What matters is that of all the dramatists, Euripides has his characters deliver the most sophisticated attacks on traditional religion, using arguments that he surely mined from the rich seam of contemporary sophistic thought. Whether he was or was not personally an atheist, he was certainly captivated by atheistic ideas and rarely missed an opportunity to articulate them.[13]

Take, for example, the bizarre prayer that the Trojan queen Hecuba addresses to Zeus in extraordinary terms: "O vehicle of the earth and possessor of a seat on earth, whoever you are, most difficult to know, Zeus, whether you are the necessity of nature or the mind of men: I pray to you." This is like no ordinary prayer: it imports pre-Socratic language into a mythological setting in the distant past, in a way that seems deliberately anachronistic. One ancient commentator thought, no doubt correctly, that he could detect an allusion to the notorious arguments of Anaxagoras that the universe is built of matter and directed by a cosmic "mind." But it also reflects a genuine question about Anaxagoras's meaning: was his "mind" supposed to represent a natural energy, like the god of the Ionian pre-Socratics? Or was it simply the underlying structure of reality, which discloses itself to human rational thought?[14]

In *The Madness of Heracles,* produced probably toward the end of Euripides's life (he died in 406 BC), the focus shifts onto the moral critique of religion. The play falls into four phases. In the first, Heracles's family—his adoptive father Amphitryon, his wife Megara, and his children—are being persecuted by the wicked Theban king Lycus while he is away on his labors. When he announces that he will kill them the second phase begins: Heracles returns just in time to slay Lycus and his agents. The third phase is all about the vengeance of the goddess Hera, who is jealous of Heracles since his biological father is her husband Zeus. She sends Lyssa (the personification of insanity) and Iris (the messenger goddess) to drive him mad; he promptly kills his own children, thinking they are his enemies. Finally, he awakens from his madness and though grief-stricken is persuaded by Amphitryon and Theseus to live on and to move to Athens. The play gives plenty of opportunities for reproaching the gods for their injustice. First of all, Amphitryon berates Zeus for not looking after his son Heracles properly: "I am only a mortal," he says, "but I outdo you in virtue, though you are a great god . . . You are a stupid kind of god, or by nature you are unjust." The fact that Zeus's son Heracles, of all people, was beset by suffering throughout his life logically implies that the gods either cannot or are unwilling to look after their own kin (a basic obligation of Greek ethics). The logical structure behind this argument suggests, again, that it is drawn from contemporary philosophical reasoning. Later in the play, Heracles, newly awoken from his trance and in a suicidal mood, also expresses skepticism about Zeus, "whoever he is." Like the chorus of *Oedipus the King,* he echoes the conventional, pious prayer's doubt about the correct naming of the god, but in a way that suggests that he may not exist at all. "Do not be angry, old man," he says to Amphitryon. "I consider you my father, not Zeus." Presently, Theseus tries to console him by saying that even the gods suffer: the myths portray them as cuckolded, punished, and imprisoned. Heracles replies that "I do not believe that the gods enjoy illicit unions, or that they chain each other up; I do not think, nor will I ever be persuaded, that one god can be master over another. A god has no need of anything, if he is truly a god. These are the wretched tales of singers." Heracles appeals to a traditional critique (going back to Xenophanes, via Pindar) of poetic stories of divine immorality but does so in terms that suggest an underlying argument against the existence of divinity: if there are such things as gods, they will be entirely blessed, but if they are blessed, they will have no need of anything; hence they will not have any need to change anything (least of all in an immoral way). Ironically, Heracles is himself at this moment caught up in such a tale of divine immorality (Hera is behind his madness). In one sense that fact disproves his argument and reaffirms the traditional conception of the gods. But it also underlines the central theological problem of the play: where is Zeus, the all-powerful king of the gods, and why does he seem to have so little control over things?[15]

The Madness of Heracles explores a version of what theologians now call the "problem of evil": if there is a god, and that god is just and powerful, how do we account for the existence of evil in the world? This paradox is expressed most strikingly in a Euripidean play that survives only in fragments, *Bellerophon*:

> Someone says that there really are gods in heaven?
> There are not, there are not—if you are willing
> Not to subscribe foolishly to the antiquated account.
> Consider it for yourselves; do not use my words
> As a guide for your opinion. I reckon that tyrants
> Kill very many people and deprive them of their property
> And break their oaths to sack cities;
> And despite this they prosper more
> Than those who live piously in peace every day.
> I know too of small cities that revere the gods
> Which are subject to larger, more impious ones
> Overcome as they are by a more numerous army.[16]

This is one of the most explicitly atheistic utterances in all of ancient culture; it is frustrating that it comes in fragmentary form, and the context is unclear and the speaker unknown. The best guess is that Bellerophon himself speaks these words. One clue lies in his family background: Bellerophon was one of those descendants of Aeolus, who are so closely associated with atheism in the *Catalogue of Women*. There are also other fragments from Euripides's play that suggest a depressive, cynical, fatalistic worldview: one, for example, reads: "I'd rather die: it's not worth living, if people see bad men unjustly honoured." We know from other sources that Bellerophon was prone to moroseness. In Homer's *Iliad*, it is said that late in life Bellerophon "wandered the plain of Aleion, eating out his heart, avoiding the footsteps of humans." Homer does not explain the source of the misery, except to comment that Bellerophon "was hateful to all the gods." There are cryptic hints here that Homer knew a story in which Bellerophon, who had been a heroic success in his earlier life, somehow offended the gods and was punished with exile, which in turn led to his disenchantment with religion.[17]

How did Bellerophon offend the gods? Homer's account gives us no clue, but later versions tell how, flush with heroic success, he attempted to fly up to Olympus on the winged horse Pegasus; Pegasus however reared and threw his rider to earth. Pindar, the famous composer of praise songs for athletic victors in the earlier part of the fifth century BC, already knew this story. It is almost certain that Euripides's play featured Bellerophon's assault on the heavens, using the theatrical crane (*mēkhanē*, or "machine") to swing him up toward the roof of the *skēnē*, or set building. This is confirmed by a parody in Aristophanes's play *Peace,* performed in 421 BC, which has a similarly melancholic figure, Trygaeus, railing against the gods and soaring up to Olympus to confront them—but in the comedy he flies on a dung beetle, not a heroic horse.[18]

If this is right, and Bellerophon speaks the words quoted above, then there are some interesting implications. Like other descendants of Aeolus in myth, Bellerophon expresses his skepticism by trying to usurp the gods' prerogatives, in this case trying to enter their very domain. Atheism is seen as an aggressive challenge to the gods, an attempt to claim immortal privileges for humans—just as, for example, Salmoneus tries to imitate Zeus's thunder using pots and pans behind his chariot. Humans cannot fly, but in myth gods can. The winged horse is like Salmoneus's thunder-generating machine, an artifice designed to mimic the effects of divinity. And the same point can be made of the theater itself: it too is a human invention that makes gods out of mortals, thanks to masking, staging, and the crane. Bellerophon flying up to heaven is a sign not just of a mythical hero overreaching himself, but also of the theater's disturbing illusionistic power, which can make a god of a human.

But in this fifth-century retelling, at a time of intense philosophical questioning of the divine, this mythical pattern seems to have been directly linked to a rational argument for the gods' nonexistence. The implicit atheism of figures from myth like Salmoneus has been transformed into explicit argument. Bellerophon's reasoning, indeed, has the structure of a philosophical syllogism: if (a) any gods who exist preside over justice in the world and (b) injustice is not rectified then (c) there can be no gods. The philosophical nature of the argument is reflected in the phrasing "consider it for yourselves; do not use my words / As a guide for your opinion": the pedagogical voice of the instructor teaches self-reliance and independence. The verb "consider," *skeptesthai,* is not a poetic word: it is more appropriate to highbrow intellectual reasoning. We also have the advice not to rely foolishly on "antiquated reasoning." The Greek says *palaios logos,* which could also be an ancient account or story: in the context, this implies that the speaker is pitching his new, intellectualized version of divinity directly against the model of divinity enshrined in Homer's *Iliad* and *Odyssey,* and in Hesiod. In other words, the speaker at this point seems to be aligning himself with philosophical critics who attack the traditional epic portrayal of the gods—in this case, the traditional portrayal of them as arbiters of justice—and base their conceptions of the universe instead on what can be derived from rational observation.

What is more, there is just the tiniest hint that behind Bellerophon's words lie a direct reference to a contemporary philosophical thinker. The evidence needs treating with some care and in some detail. The very last lines of the fragment are difficult to interpret and were not quoted above. Literally, it would translate as follows:

I think that, if a man were lazy and prayed to the gods and did not go gathering his livelihood with his hand, you would < . . . > and ill-fortune fortify religion

This clearly does not make sense, and so scholars have reasonably assumed that one or more lines have dropped out of the text (at the point marked by "< . . . >"). There is much speculation about what the missing words might be, speculation that need not distract us at the moment. The important point is the word "fortify," which corresponds to the Greek *purgousin,* from *purgos,* "tower." It looks as if something, together with ill-fortune, would fortify or "build up the towers of" religion. What is behind this particular metaphor? Why should religion be thought of in terms of "towers"? Partly, surely, because Bellerophon's own atheism is coupled with an assault on the fortifications of Mount Olympus. Olympus is a lofty mountain, rather like a city; for Bellerophon to fly up there suggests the equivalent of a siege on heaven. It is interesting to note, in passing, that one later source refers to a "tower" (*pyrgos*) as part of the theatrical set building. If this was the case already in classical times, then Bellerophon's flight, on the crane, would have been literally a flight toward a tower.[19]

But there is another reason to focus on the towers. Let us zoom out a little and think about the context. It is not known when *Bellerophon* was written, but we do know that Aristophanes's *Peace*—containing the parody—was performed in 421. It seems likely that the object of the parody would have been fresh in the minds of audiences: so *Bellerophon* had been performed at some point in the previous five years. Euripides's play will have been produced during the time of heightened anxiety that followed the impeachment of Anaxagoras in around 432. It is possible, even, that there is a precise allusion to another trial for impiety. The prosecution of Diagoras of Melos, nicknamed "the Atheist," seems to have occurred at some point between 423 and 415. Diagoras was already well known enough in 423 to be mocked by Aristophanes in his play *Clouds.* In other words, there is a distinct possibility that when *Bellerophon* was composed, Diagoras was the public intellectual whom Athens associated most closely with atheism (even if we know nothing about his actual claims).

Why does this matter? One of the few things we know about Diagoras was that he composed a work called *Apopyrgizontes logoi,* a rather obscure phrase that will take a little bit of unpacking. The title refers to *logoi*—speeches, arguments, accounts—that *apopyrgizein,* an otherwise unparalleled verb composed of two elements: *apo* (away from or off) and *pyrgos* (tower). *Pyrgos* is the very word we have discussed in connection with Euripides's *Bellerophon*. What might Diagoras's title have meant? We know of other sophists and philosophers of the era who wrote works with similar titles: Protagoras wrote *Knock-Down Arguments* (*Kataballontes logoi*), and Thrasymachus *Knocking-Over Arguments*. It is likely, then, that Diagoras's *Apopyrgizontes logoi* were *Arguments That Knock Down Towers*. They were surely claims against the existence of the Olympian deities; he may well have presented himself as metaphorically enacting a siege on Mount Olympus itself. There is no way of telling whether Diagoras specifically mentioned the example of Bellerophon's flight up to Olympus. But it seems likely, as an acute nineteenth-century commentator first guessed, that when Euripides's Bellerophon speaks of the things that "fortify" (*purgousin*), he is subtly alluding to Diagoras's *Arguments That Knock Down Towers,* a work that clearly had an immediate impact on Athenian society. I speculate, then, that Diagoras's atheistic work is likely to have presented its author as besieging, at least metaphorically, the "towers" of Olympus, and that Euripides's *Bellerophon,* produced probably in the late 420s in the aftermath of the publication of Diagoras's scandalous work, alluded to this by presenting its protagonist as attempting to literalize the metaphor and engaging in a type of siege of Olympus.[20]

This idea of atheism as an assault on the heavens was picked up in Aristophanes's comedy *The Birds,* performed in 414 BC: here two Athenians co-opt the world's birds to help them build a city in the sky ("Cloudcuckooland") and end up besieging the gods by starving them of sacrifices. There is, indeed, an explicit allusion in the play to Diagoras, and to the action taken against him by the Athenians in 416–415 BC: "Whoever kills Diagoras of Melos shall receive one talent!" proclaim the birds (one talent being a huge amount of silver). The "Melian starvation" that the birds try to impose on the gods is also surely a reference to Diagoras. In the period of ten years or so after the publication of Diagoras's atheistic book, a rich complex of ideas emerged associating fantasies of human flight with assaults on Olympus, and hence with displacing the gods.[21]

So what are we to conclude about Athenian drama and religion? There were certainly religious aspects to it: it was performed in sacred space during a festive celebration of Dionysus and introduced with sacrifices. The theater was the central place in Athens where religious themes could be explored and expounded upon; in fact, it was the only space in the city where the implications of their religious system could be pondered collectively. Most of the plays, indeed, were generally pious in their overall implications. But this left plenty of room for sympathetic and constructive exploration of the challenging ideas about the gods introduced by the pre-Socratics and the sophists. Is it possible to imagine a monotheist equivalent? Is there any synagogue, mosque, or church where the ideas of Richard Dawkins, Christopher Hitchens, and Sam Harris are expounded seriously and constructively? If such places exist at all, they are extremely rare. But then Greek religious culture had no sacred text, no orthodoxy, no clear sense of what was ruled in and out of the sacred sphere, and as a result it was not blasphemous to subject the nature of the gods to radical questioning.

8

Atheism on Trial

In January 1962, Greek construction workers on the national road that runs east from Thessaloniki along the ancient Via Egnatia uncovered a cist grave. Excavation of the area revealed a network of tombs, containing numerous grave goods. Among these was an ancient scroll, now carbonized, dating to the second half of the fourth century BC. The Derveni papyrus, as it is now known (after the nearby town), is the oldest surviving European manuscript of any length. As such it is invaluable both as an artifact and as a document. The papyrus contains a late fifth-century BC allegorical commentary, infused with pre-Socratic ideas, on a now-lost mystic poem on the nature of gods; the person buried with it was probably expected to carry it with him or her into the afterlife. This is a rare example of a Greek use of a text as sacred, although in a ritual-functional rather than a scriptural sense. Presumably the sacredness was attached primarily to the original poem, not to the commentary; perhaps that was originally included on the papyrus (much of which has been lost), or perhaps the commentary was all that was to hand at the time of the burial. At any rate, the dead person may well have been a member of one of the mystic afterlife cults that modern scholars have tended to group together under the label "Orphic," and the papyrus may have been intended somehow to ease her or his passage to the afterlife.[1]

In one of the earliest legible sections of the text, the author inveighs against those who "disbelieve" (*apistousi*). "Given that they do not understand dreams or each of the other things, on the basis of what examples would they believe? Overcome by error, and by pleasure too, they have no understanding or belief. Disbelief and misunderstanding are the same thing. For if they do not understand or know, it is not possible for them to believe." This is, to my knowledge, the earliest reference in Greek to the idea of religious belief as the foundation of a religious community, and to the labeling of outsiders as disbelievers. It offers a cautionary reminder that any picture of classical Greece as entirely free from religious discrimination should be nuanced. Much of the literary material that survives from classical and archaic times tends to be relatively nondoctrinaire; this, indeed, was a crucial factor in its survival through different eras with different religious and political ideologies. But the Derveni papyrus shows that there were those who could insist that only they and their sect had the true understanding of the nature of the divine and that all others were disbelievers. It is quite possible, moreover, that the author thought that only his group was likely to survive in the afterlife.[2]

Atheism is not just a philosophical position willingly assumed by consenting adults; it is also a social category constructed by self-styled protectors of religious orthodoxy as a receptacle for those whose beliefs they do not share. Like pirates, heretics, and terrorists, atheists constitute what social scientists call an "outgroup," a group defined in the negative by the religious "ingroup." This was true of Greek antiquity as much as it is today. The history of atheism cannot be just that of those who profess not to believe in gods; it must also account for those social forces (of the kind that can be glimpsed in the Derveni papyrus) that construct it as the other, the inverse of true belief.

The invention of atheism was, both etymologically and historically, the creation of a negative. The Greek word *atheos*, which first appears in the fifth century BC, implies the absence (*a-*) of a god (*theos*). The older meaning implies someone who has lost the support of the gods, someone who is "godless" or "godforsaken" in the archaic English senses. It was often used in a kind of hyperbolic crescendo along with other negative adjectives, in phrases such as "*atheos*, unruly (*anomos*), and lawless (*adikos*)." This kind of phrasing suggests wild, barbaric behavior that is the very antithesis of proper, civilized Greek behavior (think of Homer's Cyclopes: "arrogant, lawless [*athemistōn*] men, who place no trust in the god, and neither sow nor reap vegetation"). Within the lifetime of the classical Athenian democracy, however, it came to acquire a second meaning, referring to someone whose beliefs or practices suggest a lack of commitment to belief in the gods. "I certainly do believe in gods—I am not an out-and-out *atheos*," said Socrates at his trial in

399 BC (according to Plato). From the 430s onward we hear of *atheos* being used as a surname or nickname attached to various individuals. The pre-Socratic Hippo of Samos, active in Athens in the mid-430s, was said to be "surnamed the *atheos*"; so were Diagoras of Melos (mid-420s onward) and Theodorus of Cyrene (late fourth century). In other words, if you said "Hippo the atheist," everyone knew who you meant.[3]

A more powerful insult than *atheos* was *asebēs,* "impious." It was potent because it was legally actionable. The verb *sebein* meant to worship the gods in the traditional manner, to pay them their due (as in the modern name Sebastian). The crime of *asebeia* seems to have referred originally to any individual's failure to perform sacraments according to custom, an infringement of the local rules of a temple that would incur sanctions meted out by the priesthood. There is plenty of evidence that temples could impose fines on anyone they decreed *asebēs:* someone, for example, who cut down sacred trees or who failed to follow the proper protocols while serving as a priest. At some point in the 430s, however, a seer called Diopeithes seems to have set in motion a chain of events that ultimately changed the term's meaning irrevocably.[4]

We have met Diopeithes before: he was the religious crackpot lampooned by the comic poets and perhaps reflected in Sophocles's portrait of Tiresias in *Oedipus the King.* His significance for fifth-century atheism lies in a passage found in the historian Plutarch, who writes that he "brought in a bill providing for the public impeachment of those who did not recognize the gods, or who taught doctrines regarding the heavens." The real aim, Plutarch says, was to attack Pericles, the most powerful man in Athens, by accusing his friend Anaxagoras of illicit religious beliefs. This passage has caused scholars much consternation. Could it really be the case that the Athenians, otherwise so intellectually curious, approved a bill that banned disbelief in the gods and speculation about the heavens? What is more, the legal process that Plutarch mentions is not any old kind of prosecution: an *eisangelia* (impeachment) was the most severe form of incrimination, which in effect accused the defendant of subversion of the democratic constitution. An impeachment was tried in front not of a jury but one of the political decision-making bodies, the Council or the Assembly. A large majority of such cases resulted in the death penalty.[5]

Some modern commentators have been incredulous: for Diopeithes to have persuaded his fellow citizens to treat disbelief in the gods as an invitation to impeachment would have been a murderously intolerant act, and an exceptional instance of public legislation about religious beliefs. Yet there is no reason—apart from an anxious desire to protect the Athenians' reputation as enlightened liberals—to doubt the Diopeithes decree. There are certainly a few problems of a chronological nature with Plutarch's account at this point, but the language of the decree itself has the technical ring of Athenian officialdom. Although writing some five hundred years after the events, Plutarch was working with compilations of documentary sources from the original time, among them a collection of verbatim transcriptions of Athenian legal decrees (and commentaries on them) compiled by Craterus of Macedon in the early third century BC. The specifics of Diopeithes's decree probably came (via Craterus or someone like him) from the records in Athens's own official archive. It seems genuine enough.[6]

The decree targets two kinds of criminality. The first is not recognizing (*nomizein*) the gods. The Greek word is ambiguous and can suggest either their ritual worship or belief in their existence. Perhaps this ambiguity was intentional, so that prosecutors could use the law to sweep up both those who were derelict in their fulfilment of religious obligations and those who held heterodox beliefs. This would fit with the corresponding extension of impiety from the sphere of ritual into that of belief. The second activity outlawed is "teaching doctrines regarding the heavens," which might seem at first sight a completely different issue. What does pre-Socratic speculation about the nature of the cosmos have to do with not recognizing the gods? But that is presumably the whole point: the motives behind the decree were political in nature and designed to forge a link between Anaxagoras's speculative theories and outright rejection of the city's gods. What was even more revolutionary, however, was that this was the first time in Greek public life that legislation had sought to govern people's intellectual beliefs about the nature of the world. If you did not believe the right things about the world then you did not believe the right things about the gods, and in that case you were unlikely to be in a position to worship them effectively. Athens had its first taste of the idea of religious orthodoxy. To be a good citizen you had not only to do right but to think right too.[7]

Diopeithes, the dancing madman of the comic poets, may well have been motivated by nothing more than a fanatical religious obsession. The political machination behind the scenes, on the other hand, may have been the work of Pericles's enemy Cleon (who in the 420s would succeed him as the most influential citizen in the popular assembly). At any rate, the ability to mobilize public opinion was the most powerful weapon at anyone's disposal in democratic Athens. The new thought crime of impiety was not just a state-imposed restriction; it was also a means of manufacturing outrage against political opponents. Athens was tasting not only the concept of orthodoxy but also its politicization.[8]

This process of politicization was facilitated by the adoption of the extraordinarily slippery word *asebeia,* "impiety." Once the Diopeithes decree had unhooked it from its narrowly ritual meaning, it could be used to describe just about anything. When Aristotle tried to define it he came up with "crimes against gods and deities, parents, the dead, and the fatherland"—a definition that leaves rather little wrongdoing actually excluded. Aristotle was speaking in moral, not legal terms, and certainly the cases covered by *asebeia* that came to court tended to be more narrowly connected with religious misdemeanors. Even so, the connection to religion could be tenuous. There is, for instance, the case of a man who prosecuted his father for murder being himself accused of *asebeia* for the very act of bringing the prosecution. Sometimes the charge of *asebeia* seems to have been piled on top of an existing one, simply to intensify it. The fourth-century BC orator Demosthenes, for example, cried impiety when a political rival slapped him in the theater: because he (Demosthenes) held the official position of chorus master, he protested, and because the offense occurred within the sacred space of the theater, is Meidias not guilty of *asebeia* as well as assault?[9]

Athenian law as a rule avoided tight definitions of particular crimes and rested on the assumption that each citizen had an innate sense of natural justice. From a modern perspective, indeed, there is a troubling elasticity to Greek legal language. This was an inevitable result of the fact that unlike Rome, Athens had no professional jurists whose job was to interpret the law. Decisions were made by the populace, and so the system rested on popular, commonsense conceptions of justice rather than forbidding (but perhaps more rigorously defined) statutes. But while this meant that the law was democratized, it also opened it up to exploitation by mudslingers. Even within this malleable system, however, impiety was understood with unusual latitude. In fact, it is not even clear whether there was a specific law against impiety as such: it may have been simply that describing a particular action as *asebeia* was felt to be enough to make it actionable. Plutarch's phrasing does not mention impiety as part of the wording of the original decree. All we can say with any confidence is that in the aftermath of Diopeithes's intervention, accusations of *asebeia* became the favored means of hobbling both political opponents and intellectual undesirables, and that popular culture too (as we can see from drama) began to be obsessed with labeling certain individuals or ideas as impious.[10]

Pinning down just how many people were tried for atheism under the impiety laws is not straightforward. As ever, the problem is one of sources. In later Greek culture, the idea that Athens was obsessed with trying religious heretics became a starting point for all biographies of intellectuals. There are stories about trials of the tragic dramatists Aeschylus and Euripides, for example. Diogenes of Apollonia was a younger contemporary and former student of Anaxagoras's, a natural philosopher who believed that air was a kind of god, and was included in later lists of *atheoi;* he is said to have "almost come into danger" (whatever that means) in Athens. Protagoras is said to have been tried and to have had *On the Gods* burned in the marketplace; though condemned to death, he escaped. There are reports, too, of trials of the later fourth-century philosophers Aristotle, Demades, Theophrastus, Demetrius of Phalerum, and Stilpo of Megara. How many of these stories are true is anyone's guess, but scholars have in general not given them much credence.[11]

Four trials, however, are more or less secure. It is highly likely that Anaxagoras was prosecuted for *asebeia,* although again the exact details (when? by whom? did he stand trial or flee?) have been hotly debated. The trial is often mentioned by ancient sources and was alluded to by Plato a mere fifty or so years later. The poet Diagoras of Melos, too, author of *Arguments That Knock Down Towers,* was banished from Athens for impiety; there was also an inscription in bronze set up that offered a reward of one talent of silver for anyone who killed him. But was he actually an atheist, and was he persecuted for that reason? Or was the issue his participation in the group that in 415 BC revealed and mocked the secret rites of the Eleusinian Mysteries? Scholars have been split on the matter. On the one hand, his punishment is often associated with the profanation of the Mysteries in the sources, and there is no mention of any trial for his beliefs. The two tiny fragments of his poetry speak of gods in the conventional way. These observations have led some to conclude that he was not in fact a professed atheist at all. Yet the evidence that he was is overwhelmingly strong. He is more commonly associated with atheism than any other ancient figure: there are thirty passages testifying explicitly to this effect, beginning with a play by Aristophanes in around 418 BC in which a character proclaims that "Socrates the Melian" (that is, a hybrid of Socrates and Diagoras) denies the existence of Zeus. If Euripides's *Bellerophon* is alluding to *Arguments That Knock Down Towers* (as I argued in the previous chapter), then the association goes back to the 420s. In the mid-fourth century BC, Aristotle's pupil Aristoxenus was reading an atheistic prose text that he attributed to him: this may well have been *Arguments That Knock Down Towers*. There are, what is more, some wonderful anecdotes about his cavalier attitudes toward the divine, which may not count for much in historical terms but they do show that ancients uniformly thought of him as the fifth-century atheist *par excellence*. He is said to have lost his belief in the gods after a poet swore a solemn oath that he had not plagiarized one of Diagoras's compositions; when Diagoras saw him perform the piece, and that the gods had not punished him for his oath breaking, he drew his own conclusions. He once declared he was cold and threw a wooden statue of Heracles on the fire ("This is your thirteenth labour," he quipped). In a sea storm the crew of his ship blamed him for incurring the gods' displeasure; he pointed out another ship that was struggling and said, "Do they have a Diagoras too?"[12]

So, was Diagoras prosecuted for profaning the Mysteries or for his atheism? In fact, that is surely the wrong way to phrase the question. At the time of Diagoras's expulsion, the war with Sparta was going badly; Athens was in a state of panic and paranoia. The expedition to attack Sicily in 415 BC was a desperate roll of the dice for Athens. It was in this climate that the religious crisis that implicated Diagoras arose. Just before the ships set sail, various herms (phallic statues standing on pillars) were mutilated; according to Thucydides this was seen as an aristocratic plot, and the general Alcibiades and others were accused both of having mutilated herms in the past and of parodying the Eleusinian Mysteries at drunken private parties. It was a serious affair: the claim was that the accused were conspiring to overthrow the democracy, and large numbers were implicated (over sixty names are attested). Alcibiades suffered impeachment (*eisangelia*) for impiety. In the view of the historian Thucydides (who was alive at the time), the entire process of incrimination was a political witch hunt brought about by those who were jealous of Alcibiades's success and wanted it for themselves. Is it likely that in this turbulent environment, a sharp distinction was drawn between Diagoras's atheistic beliefs and his supposed involvement in the profanation of the Mysteries? Surely not. Given his reputation for atheism, his accusers would have found it easy to throw him in with the profaners of the Mysteries, and they would have thrown at him all the ammunition that they could find.[13]

The third of the three confirmed impiety trials is the best known of all. In 399 BC, the philosopher Socrates was charged with corrupting the young and not recognizing the gods of the state. Although he was presented with the opportunity to counterpropose exile as a penalty in the event of conviction, he chose death instead. The state execution of Socrates is a different kind of story, which deserves (and will receive) a separate chapter.

The last of the impious Athenian atheists was Theodorus of Cyrene, who came to Athens from North Africa much later, sometime around 315 BC. Details of his trial are sketchy (it may have taken place around 308 BC), but the reason to include him is that the later tradition is unequivocal in granting him the epithet "the *atheos*." As with Diagoras, it is even possible that he chose to self-identify in this way. The evidence for this needs teasing out. According to his biographer, Theodorus acquired the sobriquet Theos ("God"). The nickname, we are told, derived from a trick played on him by the philosopher Stilpo of Megara. Stilpo asked him whether he agreed with the proposition that "that which you say you are, you are." Theodorus did indeed agree. Thanks to an ambiguity in the Greek language, however, the sentence could also mean "that which you say exists, you are." Exploiting this second meaning, Stilpo asked him if a god exists; when Theodorus agreed, Stilpo declared that Theodorus must therefore himself be a god (on the grounds that "that which you say exists, you are"). Yet the transmitted anecdote makes no sense, since Theodorus famously denied the existence of gods. In the original version of the story what Stilpo must have asked him was whether not "a god *(theos)*" but "an *atheos*" exists—and thereby "proved" him to be *atheos* himself. Stilpo would have assumed that *atheos* (in the sense of "god-forsaken") was an insult. The surprise, however, was that Theodorus was actually rather pleased with his new title—presumably because it linked him to Socrates, Diagoras, and Anaxagoras. And thus he acquired his nickname: not Theos, but *atheos*. The joke, if my reconstruction is right, is evidence that he did actively self-identify as an atheist. He wrote a book called *On the Gods* (an echo, surely deliberate, of Protagoras's work); as so often is the case, it does not survive, but one ancient report says that it "entirely did away with beliefs about the gods."[14]

The trial of Theodorus marked the final stage in the process that began with the Diopeithes decree, which legitimized attacks on individuals for their impious thoughts. The dangerous idea that heterodox religious belief is enough to threaten the foundations of the state had been born and was available for unscrupulous political manipulation. Men like Cleon, who was probably behind the Diopeithes decree, and Thessalus (the son of the general Cimon), who prosecuted Alcibiades—not for the last time in history—manipulated public emotion for their own ends by appealing to moral outrage at religious impropriety.

What the Athenian example shows is that even within Greek polytheism, a flexible and adaptive system, the mixture of religion, law, and imperialism was a potentially toxic one. With so much money, fame, and power at stake, late fifth-century BC Athens offered the closest precursor in the archaic or classical Greek world to the centralized sacro-political empires of the Hellenistic and Roman worlds; it is perhaps not so surprising to find that religion became one of the levers of power. Even so, it is worth remembering that the trials of Anaxagoras, Diopeithes, and Socrates were rarities. Athens in fact traveled only a short way down the road toward theocracy. In the democratic state, the political decision-making process was ultimately too diffuse and unpredictable to allow one group or agenda to dominate for long periods.

So the invention of atheism (in the negative sense of the word) in fifth-century BC Athens was rooted in a politically influenced desire to stigmatizee certain individuals. But perhaps there was more to it than that. What if what began as an insult was in time reappropriated as a badge of honor? This is a phenomenon well attested by modern social scientists: think of "queer," "nigger," or even "geek." In such instances, the connotations of an initially negative term shift, and the label becomes associated with positive attributes. In the case of *atheos,* it is not hard to imagine how that process may have occurred. Perhaps the point of transition was Diagoras of Melos and his *Arguments That Knock Down Towers:* if I am right that he introduced the image of the disbeliever as *theomakhos,* "battler against the gods," then he may well have also argued that an *atheos* was a powerful, masculine vanquisher of the gods—someone who made the deity (*-theos*) disappear (*a-*)—rather than the wild, Cyclopic figure that the term had conventionally suggested up until that point. Modern studies of the reappropriation of stigmatizing labels suggest it is the first step in the process of countercultural group formation. It is, then, perfectly plausible that the term *"atheos"* was originally (say in the 430s) applied negatively to heterogeneous pre-Socratics and sophists who were associated with disbelief in the gods, and that a revisionist definition by Diagoras or someone like him made it a label with which others then actively sought to be associated (whether publicly or in private). If this is right, then perhaps we can suggest, tentatively, that Diagoras was the first person in history to self-identify in a positive way as an atheist, and that others like Theodorus followed him. *Atheos* had the advantage over *asebēs* in that it did not imply illegality, but nevertheless retained a certain countercultural punch. Perhaps there was indeed, as one scholar has suggested, a coherent "atheist underground" operating in Athens from the late fifth century BC onward, exchanging texts and ideas, and indeed identifying themselves as *atheoi.* This is speculative, but not implausible.[15]

One major Athenian thinker of the fourth century, certainly, became convinced toward the end of his life that a cabal of atheists was threatening to undermine society. It is to him that we now turn.

9

Plato and the Atheists

Athens in 399 BC was a fearsome place to be. In 404 the city had fallen to the Spartans, after twenty-seven bruising, bloody years of warfare. The aftermath was horrific. For thirteen months, the democracy was suspended, and a pro-Spartan oligarchy known as the "Thirty Tyrants" was installed. Their leaders, Theramenes and Critias (possibly the author of the atheistic Sisyphus fragment), were famed for their brutality. A faction loyal to the old democracy was identified, arrested, and executed. After a while, a power struggle between Critias and Theramenes saw the latter hauled off and killed. In 403 BC, their rule ended when rebellious forces led by the staunch democrat Thrasybulus joined battle near the Piraeus. After more fighting, the democracy was restored.[1]

Despite an amnesty forbidding *mnēsikakia,* "the remembering of wrongdoing," Athens in 399 BC was scarred and haunted by recent events. This was the backdrop for one of the most important events in Greek cultural and religious history, the trial and execution of Socrates. Athens's most famous philosopher had found himself reluctantly embroiled in the events of the previous five years. Critias had been one of his students, along with another of the tyrants, Charmides. Both of these were relatives of Plato, Socrates's star student and later apologist; in fact, two of Plato's dialogues featuring Socrates are called *Critias* and *Charmides.* Certainly Socrates had not been an unequivocal supporter of the junta. On one occasion he had been mandated, along with others, to arrest one Leon of Salamis; he had refused, however, because (reportedly) he had a greater fear of committing injustice than he had of the recriminations that would follow. On that occasion, he was saved by the fall of the tyrants from any repercussions of his principled insubordination. In the public's mind, however, the stain of association with that hated band, which the Athenians of the newly restored democracy were keen to drive from their memory, was hard to shift.[2]

But association with the tyrants was not the explicit basis of the charge against Socrates, which ran: "Socrates commits a crime in not recognizing the gods the state recognizes, and introducing other, new divine powers instead. He also commits a crime by corrupting the young." Diopeithes's decree providing for the impeachment of "those who do not recognize the gods" lies in the background: the shared language of "not recognizing" (*mē nomizein*) suggests this much. The vaguer charge of *asebeia*, "impiety," was also hanging in the air. But as so often in Athenian criminal prosecution, impressionistic as it was, not everything corresponds exactly to known legislation. "Corrupting the young" was not a crime on the statute book. The additional accusation was no doubt designed to influence the jurors with insinuations: this, after all, was the philosopher who had taught Critias and Charmides (and Alcibiades too) when they were young men. There was also a pederastic hint in the word "corrupt": Socrates was well known for his attachment to handsome youths. For an older man to court a younger boy was not in any sense seen as a moral offense, but it was a practice associated with the aristocratic elite and so likely to play badly with the largely working-class jurors.[3]

Whatever the underlying political motivations, the explicit force of the charge lay in the assertion that he had turned his back on the religion of the city and invented his own private mysticism. This accusation was rooted in a peculiar foible of his: he claimed to have access to a *daimonion*, a "divine thing," which he identified sometimes as a voice in his head and sometimes as a "sign from the god." He was claiming a direct communion with an unspecified deity, a form of divine engagement that cut right across the usual ideology of Greek religion, which insisted that collective ritual marked one's subservience to the social order. Believing that gods speak to us was not in itself so very strange: Greeks imagined that gods revealed all sorts of things through dreams, signs, and even direct manifestations ("epiphanies"). It was the idea of an enduring one-to-one relationship with his own personal deity that was the problem. *If* Socrates believed that he alone had been granted access to the full depths of the divine, while conventional religion merely paddled in the shallows, that would have been deeply threatening to the civic consensus. Earlier philosophers had claimed similar things: the pre-Socratic philosopher Parmenides of Elea, for example, describes a journey on a chariot, through a locked gate, to the temple of a goddess who reveals to him the ways of truth and hollow belief. But Parmenides was not unfortunate enough to have to defend this claim in the aftermath of a bloody aristocratic regime spearheaded by some of his followers. Socrates's (alleged) claim to exclusive access to divine truth could have been presented to his democratically minded peers as a dangerous attempt to legitimate the rule of the many by the elite.[4]

What did Socrates really think about the gods? Did he really "not recognize the gods of the city," as the accusation ran? Did he believe firmly in the "divine thing," or was that simply a whim of this famously ironic philosopher? How did he square this emphasis on divine revelation with his philosophical commitment to rationalism? Barring some remarkable discovery, these questions will never be answered conclusively, for Socrates—like Jesus and Mohammed (and, indeed, several other noted Greek philosophers)—wrote nothing down. Every single piece of evidence for him comes mediated through others. What is more, apart from the scurrilous portrait painted by the comic poet Aristophanes in 423 BC (in *Clouds*), during Socrates's lifetime, every major piece of evidence is carefully polished up by one of Socrates's loyal supporters, in the aftermath of the trial. Socrates is a paradox: we know all about his central importance to Athenian cultural life in the late fifth century BC, but there is little certainty about his beliefs.[5]

The two most important of these sources for Socrates's thought are also the two most vigorous polishers of the Socrates myth: Xenophon and Plato. Xenophon (ca. 430–355 BC) was an aristocratic Athenian who combined a diverse literary output with a colorful military life. An associate of Socrates in his youth, he left Athens in the turbulent years after the end of the Thirty Tyrants to join the Greek mercenary force supporting the failed attempt of the Persian Cyrus the Younger to oust his brother, Artaxerxes II, from the throne. His epic march from Mesopotamia to the Black Sea (where the soldiers uttered the famous cry "The sea! The sea!"), and thence to Greece, is recorded in his *Anabasis*.

When he returned, he began associating with his native city's other nemesis, Sparta, and even fought with the Spartan king Agesilaus II against Athens in 394 BC. This loyalty to Sparta won him a beautiful country house at Scillus, near Olympia (the site of the games); there he wrote many of his literary works, including a biography of Agesilaus, an idealized novel on the subject of Cyrus I of Persia (the sixth-century creator of the Persian Empire), and four works on Socrates: a fictionalized version of his defense speech at the trial, a collection of conversational pieces, a dialogue on household management, and a description of a symposium. Although he may have returned home in his declining years, it is fair to say that Xenophon was far from a conventional Athenian. Whether he had become alienated by the horrors of the Thirty Tyrants and the aftermath (for which his *History of Greece* is the primary source), or whether he was simply perverse by inclination, he seems to have allied himself with persons most unwelcome to Athenian ideology: Persian kings, Spartan kings, and Socrates.[6]

Plato (ca. 424–347 BC), the most famous of all philosophers, was another native Athenian aristocrat and an almost exact contemporary of Xenophon's, but whereas Xenophon's life was characterized by experimentation and adventure, Plato spent most of his adulthood beavering away at his writing (thirty-seven works are transmitted under his name, at least twenty-six of which are certainly genuine). His one big foray into realpolitik may have been a trip to the court of Dionysius II of Syracuse (ruled 367–357 and 346–344 BC). According to a surviving letter that purports to be written by Plato himself, he was invited over to Sicily on two occasions, first by Dionysius's father (during his own reign) and second (early in the new king's reign) by his philosophically inclined uncle, Dio. On both occasions, the plan was to curb the young man's lavish appetites and to put into practice the Platonic ideal of the "philosopher king." Dionysius, however, was congenitally indulgent and cruel. Dio was exiled, only to return with an army and depose Dionysius. Whether Plato's Sicilian sojourn really took place all depends on the question of the authenticity of the letter. In any case, Plato developed a reputation throughout later antiquity as a head-in-the-clouds idealist, as otherworldly as his mentor Socrates himself, and the Sicily story came to be seen as a sign of his inability to translate his ideals into practice. Lucian, the playful satirist of the second century AD, wrote a fantasy story ironically titled *The True Stories*. In it he claims to have visited the underworld and to have met all the famous figures of the past, except for Plato; for "it was said that he was living in his imaginary city in the republic and under the laws that he himself had composed." The joke is on the titles of two of his best known works, the *Republic* and the *Laws,* both blueprints for hypothetical cities.[7]

Both Plato and Xenophon wrote apologies, accounts of the trial of Socrates. Convergences between the two might be taken as evidence that they are both testaments to the actual words spoken in court, but in fact that assumption crumbles once we realize that Xenophon is responding to Plato. Xenophon was not there in person; his account is simply a blend of Plato and a now-lost version by one Hermogenes, together with an incalculable amount of his own invention. It would be wonderful to have Socrates in his own words, but in truth he is lost to us. Although there is surely *some* of the historical Socrates in Plato and Xenophon, the more valuable evidence they offer is for the creation of a myth. The paradigm of the heroic individual who cheerfully faces death for her or his beliefs has exerted a powerful grip on history ever since and offered a template for any number of heroically principled deaths.[8]

Herein lies the central critical problem with Socrates. He is, as a well-known classicist once observed, like a ring doughnut: rich around the outside but absent in the center. What was he really like? What did he really think and teach? The problem is exacerbated by the fact that an earlier but wholly contradictory picture survives, in the form of Aristophanes's *Clouds*. Given that the play was originally produced in 423 BC (and revised for reperformance at some point in the next six years), it is in fact the only substantial Socratic picture from his own lifetime. In the play, he appears as a blend of two different types of intellectual. The protagonist, Strepsiades, visits his "Thinktank" (*phrontistērion*) because he wants to learn the art of rhetorical argumentation, how to make the weaker argument seem the stronger. Socrates excels at this, naturally. But he is also the model of a pre-Socratic cosmologist like Anaxagoras, theorizing about the nature of the universe. Aristophanes has him worship the clouds of the title and disbelieve in the existence of the Olympian deities. The Socrates of Plato and Xenophon is nothing like this; in fact, in Plato's version of the defense speech, Socrates explicitly blames his public perception as a religious skeptic on Aristophanes's play. Did then Aristophanes simply invent these traits? It is far from impossible: he was, after all, a comic writer, with all the license that goes with it. Yet it is a striking fact that Aristophanes's Socrates contains *none* of the traits visible in Xenophon's account, or that of the early Plato: there he is primarily an ethical philosopher, whose primary interest is in discussing moral dilemmas with individuals. This disparity might lead us to ask whether there is not an element of artful construction in theirs too. Or perhaps over a career of some twenty-five years in the public eye as Athens's best known philosopher, perhaps he changed course? Perhaps he started out as the Aristophanic cosmologist and sophist and ended up at the ethical investigator?[9]

Most would agree that the picture of Socrates as an ethical philosopher, glimpsed dimly through Xenophon and Plato, is likely to be historically accurate, at least for his later years. But agreeing to this does not resolve the wider problem of how and why Xenophon and Plato have distorted that picture. The crucial point is that both of these authors composed in the aftermath of his trial and execution. As apologists for a man condemned as a state criminal, they were placed in a very difficult position, particularly in the matter of religion. Their central mission was, in different ways, to rescue their hero from the atheistic opprobrium poured on him by the state.

This awkwardness is visible everywhere in the opening words of Xenophon's *Recollections of Socrates*. Here Xenophon explicitly—and perhaps there is an element of protesting too much—rebuts the charge against Socrates, focusing on the accusation that he "does not recognize the gods that the state recognizes." How can this be? Xenophon wonders. He sacrificed regularly and consulted oracles. Everyone knew this. He even claimed to be guided by a *daimonion,* a "divine thing," which is hardly consistent with the idea of disbelieving in gods. What, then, is the problem? But there is indeed a problem, which Xenophon is sweeping under his finely woven Persian carpet. Socrates's *daimonion* was not simply (as Xenophon suggests) a god like any other one in the city but a personal connection to the divine that bypassed the processes of state religion. In democratic Athens that was an issue: it was tantamount to setting oneself above one's peers, in religious terms.[10]

It is Plato more than Xenophon who is responsible for transforming the picture of Socrates. Almost all of his philosophical treatises come in the form of dialogues between Socrates and one or more others. In the early Plato, as in Xenophon, the apologetic project is never far from the surface. But while Xenophon tries to present him as a regular Athenian, in religious terms, Plato takes the bull by the horns. His Socrates is a pious one—but in a wholly new way, which threatens to subvert the very foundations of conventional Athenian religious sensibility.

Euthyphro, a dialogue between Socrates and the self-proclaimed religious expert of the title, is one of Plato's very earliest dialogues (perhaps even his earliest). It is set in the run-up to the trial, and the discussion is prompted by Euthyphro's incredulity that Socrates of all people could be tried for impiety. This leads them into a discussion of the nature of piety and holiness. Euthyphro, it transpires, is being accused of unholiness by his own family, since he has decided to prosecute his own father for murder. The dialogue is really about unsettling Euthyphro's overconfident belief that he knows what piety and holiness are. Time and again he tries to define these terms, and every time he fails when probed by Socrates. At the end of the dialogue he suddenly declares himself in a hurry and rushes off, leaving the discussion unresolved. In the context of the trial, the implication of the dialogue is that "piety" is a much more complex field than most people, including Socrates's accusers, realize—and so his conviction for impiety turns on a misapprehension.

Even more explicitly apologetic is (as the name suggests) the *Apology,* which purports to be Socrates's defense speech at the trial in 399 BC. Here, Socrates is portrayed as directly addressing an accusation of atheism leveled at him by Meletus, one of the two prosecutors:

> SOCRATES: At any rate tell us, Meletus, how do you say that I corrupt the young? Is it that you think it is obvious, according to the terms of the prosecution that you brought, that it is by teaching them "not to recognize the gods the state believes in, but other new divine powers instead"? Isn't that how you say that I corrupt them with my teaching?

MELETUS: That is exactly what I say.

SOCRATES: In that case, Meletus, do tell me (I beg you by these very gods that we are talking about!) to clarify the situation for both me and the jurors. For I do not understand: Is it that you are saying that I teach people that there are indeed some gods, and the accusation is that they are not those of the city? (I can tell you I *do* recognize that there are gods, and I am not guilty of being an out-and-out atheist!) Or is it that you say I don't recognize gods at all, and I teach this position to others?

MELETUS: The second option: that you do not recognize gods at all.

SOCRATES: You are extraordinary, Meletus! Why do you say this? Do I not even recognize the sun or the moon as gods, as other people do?

MELETUS: No by Zeus, judges, he does not! He says that the sun is a stone and the moon made out of earth.

SOCRATES: Do you think it is Anaxagoras you are accusing, my dear Meletus? Do you hold these men in such low esteem and think them so illiterate that they don't realize that it is the books of Anaxagoras of Clazomenae that are full of that kind of statement? Do the young men learn such things from me, when they can sometimes buy them for a drachma—and that is when the prices are high!—in a corner of the marketplace, and mock Socrates for passing them off as his own? Especially when they are so bizarre? Is that what you think of me, by Zeus? That I do not recognize the existence of any god?

MELETUS: No, by Zeus, you do not: not in the least.

SOCRATES: You cannot be believed, Meletus. I am not even sure that you believe yourself. Men of Athens, this man seems to me to be altogether aggressive and impulsive and to have brought this accusation simply out of aggression, impulsiveness and youthful naivety.[11]

This is essentially the same argument as Xenophon's: that it is contradictory both to claim that he is an atheist and to argue that he believes in the *daimonion*, which is a form of divinity. As in Xenophon, there is an underlying flaw in the reasoning: the *daimonion* may be an altogether different kind of divinity to the gods of the city. Socrates may well be a kind of atheist, if his conception of deity is so radically different from anyone else's that no one else would recognize it as a deity at all. Meletus, at least as Plato portrays him in the ensuing exchange, was not bright enough to make that point. One modern philosopher, however, has done some of Meletus's job for him and argued that Plato's Socrates was indeed guilty of a kind of impiety and deservedly convicted. According to Myles Burnyeat, Socrates in the *Apology* can be seen to reject entirely the idea of the gods as traditionally understood, the individual gods of cult, and to replace them instead with an alternative "theology" that had but one law: humans are obliged to question the world around them, search out their own moral codes, and live by them. Socrates was famously the subject of an oracle issued by Delphi, which named him the wisest of all men. In the *Apology* his interpretation of this offers him a divine mandate for questioning everything that he comes across. "Men of Athens," he says, "I respect and love you, but I shall obey the god rather than you, and as long as I have breath and strength in me, I shall never stop philosophising or exhorting you or point things out to any one of you I meet." Significantly, for the Socrates of early Plato, this included attacking their uninterrogated beliefs about the gods. In *Euthyphro,* he protests that his prosecution is all down to the fact that he refuses to accept all the baroque mythological stories about the gods' immoral behavior. This Socrates is still following in pre-Socratic footsteps, rejecting the epic conception of gods warring and cheating one another. But what is striking is that although he claims to have divine approval for his action, his program is anything but religious. It calls for no worship, no acts of devotion: the only requirement is that the individual live her or his life in the most moral way possible. Socrates himself would probably not have understood it in this way, and Plato certainly would not have done so, but to all intents and purposes this is what we would now call a humanist ethics. Do not accept inherited wisdom about anything, question everything, live only according to principles you can justify rationally: in this sense, Meletus was right about Socrates's atheism.[12]

In his subsequent writings, however, Plato promotes an ever more powerful metaphysical agenda. In the dialogues of the middle period,

Socrates is found proposing a new theory of "forms," which are other-worldly, abstract distillations of all of the things that we witness with our senses in the world around us. We may see or touch many individual examples of a chair, for example, but the form of the chair—the specific quality that makes each one of them a chair, and not a bench or a table—is something we can only grasp with our mind. The same goes for attributes: we may be able to point to individual things or people that are (for example) beautiful or just, but to understand the quality that unites all of them and makes them beautiful or just we need to seek the abstract form of beauty or justice. This concern seems to have grown directly out of the Socratic method. In his early phase, Plato typically represents Socrates as demanding definitions. What is piety? he asks Euthyphro. What is courage? he asks Laches. Typically, his interlocutors answer initially with individual examples: so, for example, one of his victims, Laches, answers that courage consists in "not running away in battle." But, Socrates observes, that is simply an individual instance of courage. There are other types of courage that are not captured by that definition (modern examples would include telling one's parents about one's sexuality, for example, or confronting a bullying partner). These early dialogues tend to end in *aporia,* in the failure to reach any definitional resolution. This Socratic *aporia* seems to have spurred the middle-period Plato on, so that he developed a theory of abstract, other-worldly "forms" that can be accessed only by philosophical inquiry. To understand what courage is, we need to stop considering all of the individual examples and imagine what courage is in and of itself. That is the "form" of courage, the master definition that encompasses all particular manifestations of it.[13]

What does this have to do with metaphysics? Plato had by this stage begun to correlate this distinction between particular instance and abstract form with a distinction between the mundane and the supernatural. The form of courage exists not in this world, but in a higher plane, accessible only to the mind. Socrates's search for definitions had now metamorphosed into a theory dividing existence into two realms, our day-to-day environment and the higher realm of the forms. Plato built on this distinction, arguing that the world as we perceive it is a mere reflection of the truth, which is embodied in the forms. The famous cave analogy of *The Republic* makes exactly this point. The inhabitants of the cave believe that they can see reality, but in fact all they see are shadows projected onto the rock face; it is only the philosopher who can exit from the cave into the light of the sun and grasp reality for what it is. We need to journey intellectually beyond this world, the world of individual things perceived by our senses, and ascend into the sphere of pure thought. Around this time Plato also develops his theory of the immortal soul. His dialogue *Phaedo,* set on Socrates's last day, argues for a kinship between the soul and the forms. On death, the souls of the virtuous are permanently released from the confines of the body, whereas those that are beholden to bodily pleasures are condemned to reincarnation. These theories depend on a series of parallel oppositions: body/soul, matter/spirit, this world/the next, senses/mind, particulars/forms. Whereas the Socrates of the early Platonic dialogues had thought it his mission to live a virtuous life in this world, the later Socrates puts the emphasis on escaping from it into a pure, transcendent realm of the soul, free from bodily impurity.

There is nothing specifically godlike about the forms, but they do point to mid-period Plato's emphasis on the otherworldly and the spiritual—something that is barely visible in the early period Socrates. But the divine reappears in spectacular form in *Timaeus,* a late dialogue that argues for a divine creator god whom he calls the demiurge (or "craftsman"). *Timaeus* is by some distance the most theistic of Plato's dialogues—and it is no coincidence that it was the only one of his works that was read continuously throughout late antiquity and the medieval period. Here Plato takes the cosmic god of the pre-Socratics and transforms him into an active, designing, anthropomorphic deity. The demiurge forged the universe in a perfect, orderly way, with every element fitting together harmoniously. He created the celestial bodies, the world, the gods, time, animal life, and a superior race of human beings. Each human soul is paired with a star. If a man lives ethically, on death he returns to his star, but if not he is reborn as a woman (!). A badly behaved woman is then reincarnated as an animal. The *Timaeus* finally ties together all the various strands of Plato's thought into one theistic whole. His intellectual journey, which began with the project to rehabilitate an atheist, ends here: with god.

But the journey was not, in fact, quite ended. At the very end of his life, Plato returned to the traumatic topic of atheism. His very last work, *The Laws,* is an unusual text, a dialogue that—exceptionally—does not feature Socrates at all. The participants are an unnamed Athenian stranger (the central figure, who dominates the discussion), a Spartan called Megillus, and a Cretan Clinias. Their discussion is protracted and wide-ranging—this is Plato's longest work, and it rambles somewhat— and deals with the question of what laws are to be established in the new Cretan colony that Clinias has been tasked with overseeing. *The Laws* is a companion piece to *The Republic,* Plato's mid-period analysis of the ideal, utopian city, but it is much more focused on the realities of lawmaking. *The Republic* described an utopian state; *The Laws,* by contrast, offers a pragmatic second best to the ideal.[14]

Among the areas requiring legislation is theology. The tenth book is devoted to precisely this question, and Plato here develops some of his most important and worked-out ideas about the nature of deity and in particular focuses on proofs that gods exist. These take two forms. The first is a cosmological one. The regular motions of the heavenly bodies demonstrate that a divine hand is at work. Anything that moves must have something that animates it, the Athenian supposes. In the case of living beings, that is the soul. In the case of the heavens, that is god. The second argument is a moral one: if we do not accept that humans have a share in the divine, in the form of our souls, then we cannot aspire to moral perfection, which is the property of the gods alone.

These are not just philosophical arguments; they are also justifications for the legal repression of atheism. The Athenian pitches his arguments in response to "certain clever moderns," some "young men" who hold disreputable views about the gods. There are, he claims, three types of position to which such people subscribe: they assert either that the gods do not exist; or that, if they do, they have no involvement in the affairs of humans; or that they do, but they are easily swayed by sacrifices and prayers. Is he talking about a real community? Does he mean that there was a sizeable movement among the young in Athens who held these three types of beliefs? One respected scholar has argued exactly this: that there was an "atheist underground" at Athens, on which Plato is here shining a light. He may well be right. But the primary target of this designedly nonspecific attack is, surely, the phantoms that have haunted Plato ever since the trial of Socrates. Book 10 of *The Laws* is ultimately about disavowing all traces of philosophy's origins in (real or perceived) atheism.[15]

Instilling belief in the gods, the Athenian insists, is absolutely essential to the functioning of a just society. Therefore, there must be penalties laid down against anyone who insults the gods, "either in deed or in word." The qualification "or in word" is striking and reactivates memories of Diopeithes's decree, almost one hundred years earlier, which had come up with the revolutionary stipulation that piety consisted in proper belief as well as proper action. Paradoxically, the Athenian stranger ends up parroting precisely the legislation that had done for Socrates. Plato seems to be the victim of a kind of intellectual Stockholm syndrome: having spent so long psychologically trapped by the traumatic effects of Socrates's unjust execution for supposed impiety, he ended up designing a state that cannot tolerate anything other than one type of religious orthodoxy and punished disbelievers. Abuse, as they say, begets abuse.[16]

Plato laid the ground rules for Greek philosophy, and his theistic swerve toward the end of his life had a major influence. For the Stoics, *Timaeus*'s model of cosmic design was *the* proof text. The Church Fathers, too, expended much energy on blending Platonic and Judeo-Christian metaphysics and creationism. It is no exaggeration to say that the design-based arguments for the existence of God that proliferate even now were stabilized by Plato. And yet the execution of Socrates for "not recognizing the gods of the city" is an integral part of the story of how Plato came to that position. Before Plato's theism there was Socrates's playfully subversive humanism: based, to be sure, in a sort of divine revelation, but its ultimate message was that you make your own principles and you live by them.

PART THREE

The Hellenistic Era

GODLIKE KINGS AND
GODLESS PHILOSOPHERS

In the fourth century BC, a new military and political power emerged in Greece. Few would have predicted the rise of Macedonia. It had certainly been a wealthy state from the sixth century onward, headed by a royal family bent on acquiring local Thracian territories. Archaeology has revealed grand royal designs in the form of spectacular tombs dating back to this period. For most Greeks farther south, however, until the time of Philip II, Macedonians remained a marginal presence, glimpsed only in the penumbra of Hellenism.

But this northern kingdom had many advantages. It had wide, fertile plains that were agriculturally rich. Easy maritime routes led down the Thermaic Gulf into the Aegean. It also had the distinction of sitting on two land axes: to the south it faced the Greek peninsula, and to the east there was the land route between Europe and Asia. In time, the way from Thessaloniki (founded in 315 BC) and Byzantium in Anatolia would become one of Europe's major thoroughfares, thanks in no small part to the Roman road known as the Via Egnatia, built in the second century BC.

Already in antiquity, there was debate as to whether Macedonia was properly part of Greece or not. The mythical family tree of Greek ethnicity, captured in the sixth-century BC *Catalogue of Women*, recognized the existence of a man called Macedon, in the third generation of human existence. Macedon was the founder of the Macedonian dynasty. So the Macedonians were indeed acknowledged early on as part of the extended family of the Greek world. The mythical Macedon, however, is not listed as a descendant of Hellen, the ancestor of the Hellenes; he comes from a different branch of the human family. This sense that the Macedonians were not quite Hellenic was significant on the ground, too.

Herodotus has a story that captures their marginal position in the generation before his own time. Alexander I—an ancestor of "the Great"—ruled from about 498 to 454 BC. According to Herodotus, he sought in his youth to compete in the footrace at the Olympic Games, which were open only to Greeks. His rivals sought to debar him on those grounds, but Alexander "proved himself to be an Argive, and was judged to be a Greek." How he went about "proving" that the Macedonian dynasty originated in the Peloponnesian city of Argos, Herodotus does not tell us. But the important point is that it was not self-evident to all that the Macedonians were bona fide Greeks, even if the eventual decision of the Hellanodicae, the adjudicators at the Olympics, went in their favor. For most Greeks of Herodotus's era, Macedonia was known as a powerful, expansionist northern kingdom and (certainly) a handy ally for Athens in their war with Sparta—but rather remote from their own immediate concerns.[1]

Land routes can present problems as well as opportunities. When the Persians expanded into the Balkans in 512–511 BC, Macedon stood directly in their way. It capitulated quickly; the Persians' domination of the region lasted until they were finally pushed out of the mainland by the successes of the allied Greek forces in 480–479 BC. Toward the end of the fifth century BC and into the beginning of the fourth, however, Macedon became harder to ignore as a player in the political and cultural life of Greece. It was said in antiquity that the great Athenian poet Euripides spent time at the court of King Archelaus (who ruled between approximately 413 and 399 BC); whether this is true or not, he certainly produced a set of Macedonian-themed plays toward the end of his life. Athens's most famous dramatist had found the ancient mythology of Macedon a fit subject—and that is a remarkable thing, whether or not he did actually spend time in the north.[2]

From the 350s onward, Philip II ("the Great") began a series of campaigns against Athenian interests in the north. These drew the ire of the famous Athenian orator Demosthenes, whose speeches fulminating against Macedonian power (the *Philippics*) can still raise hairs. Despite Demosthenes's best efforts, however, Philip's rise remained unchecked, and he eventually won a decisive victory over a united force of Athenians and Thebans at Chaeronea in 338 BC. The following year, all of the

Greek states pledged allegiance to Macedon. Only Sparta refused to cede to the new rulers of Greece and join the so-called League of Corinth. Their resistance lasted a mere seven years.

After Philip's murder in 336, his son Alexander III came to the throne and quickly set about inheriting his father's title "the Great." Passing through the Balkans, he advanced into the territory of the Persian Empire and began his famous eastern campaigns. He captured strongholds in Anatolia (the western part of modern Turkey), Syria and the Levant, and Egypt, before pushing into the heartlands of the empire, Mesopotamia. In 331 he captured the imperial capital, Babylon, just south of modern Baghdad. He then chased Great King Darius III into what is now Iran, where the latter was assassinated by conspirators. Proclaiming himself Darius's successor, Alexander headed east into Afghanistan, Pakistan, and northern India, before finally giving in to his weary army and agreeing to turn back. He died in Babylon in 323, aged thirty-two.[3]

The period between Alexander's death and the Battle of Actium in 31 BC has been known to scholars since the nineteenth century as "Hellenistic," after the Hellenizing ("Greekifying") effects of these conquests on non-Greek peoples of the East. After Alexander's death, different generals seized different territories, and the empire fragmented into four smaller units. The descendants of Antigonus ruled much of the Greek peninsula from the heartlands of Macedon. The Ptolemies, descendants of Ptolemy, son of Lagus, built a naval empire from the new Egyptian capital of Alexandria, as well as controlling the rich Nile lands. The successors of another general, Seleucus, held Mesopotamia and Syria. The descendants of Attalus (who inherited their lands from Alexander's general Lysimachus) ruled much of western Turkey from their capital at Pergamum, modern Bergama. There were, in addition, numerous smaller confederations, including various leagues of free cities in mainland Greece.

The Hellenistic world offered a new set of models for Greek civilization: large, diverse territories were controlled imperially from grandiose capitals, dominated by royal dynasties. It was not the imperial ambitions themselves that were unparalleled (Athens had its empire) but the scale and scope of them, together with the reassertion of kingship as the normal mode of governance—and territorial expansion into the Near East.

Greeks were now heirs to political traditions not only of the mainland, but also of the older imperial states of the East: the Seleucids of Mesopotamia fashioned themselves in the guise of Babylonian and Assyrian monarchs, while the Ptolemies of Egypt adopted pharaonic iconography. To accompany this new Greco-Oriental style of kingship, moreover, the Hellenistic kings gathered around themselves outstanding figures of literary, philosophical, and artistic prowess. The Hellenistic empires, like their predecessors in Athens, Mesopotamia, and Egypt, were empires of the mind as well as of physical terrain. The royal library and museum (Mouseion, "shrine to the Muses") at Alexandria are well-known examples of Hellenistic intellectual centers, but Pergamum too had a vast library. Schools of philosophy and rhetoric flourished, first in Athens and later farther afield. Cities were adorned with magnificent temples, public gymnasia, and theaters in the Hellenic style and festooned with Greek inscriptions in prose and verse.[4]

The Hellenistic era saw the beginnings of the process of imperial centralization of the Mediterranean, North Africa, and the Levant that were fully realized only with Roman conquest. New styles of Greek kingship (based in part on Persian and pharaonic models) pointed toward the possibility of a theocratic world-empire centered on the charismatic power of the king, but political instabilities and constant interstate warring prevented this model from fully taking root. In most of the older Greek cities, life went on much as before, with the domestic political agenda dominating (the idea that larger, bullying states from without would periodically exert their influence was nothing new). Nevertheless, the idea of the king-as-god was established during this period and would come to have a decisive influence under Rome.

10

Gods and Kings

Alexander III was a lustrous king. Portrait makers reveled in trying to capture his radiance. In a wonderful Pompeian mosaic (based on a lost Greek original) of the battle of Issus, the Persian king Darius is more immediately visible: higher up, and more central, and framed against the sky by a mass of spears. But Alexander is unmistakable at the heart of the Macedonian cavalry on the left-hand side of the image, his eyes wide, unyielding, and intense, his figure taut and full of coiled power. The Persian horsemen on the right are on the point of turning to flee in panic, as if they have suddenly realized their error in underestimating their enemy. The great sculptor Lysippus portrayed him as tall, muscular, and heroic; the tilted head pointed his eyes to the heavens but also carried a hint of sadness, perhaps already suggesting the mourning of his own premature end.[1]

The royal house of Macedon claimed descent from Heracles and Perseus, and Alexander was indeed in the eyes of many like a hero reborn, combining overachievement, virility, devotion to his comrades, and obsessive ambition in the space of a short life. It was an association he did little to discourage. He slept with the *Iliad* under his pillow. When he crossed over to Anatolia, he visited Troy and sacrificed at Achilles's tomb. Even his intimate relationship with Hephaestion was reminiscent of Achilles's friendship with Patroclus. One anecdote has a poet approach him and offer to write him up so that he becomes greater than Achilles; he slaps him down, saying, "I would rather be Homer's Thersites than your Achilles," naming the ugliest, most cowardly of the Homeric Greeks. It is apocryphal of course, but it testifies to the enduring interest in weighing Alexander against Achilles.[2]

Luster mattered to the ruler of vast tracts of territory and a multilingual populace, and to the inheritor of a foreign kingdom. Alexander needed to project a clear image of power that all could understand. His heroic self-presentation demonstrated clearly to all his subjects that they had a king who was touched with divinity. Indeed, aspects of it were derived from the near eastern monarchies themselves. It had been one of the clichés among the Greeks that the Persian Great King demanded *proskynēsis,* "prostration," before him. When Alexander introduced the custom in his own court, along with Persian-style dress, his Macedonian companions bristled, but shrewder observers saw it as a political move to demonstrate to his Near Eastern subjects that he was no less awesome a ruler than his predecessor in the role, Darius III.[3]

Whether he was a god or not is a more complex question. Mortal kings in the Greek tradition had always had a divine tinge to them. The aristocrats who people Homer's epics are often said to be "divine" or "godlike." Some Greek families, indeed, traced their lineages back to gods or heroes. Sophocles's *Oedipus the King,* performed in around 428 BC, has the chorus address a prayer to their ruler as "savior" (a title for deities), while insisting that they do not want to equate him with a god (which, of course, implies that that is exactly what they are in danger of doing). In Aristophanes's *Birds,* the central character Peisetairus is sung a hymn by the birds of Cloudcuckooland that acknowledges him in divine terms ("He wields the thunderbolt, Zeus's winged weapon!"). The language of divine kingship was always there, waiting to be activated. Toward the end of the fifth century there are signs that it was put to use. Lysander, the Spartan general responsible for the defeat of Athens in 404 BC, extracted unimaginable amounts of wealth from the captive city. "Out of the spoils," one later historian writes, "he set up at Delphi bronze statues of himself and each of his admirals, as well as golden stars of the Dioscuri . . . Lysander was at this time more powerful than any Greek before him had been, and seemed to cultivate an arrogance and ostentatiousness that was greater even than his power. For he was the first Greek, as Duris [a historian] writes, to whom the cities set up altars and made sacrifices as to a god, and the first to whom songs of triumph were sung." This is not just a fantasy of later historians: there is material evidence for the cult of Lysander on the island of Samos, on the other side of the Aegean. New modalities of kingship were emerging in the late fifth century BC, pointing the way toward the grandiosity of the Hellenistic kingdoms that followed Alexander's conquests.[4]

Another ruler with divine pretensions was Dionysius I of Syracuse, in Sicily. A mercenary leader who had toppled the existing democratic government, Dionysius built an elaborate court structure around him that attracted musicians and intellectuals: Philoxenus of Cythera, the author of a still-extant poem about the love of the Cyclops Polyphemus for the nymph Galatea, the historian Philistus, perhaps even Plato himself (if we can trust the letters transmitted in his name). And like Lysander, Dionysius seems to have styled himself as an exceptionally luxurious, charismatic king. In 388 BC, for example, a deputation arrived from him at the Olympic Games and pitched camp in a tent adorned with gold and purple, "so that Dionysius might inspire the awe of Greece." This, however, prompted the Athenian orator to deliver a lusty speech comparing Dionysius to the Persian Great King, the embodiment of despotic decadence in the eyes of many Greeks. Again like Lysander, he was probably worshipped in his own lifetime with divine honors, perhaps in the likeness of his near namesake, the god Dionysus.[5]

There is, of course, no such thing as a clean break in history: all new developments, rather, are adjustments of the ratio between change and continuity. There were intimations of Hellenistic swagger already in the court of Dionysius I and in the flamboyant self-styling of the victorious Spartan general Lysander. Yet neither carried the same conviction with other Greeks. Alexander, after all, had not just sacked one city. Between 334 BC, when he led his invading force across to Anatolia, and 323 BC, when he died in Babylon, he had comprehensively routed the Persian king Darius III in a series of battles and successfully laid siege to Sardis, Tyre, and Gaza. He had subdued the whole of the Levant, Egypt, and Mesopotamia before heading through the Zagros Mountains into Persia and capturing the imperial capital Persepolis. He had journeyed east through Bactria (approximately modern Afghanistan) and into northern India.[6]

There was undoubtedly something godlike about this Macedonian conqueror. His propagandists portrayed him as more than human. He claimed as his father Ammon, an Egyptian ram god whom the Greeks treated as the equivalent of Zeus; this was confirmed to him by the oracle itself when he visited Siwah, an oasis in the western desert, in February 332 BC. To mark this ancestry he was depicted on coins wearing ram's horns (the reason why many have thought the "two-horned one" of the Qur'an—Zul-Qarnayn—to be him). In the Temple of Artemis, Ephesus, hung a painting by Apelles portraying him with a Zeus-like thunderbolt. He is often found in the likeness of Apollo or Heracles, or with the Dionysiac attributes of panther skin and (perhaps) elephant scalp. In later times he was assimilated to the sun god Helios and depicted with a solar crown (an iconographic motif that would eventually metamorphose into the Christian halo).[7]

But being godlike is not the same as actually being a god. This distinction is in fact fiendishly difficult to draw. What did it mean when cities offered their rulers "honors equal to the gods" (*isotheoi timai*)? The very phrase communicates this uncertainty: to treat rulers in the same way as gods is not to say that they are gods. In fact, it is arguably to say that they are not (for the observation that x resembles y depends upon an awareness that x is not y: you would not say a monkey is like a simian or a stone is like a rock). But few in antiquity drew such stark distinctions. No doubt the ideological system depended on precisely not demanding precise clarifications. Rulers were like gods in that they were possessed of superhuman power and charisma, but they were also demonstrably mortal and capable of error.[8]

In many cases, certainly, there is evidence of actual religious worship of rulers. Cities might set up altars in honor of Alexander or one of his successors. There might be a priest whose job was to sacrifice on this altar; processions and games might be held, hymns might be sung. In Athens, we hear of an altar and a new priesthood commemorating the roles of the generals Antigonos "the One-Eyed" and his son Demetrius "the Besieger" as saviors, after they expelled the occupying garrisons of Ptolemy I and Cassander. New tribes were created in their name. Alternatively, a ruler's statue might be placed in the temple of another god and become a "shrine-sharer" (*synnaos*): this was the honor decreed by the inhabitants of Pergamum for their king Attalus III, who was to cohabit with the healer god Asclepius. A related but slightly different phenomenon is the deification of dead kings, a phenomenon best attested to in Egyptian Alexandria, where there was a priest dedicated to the cult of both Alexander (as the city's founder) and the ancestral ruling dynasty, the "brother-sister gods" (*theoi philadelphoi*). Nor was the phenomenon limited to individual cities: in Seleucid Mesopotamia, the entire Greek population was expected to join in the veneration of Antiochus III and his ancestors.[9]

But what did this ruler cult actually mean in practice? When the early queens of Egyptian Alexandria Berenice and Arsinoe II were praised in the guise of Aphrodite, what was going on in the heads of those present? Were these monarchs worshipped as actual gods, or (once again) as godlike? Was their divinity real or metaphorical? For a long time the scholarly consensus was that this is the wrong kind of question: to pose the question in terms of inner mental process is to impose an anachronistically Christian framework onto polytheistic antiquity. In a pre-theological world, it was said, no one cared to ask such literal questions. The Hellenistic ruler cult, according to this way of thinking, was instead an idiom, a way of expressing the new political reality. The citizens of Greek states were well used to the idea that they voted honors to their top citizens (even democratic Athens had a form of this practice). From the Hellenistic subjects' point of view, then, treating their royals as gods was simply an extension of existing practice; it had no serious metaphysical implications. From this perspective, only the odd member of the intellectual elite paused to query the divinization of mortals conceptually (one poet speaks of the "impiety of granting divine honours to men"); for the rest, it was enough to perform the rituals.[10]

It may well be true that, in antiquity as now, many people lived their lives without questioning what they were told. But the idea that the divinity of Hellenistic rulers rarely presented itself as a problem seems, at the very least, intuitively wrong. Kings are not gods: they die. The issue is, as ever, one of sources. If we treat the official publications of states (which means in this case principally their inscriptions) as our evidence for Hellenistic ruler cult, then it stands to reason that we will end up concluding that it was largely unproblematic for its consumers. It was in the interests of those who ran cities to pretend that their institutions were straightforward, natural, and uncontested. If, however, we look to other kinds of sources then we can begin to disclose how the more quizzical onlooker may have felt. Recent scholars have begun to argue for a complex range of possible responses, from the accepting to the incredulous: often these will have been harmonized within the individual's mind, but not always. Religion in general, after all, perpetuates itself by drawing connections between things that are not intuitively connected and naturalizing these connections through social mechanisms. "Religion," one scholar has said, "is in the mind. It consists not so much in religious acts as in schemes of perceptions and thoughts whose meaningfulness is repeatedly reinforced by the performance of symbolic acts." The social expectation that one should view Hellenistic monarchs as gods was precisely one such scheme of perception. What was problematic about it, however, was that it risked conflict with another one, according to which gods are viewed as by definition supernatural beings. That conflict could come in and out of focus at different times.[11]

One instance where the problematic nature of the king-god comes into focus appears in a poem by the brilliant poet Theocritus, who wrote in Egyptian Alexandria during the reign of Ptolemy II (ca. 283–246 BC). His name is today most closely associated with bucolic poetry, but he also wrote, among other things, an encomiastic poem for his king, which begins with a meditation on Ptolemy's status. Zeus, Theocritus observes, is greatest of the immortals, and Ptolemy the most powerful of men. So far so good: Ptolemy exceeds other mortals in the way that Zeus exceeds other gods. But this means that Ptolemy is a man, not a god. He then, however, proceeds to move his ruler quickly up the scale:

> The heroes who in days gone by were born of demigods
> Had their wise bards when they performed excellent deeds.
> But I, who know how to speak of excellent things, would hymn
> Ptolemy; for hymns are the privilege also of the gods themselves.

This is a masterpiece of calculated obfuscation. We meet the heroes "born of demigods," who seem at first blush to offer a useful analogy for a king who sits somewhere between the divine and the mortal. But Theocritus seems to reject this comparison, suggesting that his song for Ptolemy is actually a "hymn," and so more appropriate to a god than to a hero. Yet there is still some reticence in that final sentence: "Hymns are the privilege also of the gods themselves." "Also" implies that hymns are appropriate for the gods as well as Ptolemy. He is not of their number. Or is he? Theocritus now imagines his king's father, Ptolemy I, sitting alongside Alexander in heaven: "For the father has made him equal in honour [*homotimos*] with the blessed immortals." Ptolemy's status slides around between human, hero, and god. For some listeners the general point will have been clear enough: their king is more than human, in a way that mere language cannot quite capture. For others, the failure to specify exactly where Ptolemy sits in the hierarchy will have been a sign that Theocritus himself was not sure.[12]

Another hymn to a deified ruler is even more potentially subversive. Demetrius "the Besieger," who liberated Athens in 308 BC along with his father Antigonus, was acclaimed as king in the city and accorded divine honors. When he made his final visit in 290, he was welcomed with incense, libations, dancing, and hymns. One of these hymns, written in the ithyphallic meter by a certain Hermocles of Cyzicus, was recorded and has partially survived. It is an extraordinary document for anyone interested in the question of whether the Greeks believed their gods:[13]

Oh, the greatest and dearest of the gods
Are present for the city!
For the situation has brought among us
Both Demeter and Demetrius.
Demeter has come to perform
The most holy mysteries of Persephone;
But he, serene (as a god should be), handsome
And smiling: he is here.
It seems a solemn thing: his friends surround him,
And he himself is in the centre,
As if his friends were the stars
And he the sun.
Welcome, son of a god, mightiest Poseidon,
And of Aphrodite!
The other gods are either far away
Or they have no ears,
Or they do not exist, or they pay no attention at all to us;
But you we see present:

You are made of neither wood nor stone. You are real.
We pray to you . . . [there then follows a prayer for peace with the
    Aetolians][14]

What is truly amazing about this hymn is that it reverses the anticipated direction of skepticism. One might expect the existence of the
Olympian gods to be unquestioned and the arrival of Demetrius, the
newcomer to the pantheon, to be awkward. But in fact it is Demetrius's
visible presence ("the greatest and dearest of the gods / Are present for
the city . . . he is here . . . you we see present") that guarantees that he
is a true god ("You are real"). The Olympian gods, by contrast, are presented as unreal, mere human artifacts ("wood and stone"—a reference
to statues). Three options are imagined to explain the absence of the
Olympian gods: either they cannot intervene in human affairs (they are
"far away / Or they have no ears"), or they will not ("they pay no attention at all to us"), or "they do not exist" at all. One exception is made
for Demeter, the goddess of agriculture (and of the nearby Eleusinian
Mysteries)—but only because her name is embedded in Demetrius's own
name. The hymn in effect argues that Demetrius is the only god worth
bothering about.[15]

Hermocles's hymn is exceptional. There is no other instance in which
earnest belief in the reality of a ruler-god is so obviously bartered in
exchange for belief in the Olympian gods. It probably should not be
taken as evidence that the introduction of a ruler cult caused a mass outbreak of atheism toward the Olympians. But it does underline the general point, that when new religious "schemes of perception" come into
play they can interfere with existing ones, and there is no guarantee that
the older ones will survive better.

Nowhere is this more evident than in the writings of one of the most
striking figures of the early Hellenistic period, Euhemerus of Messene.
Euhemerus wrote an account of a trip he supposedly took to the Ara-
bian Ocean on the orders of King Cassander of Macedon, who ruled
between 305 and 297 BC. The *Sacred Inscription,* as this work was
known, became one the most famous of all ancient texts expressing religious disbelief. Euhemerus is found in every list of *atheoi* (atheists) that
survives from antiquity. His name has even found its way into modern

English, admittedly at the rarefied end of the spectrum: "euhemerism" is the retelling of myths so as to exclude or explain the supernatural elements. In fact the English word is a misnomer. This kind of rationalizing, which had its roots in the classical writers Hecataeus of Miletus and Palaephatus, continued apace, but what Euhemerus offered was something far more radical.[16]

Euhemerus's words do not survive verbatim, but we have a detailed summary courtesy of a later writer, Diodorus of Sicily (first century BC). Euhemerus's claim was that he visited an island called Panchaea, an island of extraordinary beauty and fertility, where humans live in a utopian society. Of the three social orders, the priests, the farmers, and the soldiers, it is the priests who are the ultimate arbiters. The picture that is painted is of a people joyously submissive to a benign theocracy. "The priests are the rulers of all the others, and they adjudicate when there are disputes, and have authority over all public matters." As the narrative progresses, we come ever closer to the beating heart of Panchaean society, the temple of Zeus Triphylios ("of the Three Tribes") that stands on an acropolis. Euhemerus has much to say about the beauty and the grandeur of the temple. But, he says, it concealed a surprise: a golden pillar, inscribed with a record of the deeds of Uranus, Cronus, and Zeus. The inscription revealed that the Olympian gods were originally human beings and an exceptional generation of rulers of Panchaea. It was Zeus himself who traveled around the world and instituted his own cultic worship. In other words, Panchaean society is sustained by a religion based upon the worship of a "god" who is no more a god than you or I.[17]

In its original form, the *Sacred Inscription* was probably a mixed-genre work: a fast-paced travel story, a fictional proto-novel, a philosophical experiment with a utopia (rather like Plato's *Republic* and *Laws*), and a vehicle for exploring the further implications of atheistic theories canvassed by the sophists of fifth-century BC Athens. Euhemerus was particularly impressed by Prodicus's theory that divinities were named after human innovators: Demeter was the inventor of bread, Dionysus of wine, and each thereafter came to be treated as a god. Viewed in its historical context, however, it looks to have been a very different kind of theological critique than anything that went before: it seems hard to imagine that Euhemerus was not responding to the trend toward making royals divine. If Alexander and the Ptolemies could be made divine, why rule out the possibility that all of the gods are deified humans? Could it be that Zeus and his family founded their own ruler cults in much the same way that Hellenistic monarchs did?[18]

Euhemerus almost certainly knew all about ruler cult. At this point we need to detach the author from the narrator of the *Sacred Inscription*. The narrator claims to have been sent out by Cassander of Macedon. There is no evidence of any ruler cult for that king. But it is likely enough that the whole story about Cassander is a fiction, like the rest of the story. The one piece of contemporary biographical evidence for the author Euhemerus comes from Callimachus, the poet of Hellenistic Alexandria, who refers malevolently to a temple just outside the city "where the chattering old man who invented / Panchaean Zeus scratches out his criminal books." Euhemerus therefore probably wrote his *Sacred Inscription* in Alexandria, one of the locations where early Hellenistic ruler cult was practiced most intensely.[19]

Euhemerus was not alone in reflecting on the implications of ruler cult. The third century BC also saw the foundation of one of the most famous philosophical schools. Stoicism was named for the Stoa Poikile, the "painted porch" in Athens where its founder, Zeno, taught. (This Zeno is not to be confused with the other philosophical Zeno of Elea, the pre-Socratic whose famous paradoxes were designed to show the impossibility of motion.) Zeno was from the city of Citium on Cyprus. In about 276 BC, he received a request to move to the Macedonian court at Pella, to become an advisor to King Antigonus "the Knock-Kneed" (the Macedonian Antigoni specialized in evocative nicknames!), who ruled from 277 to 239 BC, and to teach his son. Zeno declined but sent along his student, friend, and companion, one Persaeus, also of Citium. Like so much from this era, Persaeus's philosophical output survives only in snippets. We do have a list of his books, however, which suggests that his primary interests were in political and sexual themes. In later antiquity, however, he was most remembered for his theory of religion. Cicero, the Roman orator and thinker of the first century BC, summarizes his views in his *On the Nature of the Gods:* "It was men who had discovered some great aid to civilisation that were regarded as gods, and that the names of divinities were also bestowed upon actual material objects of use and profit." A fragmentary papyrus, recovered from the beneath the volcanic debris of Vesuvius, clarifies that Persaeus saw the development of religion as occurring in two stages: first the human inventors of various technologies were deified, then the objects themselves. He may have taken over this idea from the fifth-century BC sophist Prodicus, but he certainly lent them a new forcefulness in the changed cultural context of the Hellenistic kingdoms. Persaeus, unlike Prodicus, actually knew of cases in which exceptional humans had been granted divine cult (although there is no evidence to suggest that knock-kneed Antigonus himself was worshipped). Some scholars, it is true, have argued that Persaeus's critique of religion was milder than this: either he was merely denying the gods of popular religion (and promoting instead a Stoic view of a cosmic intelligence), or he was claiming that the popular view of the gods, though misguided, contains a measure of insight into the true nature of divinity. But the Herculaneum papyrus seems to rule this out: "It is clear that Persaeus actually does away with and gets rid of the supernatural, or perhaps thinks that nothing can be known about it." This evidence is hard to argue away. Persaeus saw all divinity as a human construction, and although there is nothing that can prove it conclusively, it is likely that he was inspired to claim this by the unfamiliar sight of humans who were treated like gods.[20]

Philosophically speaking, Persaeus and Euhemerus built on the atheistic foundations laid by the sophists of fifth-century BC Athens. But on these foundations they constructed a new, contemporary edifice, one that reflected the changed political realities of the world in which they lived. For a mortal to become a god—or to become "godlike" in ways that defied specification—was now no longer the preserve of ancient heroes. Deification was now a cultural trope through which Greeks understood the world around them, a meme rather than a mytheme. But the possibility of humans becoming gods also challenged the divide between mortal and immortal, eroding further the idea (which had been assailed already by the "god battlers" of myth) of a special divine privilege.

11

Philosophical Atheism

The Hellenistic era saw the dissolution of Alexander's vast but thinly stretched empire into smaller units seized by his power-hungry successors. The Seleucid Empire, named for its founder Seleucus I Nicator ("the Conqueror," ca. 358–281 BC), was centered on Babylon in Mesopotamia (modern Iraq). The Ptolemies, who looked back to Ptolemy I Soter ("the Savior," ca. 367–283 BC) were based in Egyptian Alexandria. The Antigonid dynasty, in Macedonia, was inaugurated by Antigonus I "the One-eyed" (ca. 382–301 BC). In time a fourth empire would emerge, the Attalids of Pergamum (on the western coast of what is now Turkey), after Attalus I claimed power in the 230s.

The intellectual world too was reshaped: powerful, international philosophical schools vied for dominance in the way that their rulers did. The idea of rival philosophical sects dated back to fourth-century BC Athens, when Aristotle split from Plato's Academy and set up his Lyceum. The two names refer to physical locations, in fact to gymnasia, where young men would congregate to hear the masters; one was named after the mythical Academus, from the cycle of stories connected to the Athenian hero Theseus, the other after Apollo Lyceus ("the Wolf").

In the Hellenistic age, new schools sprang up alongside the Academy and the Lyceum, centered initially in Athens but with a huge geographical reach. Many of the Hellenistic philosophers came from the farthest corners of the Greek-speaking world: from the Black Sea area, for example, and from modern Iraq and Tunisia. The labels attached to these various philosophical groups are no less resonant today: Cynics, Stoics, Epicureans, Skeptics. Modern, Western ideas about how life should be lived were largely formed in the laboratory of Hellenistic philosophy. Do you believe in a countercultural existence that defies society's conventions? You are a Cynic. Or is life best when we dutifully play the hand that fate gives us, whatever it is, to the best of our abilities? In which case you are a Stoic. Or is the aim to remove the stress and anxiety that comes with society's false demands? You are an Epicurean. Or do you reject any kind of dogma whatsoever? In that case you are a Skeptic.[1]

These philosophical schools insisted primarily upon the values and ethics of lived experience: in this they followed the lead of Socrates rather than any of his rivals. Philosophy should be therapeutic, it was believed: it should make the user's soul better. By placing the emphasis on the practical problems of existence, the Hellenistic schools created a less rarefied, more inclusive environment, at least for the male elite. By the first century AD most educated Greeks and Romans had at least a smattering of philosophical education, and many publicly identified with one school or another. Philosophy continued to fulfil many of the needs that we today think of as belonging exclusively to religion: it offered consolation to the suffering and bereft, it helped the perplexed understand their place in the cosmos, it explained why it was important to be good even if the world was not always good in return. The movement of philosophy into the mainstream also prepared the way for Christianity later to spread among the ruling elite of the Roman Empire, for it was initially taken as another form of philosophy of life. This process, indeed, was helped by the fact that the early Church Fathers, in the third and fourth centuries AD, largely reformulated Christianity so that it looked much more like a Greco-Roman philosophy.

What role did the gods play in this philosophical revolution? It was the Stoics, most of all, who embraced and developed the theistic philosophies of Plato and Aristotle. Stoicism was founded in Athens by Zeno of Citium (on Cyprus) in the third century BC. Of all the Hellenistic philosophies, it most resembled a guidebook for living in the new historical reality of international empires. Orthodox Stoics believed in a world governed by an intelligent, designing deity, composed of matter but also identified with fire. True happiness comes from aligning oneself to the plan of that deity, to a life according to nature. Stoicism in effect advocated submission to a god who looks very much like an all-powerful cosmic king. And conformity to the divine plan, the Stoics taught, is the only form of moral virtue. In fact, they argued that it was not submission at all but liberation from the petty concerns of mundanity. The things that conventional society tells us are good—wealth, health, success in the eyes of others—are neither good nor bad, merely indifferent. If I fall ill, so be it: rather than bewailing my lot, I should respond virtuously to it. I may prefer to have good health than bad, and it is right to seek it out as much as I can, but if the divine plan necessitates my illness, so be it.[2]

Stoicism was a comprehensive theory of life and the universe, covering gods, nature, matter, time, language, logic, and perception. In terms of ethics, however, it has always been associated with fortitude and endurance and indeed has inspired many (from antiquity to the present day) to resist terrible conditions. The famous teacher Epictetus (ca. AD 55–110), for example, was born into slavery. In one account he was crippled when his master deliberately twisted his leg till it broke. Epictetus is said to have smiled during the torture and to have calmly described the progress of the breakage. If this happened in Rome, his master will have been Epaphroditus, Nero's henchman, who in the end conspired against the emperor and slit his throat. Epictetus was freed after Nero's death but later suffered banishment under the equally feral Domitian. It was Stoicism that kept him smiling through those dark days. His teachings are preserved in the *Discourses* and *Handbook*, ghostwritten by the military historian and Roman consul Arrian (better known as the author of the best ancient account of the campaigns of Alexander the Great). Epictetus's influential example has resonated throughout the ages and given us the modern idea of "stoic" behavior in the face of adversity. Take the case of James Stockdale, shot down above Vietnam on September 9, 1965. As his plane caught fire, he recalled reading Epictetus's *Handbook* as a student at Stanford University. "I'm leaving the world of technology," he told himself, "and entering the world of Epictetus." Epictetus taught that we should not concern ourselves with what is beyond our control and focus only on what is *eph' hēmin,* "up to us." It was this message that saw Stockdale through nearly eight years of prison in Hanoi, which saw him tortured, shackled, and confined in isolation.[3]

Stoicism urged more than the stiffening of the upper lip. Fundamentally, the Stoic ethical system taught its practitioners how to live in a world in which their power had been radically reduced. This is why an exiled former slave or, equally, a prisoner in 1960s Hanoi could find it so helpful. But it had a wider applicability in the Hellenistic and Roman worlds, where individuals, and indeed entire communities, were often subject to the dominion of distant imperial forces. There was an implicit structural analogy between the divine governance of the cosmos and the worldly governance of kings and emperors. It is no surprise that one of the greatest Stoic philosophers of antiquity was also a Roman emperor, Marcus Aurelius (AD 121–180). Not that Stoics were always on the side of mundane authorities when their values clashed with those of the authorities. In the dark days of Nero's reign, the Roman senator Thrasea Paetus, fortified by Stoic principles, opposed the emperor to the point where he was tried and ordered to commit suicide. The famous Stoic philosopher Seneca the Younger suffered the same fate at around this time, swept up (perhaps unjustly) in the recriminations that followed the anti-Neronian conspiracy of Gaius Calpurnius Piso in AD 65.

In general, however, Stoicism encouraged obedience. This applied to religious practice too, even though this was not a position that followed necessarily from their idea of deity. The notion of a god who was a fiery cosmic intelligence could have been a deeply heretical proposition. The Stoic god was an amalgam of many of the most radical ideas of the pre-Socratic philosophers (Heraclitus's fire, Anaxagoras's nous or "mind"), blended with Plato's idea of the cosmic craftsman. This could have led to a rejection of the existence of the Olympian gods, and hence of all civic cult. But in fact the Stoics took the opposite tack, claiming that the figures that we call Zeus, Hera, Athena, and the like are all different aspects of the cosmic deity: Zeus is associated with life (*zēn*), Athena with the rational faculty that stretches into the ether (*aithēr*), Hera with that in the air (*aēr*), and so forth. This kind of wordplay springs from the deeply rooted Greek idea that myth, however mythical, contains a grain of truth. But it was enough to ensure that the Stoics remained committed to civic religion. Among the Stoics only Persaeus of Citium, the friend of the founder Zeno, denied the existence of gods—and even he still insisted that the gods of the city should be worshipped in the normal way. In general, Stoicism preached submission to an all-powerful god of the cosmos.[4]

Other sects were less pietistic. Amongst the most colorful were the Cynics ("doggish ones"), inspired by Socrates and his contemporary

Antisthenes but thoroughly opposed to the highbrow intellectualism that Plato promoted. Cynicism was a philosophy of life, rather than of the mind. The only true path for the Cynic was the life "according to nature" (to use a phrase they favored): in other words, material goods are worthless, conventional society is there to be mocked, and power is there to be laughed at. It is hard to compile a list of Cynic beliefs as their writings were few and none have survived, and they were in any case comfortable with self-contradiction, having no time for dogma or rule books. All we have are the testimonies, usually either bewildered or amused, of others. Typically, however, Cynics mixed austerity in their personal habits with a refreshingly experimental approach to life. They did not believe in slavery; they mocked the powerful to their faces; they saw animals as moral exemplars, rather than tools for human exploitation; women were welcome (one important early Cynic was Hipparchia of Maroneia); in the ideal society, women and men would live intermingled and raise children together. The good life required escaping the false prison of social expectation, the *tuphos* (humbug). A well-known story has Diogenes of Sinope, a leading light of early Cynicism, masturbating in public, capping his performance with the witticism "if only it were possible to relieve hunger so easily." Cynics, indeed, were also known for their mischievous sense of humor. There are huge numbers of jokes attributed to Diogenes. When Plato defined a human as a featherless biped, Diogenes offered him a plucked chicken. Seeing temple officials arresting a thief, he commented that "the big thieves are taking away the little ones." With witty, pungent gags like these, the Cynics satirized convention without being drawn into a dogmatic position of their own.[5]

As one might expect, the Cynics had no explicit doctrine on religion— after all, they had no explicit doctrine on anything. As a result, scholars wanting firm answers have struggled with them. Certainly, Diogenes mocked sacrifice and dedications to the gods for their ineffectiveness. His position on the gods seems to have been contradictory. On the one hand, he is said to have pointed (like Bellerophon in Euripides's play) to the fact that the wicked often prosper as evidence for the nonexistence of gods. On other occasions he seems to have presumed their existence: "When the pharmacist Lysias asked him if he believed in the gods, he replied: 'How could I not believe in them, when I consider that they despise you?'" The most probable conclusion is that the Cynics did not care much about gods, except when they offered good material for poking fun at the self-righteous or the immoral. There was no place for gods in their radically anti-dogmatic view of the world and no place for organized religion in their anti-establishment utopia. But nor, on the other hand, were they interested in grand assertions of the nonexistence of gods. Their stance toward life had strongly agnostic implications, even atheistic, but metaphysical reasoning would have struck them as pretentiously irrelevant. A poem by the Cynic poet Cercidas (third century BC) sums up this position beautifully. After airing the familiar complaint that the gods fail to punish the wicked and reward the good, and meditating on the inconstancy of fate, he concludes: "Better to leave all these things to those who gaze on the heavens . . . let our concern, rather, be worldly: with Paian [the god of health], Redistribution—yes, she is a goddess—and Nemesis [vengeance]." Cynics had their feet planted firmly on the ground; metaphysics were an irrelevance rather than an object of discussion.[6]

The more robust challenge to conventional theology came from another philosophical movement that has left its mark on modern languages, now known as Skepticism. The Skeptics developed within Plato's school, the Academy; they were inspired by the example of Socrates, who often debated with people to prove the fragility of their views rather than any positive claim on his own part. Skepticism took aim at belief systems or dogma (the modern English word can be traced back to the Skeptics). Any beliefs, it asserted, rested on shaky foundations. The aim of philosophy, then, was to challenge dogma and to reduce dependence on weak argumentation. Indeed, one group of Skeptics (the Pyrrhonists) argued that *epokhē*, "suspension of judgment," was the route to happiness and tranquility. (Here we see a problem that always bedeviled Skepticism: Is this not a dogma itself? How, from a Skeptical perspective, can any positive belief be put forward, even about the benefits of suspension of belief?)[7]

Religion, of course, is a form of dogma. The very existence of multiple, competing views about gods (what form they have, where they live) already shows the impossibility of secure knowledge. Arguments against conventional theology were promoted by one Skeptic in particular, Carneades (ca. 214–129 BC), the magnetic and influential head of the Academy. He was such an impressive speaker that even the teachers of rhetoric, traditionally contemptuous of the complexities of philosophy, would leave their schools to admire his performances—despite the unkempt hair and overlong nails, the result of his obsessing over his studies at the expense of personal grooming. He won a place in history by showcasing the potential of Greek philosophy for the first time in Rome. In 155 BC, at a time when Rome was now the power broker in Greece, he was part of a delegation sent by the Athenians to try to reverse a massive fine that had been levied on them. One report compares the effect of his arrival to a tornado ripping through the city: "Carneades' charisma had extraordinary power, and a fame no less than its power; this gripped large and sympathetic audiences, and filled the city with hubbub, like a wind." Thrillingly, and controversially, he made two speeches to the Senate on consecutive days: the first argued for the sovereignty of Roman justice, while the second proposed the essential bankruptcy of the very same notion. Only the venomously anti-Greek Cato stood against the winds of philosophical change: fearing that the young men would prefer gilded words to deeds of war, he inveighed mightily (and not without a certain rhetorical polish of his own) against these Siren-like visitors. "Rome will lose her empire," he opined, "once she has become infected with Greek letters." Whether as a result of pressure from Cato or not, the Senate expelled two Epicurean philosophers from Rome. But history was not on Cato's side: the gusts howling through the city were winds of permanent change.[8]

Part of the reason for the attraction Carneades still exerts is the mystery around his views. Like Socrates, he wrote nothing down. This absence fed the wonder, curiosity, and contentiousness of his acolytes. Nowhere was the debate more intense than in discussion of his views about the gods. The later tradition knew him best for his arguments that belief in gods is illogical.

His first went as follows. If gods are superior to humans, then they must be able to sense things, because they cannot lack any capacity that humans have. In fact, they must have more senses than humans, because they are better than us. Yet sensation is a form of vulnerability to outside influence: if the gods can taste sweet things and bitter things, they can experience pleasure and distress in response to factors beyond their control. This means that gods are vulnerable, in that other forces can make them feel pain, and if they are vulnerable, they are in principle subject to decay.[9]

Another of Carneades's arguments attacked the idea that divinities can be morally rational. Its central principle was that the gods cannot be both entirely good and moral, since morality depends upon the possibility of doing wrong. If a god is good, Carneades reasoned, he cannot be prudent, because prudence implies the ability to choose among different available courses. If the god is entirely good, the wrong course will never occur to him. He therefore has no capacity to make rational moral choices. The same goes for justice: only humans can be just, since justice depends on the capacity to make wise judgments between options that present themselves. A perfect god simply would not have the option of taking the unjust path. Similarly with the avoidance of bodily pleasures: gods, surely, never display temperance because they are never tempted. Nor can they be brave, since they can never feel pain or suffering. The target of this argument was the Stoics, who saw rationality as defined by the capacity to make correct moral judgments. Since the argument proves that the gods cannot make moral judgments, it follows that the gods also (on the Stoic model) lack rationality.[10]

His most famous argument, however, sought to show that gods cannot exist at all. It is a variant of the so-called *sōritēs* or "heaping" argument, which seeks to destabilize our belief in categories (such as the idea of a heap) that we normally take for granted. In its most basic form it goes as follows. I can get you to agree that a single grain does not make a heap. I can also get you to agree that two grains do not make a heap. Nor three. We then proceed like this sequentially, never reaching a cutoff point between a pile of individual grains and a heap. It is not the case, for example, that 300 grains are a heap, whereas 299 are not. I can get you to accept that there is no point where adding a single grain makes the pile become a heap. And the reverse is also true: if we begin with what we both agree to be a heap, there is no point where removing a single grain will cause the heap to stop being a heap. Therefore, since we feel we know what a heap is but cannot define it systematically, any claim that "this is a heap" is neither true nor false. The concept of the heap cannot be securely defined. Similarly if I have one coin I am not rich, nor if I have two, and so forth, so richness is not securely defined either. Carneades ingeniously applied the *sōritēs* argument to gods. If we accept that the Olympians are gods, then what about nymphs? And if we accept nymphs, then what about Pan? And what about the satyrs that follow Pan? But no one would call satyrs gods. So where does the dividing line exist between one kind of immortal and another? Or take water. Poseidon, identified with the ocean, is a god; so are many rivers; but would we say that every trickling stream is a god? How much water is required to qualify for divinity? As with the classic version of the *sōritēs*, there is no single point where adding an ounce of water will convert a mere stream into a deity. No secure definition of "god" is possible, since there is no sharp boundary that separates the divine from the nondivine.[11]

It is often assumed by modern scholars that Carneades was not atheist, merely a Skeptic wishing to prove the weakness of traditional arguments for the nature. This, indeed, is what the great Roman statesman Cicero, who preserves many of his arguments, thought. Late in his life, in the midst of the plot to assassinate Julius Caesar (he played a major role behind the scenes), he took time out to write a philosophical dialogue, *On the Nature of the Gods*. The three speakers are Velleius (representing the Epicureans), Balbus (the Stoics), and Cotta (the Skeptics, with whom Cicero affiliated). "Carneades used to say these things," says Cotta, "not in order to remove the gods (for what could be less fitting for a philosopher?), but to convict the Stoics of explaining nothing about the gods."[12]

But should we necessarily be taking Cicero at face value? After Carneades's death, the Academy split two ways. In the one camp were those who cleaved to what they saw as the older, more fundamentalist form of Skepticism: these, led by Carneades's successor in the Academy, Clitomachus (ca. 187–110 BC), argued that suspension of judgment (*epokhē*) was the ultimate aim of Skepticism. The other, led by Metrodorus of Stratonicea, believed that it was in fact legitimate for Skeptics to take reasoned positions on issues, as long as they accepted that these positions were in principle fallible. Now, Cicero was taught by Philo of Larissa, an adherent of the Metrodoran position. So it is unsurprising to find him arguing (through the mouthpiece of his character Cotta) that Carneades held the view that gods exist despite his arguments. Clitomachus, on the other hand, would probably have made a very different reading; he would surely have argued that Carneades meant to show that belief in the gods was impossible, and we should not commit either way.[13]

Clitomachus himself was an interesting and important figure. He was born in Carthage (in modern Tunisia) with the name Hasdrubal, like the father of Hannibal, Rome's famous assailant. Initially he taught philosophy at Carthage in Punic, a Semitic language originating in Phoenicia (modern Lebanon) and closely related to Hebrew. He then relocated to Athens and was recognized for his talent by Carneades, who took him under his wing; eventually, Clitomachus succeeded him as head of the Academy. If Carneades's fame was built partly on the absence of writing, then Clitomachus more than adequately compensated: he was said to have written more than four hundred treatises. Not one of these has come down to us, but it is clear from later sources that Clitomachus was deeply interested in the question of atheism, and indeed that he compiled a compendium of philosophical atheists: they included Protagoras, Prodicus, Diagoras, Critias, Theodorus, Euhemerus, and Epicurus. It is not too much of an exaggeration to say that Clitomachus, building on Carneades's collection of anti-theistic arguments, may have invented the idea of atheism as a coherent movement with its own deep history. It is likely that he wrote a book called *On Atheism,* which distilled the history of religious skepticism up to his own day. Clitomachus can claim one of the foremost places in the history of religious disbelief: he not only identified and named atheism as a distinct philosophical position but also mapped out its different varieties.[14]

The formative role of Skepticism in the creation of philosophical atheism cannot be overstated. Since there were swaths of arguments for the existence of gods (the Stoics were particularly fond of these), and since for the Skeptic every argument had to have a counterargument, they dedicated themselves assiduously to proving that gods cannot exist. It is a great shame that Clitomachus's *On Atheism* does not survive, but its influence can be felt in the writings of a major Roman philosopher. In the late second or early third century AD, a man called Sextus wrote several huge works in Greek on Skepticism, which have survived largely intact. These, collectively, are the most important compendium of Skeptical arguments. About Sextus himself little is known. He followed the Pyrrhonian tradition of Skepticism rather than the Academic (that of Carneades and Clitomachus); the distinction is, fundamentally, that whereas the Academics can tolerate the belief that nothing can be determined, the Pyrrhonists reject even that as dogma (in fact, they would not even be willing to commit to the belief that they do not believe in dogma!). Sextus was a doctor, a fact reflected in the nickname Empiricus that still attaches to him today. (The *empeirikoi,* "Empiricists," believed that observation and trial were a better guide to medicine than theory.) But beyond that, his value to us is primarily as a repertory for Skeptical ideas on all sorts of topics.[15]

Sextus was an aggressive opponent of the dogmatists, those philosophers who believe they can say things confidently about the world (i.e., all philosophers apart from the Skeptics). Dogmatic views of the gods drew his particular attention, since it is assertions about the supernatural that tend to be proclaimed with the most confidence and the least rigor. He devotes 180 dense chapters to arguments against the existence of gods. Many of these arguments, in all likelihood, reflect the pioneering work done by Carneades and Clitomachus in establishing atheism as a philosophically reputable position. Sextus's point is not, of course, to prove that gods do not exist, just to prove that you cannot decide the matter one way or the other. "The Skeptics," he opines, "have declared that, because the arguments on either side are equally strong, the gods exist no more than they do not." The Skeptic, he asserts, follows the ancestral practice of public ritual but finds that he cannot commit philosophically to believing in any form of deity. To this end, he also lists the claims of the believers, equal weight being given to both. There is no presumption in favor of the religious. In this respect, Sextus really does stand at the dawn of modernity. His catalogue of arguments on either side is arguably the most important evidence for a sustained, coherent attack on the existence of the gods in antiquity.[16]

Sextus pitches theist and atheist arguments against each other and lets them slug it out inconclusively. To get a flavor for these claims, and a sense of how influential they have been on the ways in which atheist critique still operates, we should pick our way through them in some detail.

He begins with theories about the origins of beliefs in the gods. First of all he considers the fifth-century BC notion that religion derived from primitive humanity, in its wild and bestial phase. Seeing the need to check wrongdoing, early lawmakers invented the idea of gods as a moral police force (this derives from Critias's Sisyphus). This argument Sextus dismisses, for it does not explain how all peoples across the Earth came to a similar conception of deity. He then considers the theory, which derives from the sophist Prodicus, that humans began to ascribe divine qualities to things that benefited them, like the sun and the moon, bread (Demeter) and wine (Dionysus). Here too Sextus is unconvinced, since this view attributes too much naïveté to primitive humans, particularly when it comes to things like water and food: Who would think of perishable items as divine? Finally, there is Democritus's idea that humans are susceptible to *eidōla,* impressive images that contain intimations of future events; early humans confused these *eidōla* with gods. Others attribute thoughts of the divine to dream apparitions, or more generally to the awe that follows from observation of celestial marvels: thunder, lightning, meteors, eclipses. Here Sextus's primary objection is that this doesn't explain why people associate these visions with gods in the first place: they will need to have had a sense of the divine in the first place in order to do this. So it doesn't get to the root cause. The older, sophistic arguments about the invention of religion, then, are in his view not credible.[17]

Sextus now proceeds to list the atheists throughout history, probably following the catalogue of Clitomachus: Protagoras, Diagoras of Melos, Prodicus, Theodorus, Euhemerus, Critias, Epicurus. He does not delve into their views into any great detail, except to cite the Sisyphus fragment in the most complete form in which we have it. (This is the snippet of Athenian drama that proposes that the police-force view of the gods was the work of a cynical lawgiver.) He pits the atheists against the views of philosophers who assert the existence of gods. These come in four different types.[18]

First of all in this section is the question of whether the fact that most cultures have a concept of belief in gods is evidence for their existence. (The modern descendant is the claim that humans are neurologically "wired" for religion.) The atheists, however, reply that there are all sorts of misconceptions about the world that are widespread, such as the idea of eternal punishment in the afterlife (how can a body be damaged—presumably progressively—for eternity?). The fact that many people believe in something does not make it true. Some dogmatists (he means the Stoics) come up with the counterargument that popular belief, even if it correctly pinpoints divinity as a higher entity, is simply wrong in this kind of mythological detail. Sextus postpones any direct rebuttal of this claim. The important point for now is just that the Stoics actually agree that popular views of divinity are misguided, and so, he implies, they actually undermine any argument that the near universality of belief offers evidence for the existence of gods.[19]

Second comes the theist argument from the orderly design of the universe, which Sextus confects from a variety of different sources, mostly Stoic. This is an early version of William Paley's watchmaker analogy: when we see apparent perfection in the orbiting of the heavenly bodies, for example, we cannot but posit a supremely gifted and benevolent creator behind it. In antiquity this idea was most associated with the "craftsman" of Plato's *Timaeus*. Sextus's example is (naturally) not a watch; he chooses as his analogy the orrery invented by Archimedes (of eureka fame), a mechanism that enacted the orbits of the planets and stars around (of course) the Earth. When we see this, we praise Archimedes; by the same token, when we observe the heavenly bodies in perfect motion we should praise the creator of the universe. Sextus also adds some Aristotle into the mix: what explains the orderly movement of the celestial bodies must be a force that is itself not moved by any other thing, in other words the Aristotelian "prime mover." He then stirs in a generous helping of Stoic cosmology. The explanation for regular movement and for the rhythms of nature is that there is a "power" pervading all things and unifying them into a harmonious entity directed toward a good purpose; this power should be identified with the god of the universe. The recipe is topped off with the argument that the regular order of the universe is similar in kind to the reason that we possess as humans; therefore a rational order pervades the universe, and the reasoning capacity of each one of us is a tiny fragment of that divine totality. In Stoic language, reason is the ruling or "hegemonic" part of us, and what rules the universe must be the cosmic god.[20]

The next argument for gods is more pragmatic, and once again familiar to modern eyes. Without a sense of divinity, it is argued, we cannot have various forms of moral behavior: piety, holiness, and justice, all of which are types of action directed toward the gods. If there is no belief in the gods, there is no belief in a universal criterion of moral goodness; ethical behavior will be impossible. What is more, if gods are held not to exist, then nor can prophecy—in which very many people believe. Atheism, then, threatens the moral fabric of society.[21]

The final set of theistic claims is based on a logical syllogism, which is to say a three-step argument from premises to conclusion. Typically the syllogism takes a form such as: "All mammals breathe air [premise]. Kangaroos are mammals [premise]. Therefore kangaroos breathe air [conclusion]." Zeno, the Stoic founder, had argued, "It would be reasonable for someone to honour the gods [premise]. It is not reasonable to honour beings that do not exist [premise]. Therefore gods exist [conclusion]." Sextus, however, disputes the logic of this syllogism, offering a counterexample, which depends upon exploiting a peculiarity of Stoic belief. Stoics maintained that the ideal for a human is to become truly wise, but that this state has never been attained by anyone. Here, then, is the contrary syllogism: "It would be reasonable for someone to honor a truly wise person; it would not be reasonable to honor someone who did not exist; therefore truly wise people exist." (To update the example in contemporary terms, we could substitute a morally perfect person.) The point of this alternative syllogism is to show the weakness of the original, by parodying an opponent's argument so as to produce an unpalatable result. Zeno's successor, Diogenes of Babylon, responded to such criticisms by amending the second premise of Zeno's syllogism to "it is not reasonable to honor those who could not, in their nature, exist." The revised version rules out the existence of the truly wise (who could not exist) and rules in the existence of the gods (who could). Eagle-eyed Sextus, however, notes that the assumption that it is possible for gods to exist is simply asserted here; it remains entirely unproven. So the syllogism demonstrates nothing if we are not already inclined to believe in gods. Sextus adds an additional objection: honoring gods, in the sense of performing ritual activities, is not the same as believing that they exist. We may remember that he has already argued that the Skeptic should take part in religious activities without actually committing philosophically to believing in gods. It might in fact be perfectly rational to honor the gods publicly without believing that they exist (which is in fact exactly what the early Stoic Persaeus did).[22]

Sextus now switches to arguments on the other side, against the existence of gods, beginning with a series of attacks on the notion of a divinity as an absolute ideal. The first we have already met: it is Carneades's proposal that if the gods are capable of sensation then they are capable of sensing negative stimuli, so they are subject to change for the worse, and hence decay. Next: Is a divinity finite or finite? If it is infinite, then it cannot move, since it encompasses all the space into which it could possibly move. If it is infinite, moreover, it must lack intelligence (or "soul"), since intelligence is a form of motion from the mind to the rest of the organism. But the idea of a deity that cannot move or think is counterintuitive. Conversely, however, we cannot imagine a god that is less than infinite, since that god will then be lesser than the cosmos around it.

Sextus's following atheistic argument depends upon commonsense Greek assumptions about the nature of the body. Does the god have a body or not? Sextus asks. If not, then it cannot have a soul (and hence the ability to reason), for only bodies can have souls. But if it does, then it is subject to decay, for that is the nature of bodies. Next comes an extended version of Carneades's argument about morality. If the gods are perfect, then they must be moral. But morality depends by definition on the suppression of nonmoral impulses: you cannot, for example, display bravery in a situation where you are not threatened; you cannot display sexual continence unless you are experiencing sexual temptation. So if the gods are moral they must also be morally fallible. Similarly, if the gods are capable of reaching good decisions, they must have the capacity to make bad ones (since decision making necessarily involves selecting the best option from a range of possibilities). In fact, gods cannot even possess any kind of virtue. Virtue is not born in us. We do not call the ability to breathe or eat virtuous. It is only when we carefully and laboriously develop certain features in our character—say, the ability to resist temptation, or self-sacrifice for others, or a rigorous training regime or work ethic—that we can be said to be virtuous. But gods, in their very nature, can see or do anything. They cannot be virtuous, because they do not need to work on anything. If, however, a deity can be said to lack virtue, it is morally deficient and therefore not a god.[23]

Sextus is not finished yet. If gods possess moral virtue, would we not say that virtue is separate from them? After all, you cannot be said to "possess" something if that thing is actually identical to you. But virtue must exist on a higher level than its possessor: we would not say that any individual is as courageous as courage itself. The abstract virtue of courage is always more courageous than anyone who possesses it. So gods are deficient in that they are less virtuous than the virtues themselves. This argument is a rather specialized one and depends on an idea that ultimately goes back to Plato's metaphysical theory according to which qualities like courage, beauty, and so forth exist as abstract "forms," whereas individual courageous and beautiful beings and things have only a share in the forms themselves.[24]

The next stage in the demolition, however, is more familiar from modern atheistic arguments: it involves subjecting the claims of the religious about their gods to the laws of the known, physical world. Sextus concentrates, initially, upon language. We all think of the gods as speaking, both to one another and to us (through prophecy, dreams, and so forth). Do they, then, have lungs, windpipes, tongues, mouths? How, otherwise, would they speak? Exactly what kind of anatomical endowments do we imagine that gods have? (We could extend Sextus's line of reasoning further: Do they have saliva? Do they then spit? And do they have teeth? Do these teeth accumulate plaque? And so forth.) And then again: What languages do they speak? And which dialect of that language? Do they need interpreters when they communicate with different language groups? Indeed, what is a god's body made of? Is it formed from one single substance, or is it a compound of many different ones? If it is a compound, surely it is capable of dissolution? After all, any process of compounding is capable of being undone. But if the god's body is made of a single substance, then that substance must be one of the elements, which Sextus takes to be earth, fire, air, or water. If that is the case, then the god cannot have a soul or a rational faculty. A god without the ability to reason is unthinkable.

Sextus completes his anti-theist barrage with Carneades's "heaping" argument, which he clearly considers the jewel in the crown of the atheist claims. Sextus's stated intention, naturally, is to prove that the Skeptics should suspend judgment on the question of the gods. In doing so, however, he provides the earliest surviving compendium of arguments against the existence of gods and the earliest surviving treatment of atheism as a unified philosophical tradition. Yet these arguments almost certainly did not all originate with him: many of them, if not all, must go back to Clitomachus in the second century BC, that prodigious figure in the history of atheism.

12

Epicurus Theomakhos

For most of antiquity, if you had asked anyone "Who are the *atheoi*?" the answer would have been immediate: the Epicureans. The modern Hebrew word for "atheist," *apikoros,* testifies to the enduring nature of this association.

In around 306 BC Epicurus (whose name means "helper") moved from the island of Samos to Athens and bought a plot of land just outside the city walls, not far from Plato's Academy. This plot was to be known as the *kēpos,* "garden," and it symbolized Epicurus's philosophy. The aim of Epicureanism was to remove psychic disturbance and find *ataraxia,* "tranquility." Epicureans were not seekers after bodily indulgence, as the English word "epicurean" suggests, although plenty of their ancient enemies accused them of that. Rather, they sought to avoid activities that led to stress and conflict—"Live unnoticed" was a famous motto—and adjust their attitudes so as to remove from their souls all turbulence and fear. Anxieties, Epicurus taught, spring from *kenodoxiai,* "empty opinions."[1]

Chief among the false opinions are misconceptions of the supernatural. Epicureans were strict naturalists. Developing the doctrines of the fifth-century BC atomists Leucippus and Democritus, they insisted that everything in the universe is composed of an infinite number of indestructible, unbreakable particles of matter, the atoms, which are continually in motion, albeit not always predictably (thanks to the famous "swerve"), and of an infinite stretch of void. There is nothing beyond the universe (for it has no outer boundary). The human soul, too, is made of atoms, fine atoms that resemble wind and heat. When we die, our souls immediately dissolve, as the body will in time. There is, therefore, no afterlife. This theory of matter is also allied to the larger aim of generating tranquility, since misunderstandings about the nature of death are the biggest cause of anxiety. "Death is nothing to us," Epicurus wrote, "for that which is dissolved has no feelings, and that which has no feelings is nothing to us." Death is not painful, for the dead cannot feel anything; it is simply the dissolution of one particular cluster of atoms.[2]

What of the gods? At first sight, the Epicurean view of the universe has no need for divinity, since everything can be explained in purely material terms. Yet for all that, Epicurus was insistent that gods do exist and was fiercely critical of atheists. "First, reckon that the god is an indestructible and blessed being . . . do not impute to him anything that is incompatible with indestructibility or blessedness." ("The god," to be clear, does not imply monotheism; it is a common philosophical shorthand for divinity in general.) But, he continues, the gods are not as the many believe them to be; in fact, it is more impious to believe in the gods of popular tradition than to deny them. The most destructive misapprehension is the belief that they intervene in the world of humans. Gods did not create the universe, nor do they order it. We can understand nature only if we grasp the physical laws of the world. And when it comes to the way that human beings live their lives, we must take responsibility for all of our choices and not hide behind excuses of external compulsion. The gods live remote from our lives and take no interest in them.[3]

Epicurus believed that perceptions that we have of the world around us are accurate; they are caused by atomic flow into our sensory organs, and atoms (along with void) are the constituents of reality. Given that the majority of people, in all cultures, have a conception of a divinity of humanoid form, and indeed perceive gods in their dreams (and occasionally in waking visitations), that conception must—so he reasoned—be true. We must have a built-in, natural ability to grasp the divine. In other words, it is Epicurus's theory of perception that leads him to believe in gods. If people see gods in dreams and epiphanies, they must be real.[4]

But what does it mean to say that gods are real? They are obviously not real in the sense that you could choose to visit them or touch them. They are not empirically testable or tangible. For a philosophy predicated on the idea that reality consists entirely of matter and void, this is a serious problem. Epicurus and his successors struggled with this. The perception of gods, they held, was different in kind from other forms of perception. We see gods not with our senses but with our minds alone; that explains why we witness them predominantly in dreams and imaginative moments, when our minds are working but not our eyes. Now, Epicurus thought that we perceive the material world around us because objects emit atoms, which enter our sense organs. To explain the perception of gods, via the mind rather than the senses, he offered an extension of that model: unlike regular matter, gods consist of superfine particles, which can be detected only by our minds, not our senses. Thanks to our natural, built-in capacity to conceptualize gods, the mind processes this atomic flow as indicating divinity.[5]

There are all sorts of philosophical difficulties with this idea. If Epicurus's view is that everything in the world is made of matter and void, and that matter can be perceived by the five senses, how are we to accommodate the fact that gods are not corporeal in the normal sense and cannot be perceived through the senses? The solution that we see them in our mind's eye while dreaming seems unsatisfactory, for not all things that we see in dreams are real: we may dream, for example, of ourselves flying, or of an animal changing shape. Are the gods any more real than all of the other oddities we dream of? At issue here is the question of whether we perceive anything real in our dreams and imaginations. Epicureans believed that all perception is true, in the sense that all sensations are caused by the impact of material atoms. But even on that account, there must surely be some room for brain malfunction through madness or drugs, or for failure of the sensory organs. What is more, on Epicurus's own account, the nature of the gods can be misunderstood (as it is by poets and the majority of people): the idea that we can encounter gods in our world, in particular, is seen as a fundamental error. Epicurus would no doubt say that in such cases our perceptions are accurate but that our interpretation of them is wrong: we have formed a false belief about the gods on the basis of them. But this leaves open the further problem, which he does not seem to have addressed: Who is to say that these things that we witness in our dreams are gods at all? Could we not simply have misinterpreted a true perception of something quite different? A version of this issue, indeed, is still with us. One of the standard arguments for the existence of divinity is the claim that many the world over have spoken of encountering the divine. The question then becomes whether such encounters mark a real experience, however remote, of the divine (like Epicurus's dreams) or (as Richard Dawkins and others would put it) a malfunction caused by some combination of psychosis, culturally conditioned expectations, and wishful thinking. What exactly is the status of religious experience? Is it evidence for the truth of religion or for the befuddlement of the witness? Who has the right to judge such matters? These questions will not go away.[6]

Another problem for Epicurus's account is the imperishability of the gods, for in the atomistic worldview the only things that are indestructible are the atoms themselves; the clusters into which they form are all destined to dissolve. How, then, can Epicurus instruct us not to "impute to [the god] anything that is incompatible with indestructibility"? Surely the stringent rules of a materialist conception of nature are being bent?

Even more difficult still is the question of where they are located, for if they are material beings, they must exist in real space. Yet if they exist in real space, there remains the awkward question of where they are. Could you go there and meet them? Lucretius (ca. 100–55 BC), the great Roman poet of Epicureanism, would frame the question with admirable clarity: "Here is another thing that you should not possibly believe: that the sacred abodes of the gods exist in any part of the world. For the nature of the gods, which is super-fine and far removed from our senses, is dimly seen by the mind; and since it eludes the touch and pressure of the hands, it cannot touch anything that we can touch (for anything that cannot be touched cannot itself touch). For this reason, their abodes must be different to our abodes, and must be super-fine in the manner of their substance." Gods, then, are different in kind from the rest of matter and do not exist in our world. But even so they are still made of real matter, and they still exist in space. How can this be? Is this not more bending of the rules? Epicurus's followers came up with an ingenious explanation. Epicurus himself believed in an infinite plurality of universes—in what we would now call a "multiverse." The gods, these later commentators concluded, must live in the places between them, which they called in Latin the *intermundia* (the "between-worlds"). An ingenious explanation, yes, but an unsatisfactory one, because it simply displaces the problem. What are these *intermundia* like? How do the atoms emanating from the gods manage to travel from them to us and into our dreams and imaginations?[7]

The loss of key works makes it difficult to be certain what Epicurus himself thought. From among his many writings, only three summary letters and a vade mecum of "chief tenets" (*kyriai doxai*) survive, along with quotations and references in later authors. Still, there is enough Epicurus to allow us to piece together some kind of picture of his religious beliefs. He clearly thought that conventional religious ritual was a waste of time. Worshipping, praying to, swearing by, and making statues of the gods, he thought, is ineffectual. We should do these things because our happiness depends in part on living in peace with our fellow citizens, but we should not expend much of our precious emotional energy on these matters. Epicurus, then, seems to have thought that the popular conception of divinity is harmless but misguided. The wiser amongst us, he says, have the truth of the gods—but what that truth is, frustratingly, we are not told.

All of this suggests that Epicurus's own writings were evasive to the point of obscurity on the matter of the gods. Conventional religion is false but should be followed. We must believe in gods but not gods as usually understood. Gods do exist but not in reality as we otherwise understand it. It is a puzzle, then, why Epicurus insisted so firmly on the existence of gods, when his theories of reality not only had no need for them but also struggled to accommodate them. Part of the explanation may lie in the cultural context. Even a century later, the trial of Socrates still resonated: the charge of "not recognizing the gods" could still hurt a philosopher, as Theodorus of Cyrene found out to his cost when he was exiled from Athens in the later fourth century BC. Perhaps it is as simple as that: having seen the theological implications of his materialist model of the universe, Epicurus realized that he had better arm himself against the counterblast that had swept away earlier thinkers like Diagoras of Melos and Socrates. Scholars of classical philosophy tend to dislike explanations of this kind, partly because they are hypothetical and not especially highbrow and partly because they imply that sordid political reality has intruded distastefully into the life of the mind. Classicists have much invested in the idea that their texts are the product of pure reflection and that ancient cities were spaces of free intellectual expression. It goes against the grain to argue that the magisterial Epicurus might have been motivated by fear of persecution, but that is no reason to discount the possibility.[8]

There is, however, another way of interpreting Epicurus's theories of divinity. According to one school of modern criticism, the gods he believed in were not real deities, but idealized abstractions symbolizing the happiness to which we should all aim. Divinity represents a mental image of serenity and tranquility to which the philosopher aspires—and nothing more. Now, this was clearly not the view of those later followers of Epicurus who saw the gods as real beings who lived in the spaces between universes. But perhaps they misunderstood the words of their leader? Did Epicurus in fact believe that gods only exist as expressions of human potential? The best evidence in support of this interpretation lies in the treatment of Epicurus himself, who was venerated with godlike honors by his followers. His will (which survives) made provision for *enagismata,* "sacrifices to the dead," performed in honor of his parents and siblings, and the community was to celebrate him annually on his birthday on the tenth of Gamelion (late January). They were also to meet monthly to revere his memory and that of his friends. These clauses do not explicitly mention cult, but they certainly do have a close resemblance to the ritual calendar of a Greek city. Epicurus's garden was, in effect if not explicitly, to secede from Athens and set up its own civic structures, including a polytheistic "religion" based on himself, his family, and his friends. Just as the Ptolemies were doing at the same time in Alexandria, Epicurus was establishing divine credentials for his rule over his "city." Epicurus seems to have conceived of divinity as something that can be attained by humans.[9]

But it seems, ultimately, unlikely that Epicurus thought that gods were only role models for mortals. When he writes that "the god is an indestructible and blessed being," it suggests something superhuman, something divine in the conventional sense of the word. We have to face the fact that the role of divinity in his thought seems to have been ambiguous—perhaps indeed, as we have said, because of the travails that he anticipated for any philosopher who dared to deny the gods altogether.

Despite his opacity on the matter of the gods, however, there was enough that was heretical about Epicurus's thoughts to win him a reputation throughout antiquity for atheism. In particular, his aspirations to divinity set him on a collision course with conventional civic religion, thanks to the familiar association—which went back to earliest myth—between humans aspiring to divinity and humans denying the existence of divinity. Like Salmoneus and Ceyx in the epic *Catalogue of Women,* or Bellerophon in Euripides's play, Epicurus was perceived to be a *theomakhos,* a "battler of the gods."[10]

Nowhere does he appear more theomachic than in Lucretius's great poem *On the Nature of Things.* Written in Rome in the midst of the civil wars of the early first century BC, it is the earliest surviving complete epic poem composed in Latin (epic in the sense that Lucretius uses the hexameter meter). It has been hugely influential since antiquity, not only for its sublime poetic craft but also for its embodiment of Epicurean doctrine. Stephen Greenblatt has famously argued that its recovery was responsible for European secularism and the Renaissance. As late as the nineteenth and early twentieth centuries it was heralded as the foundation stone of a European intellectual tradition based on science and observation rather than theocratic dictates.[11]

Epicurus makes a stirring entry in Lucretius's poem, in lines that will quicken the pulse of any humanist:

When human life lay on the ground, foully oppressed
For all to see under the weight of Religion,
Who showed forth her head from the regions of heaven,
Standing over mortals with terrifying aspect,
Then first a Grecian man dared to raise
His mortal eyes to meet hers—the first to dare to confront her.
For neither the stories of the gods nor thunder nor heaven
With its threatening growl deterred him; no, all the more keenly
Did they arouse his soul's virtue, so that he, first of all,
Should desire to shatter the narrow confines of nature's gates.
And so the vivid vigor of his soul was victorious, and far
Beyond the flaming walls of the world did he march.
He ranged the expanse of the universe in his mind and soul,
Whence he returns victorious, bringing us report of what can
   come to be

And what cannot; in sum, by what reason each thing has its
  power
Defined, and its deeply fixed boundary marker.
And so Religion now in turn lies beneath our feet,
Trampled, and his victory raises us to heaven.[12]

Just like Euripides's Bellerophon, Lucretius's Epicurus is imagined as leading a military assault on *religio*. The imagery here is largely drawn from siege works. In the first half of the passage, Religion is imagined as towering above an oppressed mankind, like an intimidating fortress of the kind that Romans built to instill fear in their subjects; myths, rituals, and conventions are the weapons that she uses to keep her subjects in check. Then the image is reversed, and Epicurus is envisaged not as the assailant but as the besieged, now leading a breakout from the "narrow confines" and marching beyond the "flaming walls of the world."

What does Lucretius mean by the Latin word "*religio*"? Not, to be sure, "religion" in our sense, which is to say the institutional apparatus promoting a particular way of worshipping the gods; the sense is more of pious devotion, a moral quality. It is psychological bondage that he sees as the enemy of human freedom. (Bondage, indeed, is an appropriate image: elsewhere he speaks of "loosing the mind from the constricting knots of religion," apparently deriving *religio* from *religare*, "to tie.") Lucretius's Epicurus is a crusader not so much against rituals and state institutions as against the false beliefs that oppress us with fear of death, punishment, and the afterlife. Liberation will be found not in smashing organized religion (no Epicurean ever suggested that) but in rejecting the received, mythical view of the gods as aggressively vengeful and accepting that in the materialist view of things they have no influence over our lives.[13]

Epicurus's war on religion was not imagined as an effort to promote secularization at the state level. But it is a more radical claim than is often admitted. The implications of denying religious truth are profound and far-reaching. Lucretius follows the description of Epicurus with an instance of the destructive effects of such beliefs: "Religion has given birth to wicked and impious deeds," he opines (mischievously repurposing the word "impious" to describe the actions of the religious rather than their foes). His example is the mythical story of Agamemnon sacrificing his daughter Iphianassa (more commonly called Iphigenia) to Artemis at Aulis. In the myth, his fleet had been stayed by a calming of the waters, which Artemis had imposed because Agamemnon had killed a deer on land sacred to her. "Such is the terrible evil that religion was able to urge," concludes Lucretius: *"Tantum religio potuit suadere malorum,"* one of the poet's most famous lines (Voltaire, for example, sent it to Frederick II of Prussia in 1737 when urging the cause of secularism). Lucretius's point is that this misunderstanding of the shifting nature of wind (which he explains elsewhere in purely material terms) is more than simply an error. When we fail to understand the truth about nature, and more particularly when we substitute religious for scientific understanding, terrible consequences can ensue. It is particularly striking that Lucretius chooses an instance of sacrifice, the central component of all ancient ritual activity: although of course the particularly horrific aspect of this sacrifice is that the victim is human, the additional implication is that any kind of blood sacrifice is both ineffective and likely to generate physical and mental pain. Without saying as much explicitly, Lucretius exposes the truth that destructive acts condoned in the name of the gods would be utterly condemned in other areas of life.[14]

So there is more at stake in true and false belief than unnecessary psychological anxiety. False beliefs have consequences, sometimes bloody ones. Lucretius is well aware that in talking of the impieties of conventional beliefs in the gods he is setting his truth up as a powerful rival to that of established theology. He predicts to his addressee Memmius that

There will come the day when you will seek to withdraw
From our community, overcome by the terrifying utterances of the
    priests.
Yes indeed, for how many dreams can they concoct for you
Even now, dreams that can turn on their head the principles of
    existence
And by terrifying you throw all your fortunes into chaos!
And with good reason: for if people saw that there is a set limit
To our sufferings, they would by some means find the strength
To stand against the threatening pieties of the priests.[15]

At stake here is the question of authority in speech. Who speaks the truth, the priest or the philosopher? "Priest" (*vates*) is a term that in Latin covers both specialists dedicated to particular cults and traditional poets. Lucretius's attack, then, is on both the established structures of state religion and on the storehouse of traditional myth. Stories are weapons, "threatening pieties" that the true philosopher should "stand against." Lucretius never sounds more modern than here, when pitching scientific materialism as a truer and more socially enlightened alternative to the "dreams" concocted by traditional religion.

The irony is that Lucretius expresses all of this using the very poetic form traditionally associated with theology: the epic poem consisting of hexameters, lines of six metrical feet. This is the form in which Homer and Hesiod had composed their ancient stories of gods and humans and the form adapted for Roman culture in the second century BC by the brilliant and highly influential poet Ennius. An example, perhaps, of using the master's tools to dismantle his own house. But the paradox runs deeper than this. In pitting Epicurus as *theomakhos*, battling the gods of traditional religion, he ended up assimilating the two. Epicurus himself became a kind of god in his own right:

> For if we must speak as that majesty of nature that we have come
>   to understand
> Demands, he was a god—a god, famous Memmius,
> Who first uncovered those rational principles underlying life
> That we now call "wisdom," and who through his art
> Brought life out of the deep currents and dark shadows
> And into such tranquillity and such clear light.[16]

It is common enough in the modern world for atheists to have their anti-religious rhetoric turned back against them: science is "just another belief system," a religious skeptic is mocked as the "high priest of atheism," and so forth. But Lucretius's words go well beyond a loose sense of equivalence, and emphatically claim divinity for Epicurus. "He was a god—a god, famous Memmius." What did Lucretius mean by this? At one level, he was merely developing Epicurus's own instructions in his will that his community of followers should treat him with honors that bordered on worship. Lucretius himself was surely aware of the cult-like reverence that the charismatic figurehead enjoyed. But in fact his words nowhere mention actively worshipping Epicurus: the point is, rather, that thanks to his achievements he deserves to be ranked among the gods. This is in fact a deeply, albeit subtly, subversive claim, since it converts the idea of "god" from a metaphysical to a metaphorical one. A god is simply a high-achieving mortal who has attained a perfectly happy existence—which, incidentally, must involve acceptance of mortality (which contradicts the very premise of deity in the literal sense). Epicurus's victory over *religio* is so complete that he has eviscerated the very idea of divinity as a special category of existence.

The poet proceeds to expand on the theme of Epicurus's divinity by adopting a line of argument that goes back to the fifth-century sophist Prodicus, via Euhemerus. Ceres (the Roman equivalent of the Greek goddess Demeter), Lucretius argues, introduced the cultivation of corn to mortals; Liber (the Roman Dionysus) invented wine. Prodicus too had interpreted Demeter and Dionysus as mortals who had been granted divine status as thanks for their beneficence toward their fellow humans; that Lucretius uses the same two examples suggests that he intends a direct allusion. Epicurus's divinity, then, is of this kind: he is to be understood not as a supernatural being (for nothing exists outside of nature) but as a human who has achieved superhuman things. In fact, by removing the necessity of fear and anxiety, he performed an even greater benefit than inventors of nonessential foodstuffs: "For that reason, he is all the more entitled to his reputation among us as a god."[17]

Where, then, did religion come from? Why did such a monstrous deception arise? Lucretius gives an answer in the midst of a long section that recalls the "culture narratives" of the fifth-century Athenian sophists, telling of humans' emergence from a state of nature into their civilized state. Even in those days, he writes, people saw both in sleep and occasionally while awake images of larger-than-life individuals of stunning appearance. (Are these dim glimpses of real gods, or just phantoms? He makes no comment at this point.) These primitive beings assumed that these individuals must also have superhuman powers and intellects, eternal life and a blessed existence. Next they perceived the orderliness of the heavens and the seasons and assumed that these beings must have been responsible for the universe's intelligent design—and that natural disasters were therefore signs of displeasure. This theory provokes another lament on human folly:

> O unhappy human race, who attributed
> Such deeds to the gods, and gave them bitter wrath too!
> What weepings and wailings did they produce for themselves, what
> Injuries to us, what tears for future generations!
> It is no "piety" to parade yourself often in public wearing a veil,
> Nor to turn towards a bit of stone and go up to every altar,
> Nor to stretch yourself out on the ground and raise your hands
> Before the shrines of the gods, nor to spatter altars
> With the blood of beasts, nor to make vow after vow.
> Piety, rather, is the ability to survey the universe with untroubled mind.[18]

True piety, then, should consist not in petty conformity to human religious convention but in the power to comprehend and marvel at nature's immense power. Divinity is a quality not of transcendent beings but of the world we inhabit: it is there in the sublime stuff of things, from the star-studded ether to the thrill of thunder to the charging stream. Lucretius was famous in antiquity for his magnificent, Turneresque depictions of nature's grand power, but there is more to such purple passages than vivid displays of poetic skill: he wanted his verse to capture the magic of the world around us and to teach us that we should seek "divinity" in matter, not in some imaginary god.

For all this, though, Lucretius, like his master Epicurus, can still insist on the reality of gods. The most famous instance is the prayer to Venus—"First of the line of Aeneas, the pleasure of humans and gods alike"—that opens the poem. It seems mightily disquieting to have a deity presiding over an Epicurean poem, until we realize that Venus—the Roman equivalent of the Greek Aphrodite—is not literally the goddess of myth but a symbol of the generative power of nature. As in the description of Epicurus as a "god," he is using divinity as a metaphor, eviscerating it of its conventional meaning. But elsewhere he certainly speaks of gods as if they are real, or real in a sense. Epicurus, he says, opened up to him a vision of the gods in their "tranquil abode," untroubled by the seasons and provided for by an unfailingly bounteous nature. We might take these gods too as figurative, merely as embodiments of the serenity toward which Epicurean philosophy steers us. Yet he seems also to locate them in real space, in the "void." At another point, he speaks of the gods existing outside of our world; they cannot come into contact with us, their nature being "thin" and fundamentally different from ours. He promises to explain what he means by this at a later point, but (frustratingly) does not.[19]

But perhaps we should take this broken promise not as a sign of Lucretius's forgetfulness or of the unfinished state of the poem, but as a token of Epicureanism's general slipperiness on the question of the divine. When it came to the gods, the Epicureans' contract with their readers was never quite fulfilled. From earliest times, this philosophy had always promised a little more than it had delivered in theological matters. There had always been a fundamental incompatibility between Epicurus's claim that "the god is an indestructible and blessed being" and a view of reality as composed of impermanent combinations of matter. The Epicureans' gods are indeed, as Lucretius put it, "thin" in nature: thin to the point nearly of disappearance, but not quite. Like distant traces of memory, they stubbornly refuse to be erased entirely. Were the Epicureans atheists, as their opponents often held them to be? Certainly atheism was the logical extension of their worldview, and certainly they felt themselves to be at loggerheads with conventional religion. But for some reason they felt unable to sever the ties completely.

PART FOUR

Rome

THE NEW WORLD ORDER

The Hellenistic period also saw the expansion of Rome from a regional capital to the dominant force in the Mediterranean. The decisive events for Rome were the Punic Wars, fought between 264 and 146 BC against Carthage, the Phoenicians' capital in North Africa (in modern Tunisia). It was the utter destruction of Carthage—famously urged by Cato the Elder, who ended every speech *"Carthaginem esse delendam"*—that left Rome as the unrivaled superpower controlling the center of the Mediterranean, and thus the profitable trade routes between West and East. Rome began gobbling up other kingdoms and states. The first overseas territory was Sicily, a dividend of the First Punic War (264–241 BC); from then on, the Empire grew steadily, more typically by annexation of client kingdoms than by conquest. In 133 BC, the Hellenistic ruler Attalus III bequeathed his territories to Rome; the Bithynian king Nicomedes IV did much the same in 74 BC. Brutalities of the most terrifying kind certainly did occur, however. When, in the aftermath of the Third Punic War the Achaean League (a union of independent Greek states based in the Peloponnese) reacted against Roman intervention in Greece, the response was uncompromising: in 146 BC the general Mummius destroyed the entire city of Corinth. The remains that partially stand today are all of later date, after Julius Caesar refounded it as a colony for his veterans in 44 BC. More Greek blood was shed in the first century BC, when Mithridates of Pontus, a kingdom on the shore of the Black Sea, expanded his territories rapidly, annexing parts of Anatolia and pushing into the Aegean Sea. The Greek cities on the Ionian coast and on the mainland were forced to take sides. Some chose the party that history favored: one such is Aphrodisias, whose splendid remains testify to this day to Rome's gratitude. Others were less fortunate: among them was Athens itself, ruled by a puppet tyrant in liege to Mithridates, until it was sacked by the Roman general Sulla in 87–86 BC.[1]

As Rome gradually took control of the Mediterranean, it quickly learned from the Hellenistic empires it displaced the style and ceremony of an imperial power. From the Greeks they took grandiose architecture, idealizing artwork, and ennobling literature. Sometimes they took these in a quite literal sense: after the sack of the Sicilian city of Syracuse in 212 BC (despite the ingenious defensive weaponry pioneered by Archimedes), the parade of loot through Rome took four days. Rome took everything it could from the Greek world, including thousands of slaves, many of whom gave the aristocratic Roman young their learning.[2]

A decisive moment in the expansion of Roman power came when Octavian, the adopted heir of Julius Caesar, defeated the navy of Mark Antony (Marcus Antonius) off the western coast of Greece at the battle of Actium, 31 BC. Although a small affair in military terms, it was a highly significant event symbolically. In the first place, it put an end to the civil wars that had raged between different Roman factions throughout much of the first century BC. Second, it began the process that led to a political revolution, whereby one man—an emperor, but the Romans would call him *princeps* rather than *imperator*—ruled much of the known world. Third, it meant that the entire Mediterranean basin was now in effect subordinate to Rome, since the defeat of Antony meant also the defeat of Cleopatra, the last of the Ptolemies of Egyptian Alexandria and the last of the Hellenistic monarchs to hold out against Rome. Octavian quickly changed his name to Augustus, and with that changed the course of history.

The eastern frontiers of the empire continued to shift over the coming centuries, but the vast majority of the Greek-speaking world was now subordinate to Rome. Having taught Rome the language of power, the Greeks now learned what it meant to be imperial subordinates. Yet many of the elite, at any rate, actually prospered in the new world, acquiring citizenship, power, and prestige. The empire brought a measure of political stability and peace and so allowed for the creation of a vast marketplace, of ideas as much as of material stuff. Different religions, in particular, prospered: Mithraism, the cult of Isis, Judaism, and eventually Christianity. In the course of the fourth century AD, in an extraordinary development that could scarcely have been predicted even one hundred years earlier, the youngest of these became the official cult of the Roman state.

The interconnected, centralized, bureaucratized world of the Roman Empire was entirely different in kind from the loose agglomeration of city-states that made up archaic and classical Greece. The structural challenge presented by a vast empire was how to bind together all those diverse regions into one whole. This was achieved with phenomenal success. In its Augustan guise, the empire survived for three hundred years; once refounded by Constantine in Byzantium, it lasted until the Ottoman conquest in 1453. The Romans were experts in governance: the empire owed its perdurance to a number of finely honed techniques. Unlike the Hellenistic monarchies, the Romans co-opted regional rulers and aristocratic elites, persuading them that their own interests were identical to those of the ruling power. One mechanism for doing so was the sharing of Roman citizenship, which also gave the beneficiaries access to Roman law. In AD 212 (under the emperor Caracalla) a decree was passed extending that citizenship to all male inhabitants of the empire, while all women were to have the same rights as Roman women.

The empire was also integrated by a number of symbolic mechanisms that connected the center to the periphery: images of the emperor, inscriptions detailing his responses to the city's requests, public postings of news from Rome. Above all, the army and the law were ever-present reminders of the Roman order. One Greek orator in the second century AD compared the whole world under Roman rule to a single city on a feast day: "It has laid aside its old dress and the carrying of weapons, and has been allowed to turn to adornments and all kinds of pleasures." Regional variety had not in fact disappeared (there is some rhetorical exaggeration here), but it was constantly weighed against the norms demanded by Rome. One neat illustration of this process is naming. Greeks with Roman citizenship often adopted the Roman habit of taking a forename (*praenomen*), a family name (*nomen*), and an individualizing name (*cognomen*). For Greeks, the first two were typically Roman (the *nomen* reflecting the Roman who had granted the family citizenship), and their regular Greek name became the *cognomen*. Hence Plutarch's full name was Lucius Mestrius Plutarchus, and the historian, philosopher, and politician Arrian was Lucius Flavius Arrianus. Those Greeks with citizenship had Romanness etched into their very identities.[3]

Religion provided the most powerful mechanism of symbolic integration. As they had done under many of the Hellenistic kingdoms, the Greeks treated their ruler as a god, building temples to him and holding festivals and sacrifices in his honor. In this way, cities came together as civic communities, as they had always done, but also validated their participation in the wider empire. Worship of the emperor was an important test of provincial loyalty to the Roman cause. The Jewish rebellion against Rome was presaged by a refusal to offer sacrifice to Nero. In 250, the emperor Decius precipitated the first major wave of Christian persecutions (perhaps unintentionally) by insisting that everyone in the empire should be certificated by a magistrate as having performed a sacrifice to the Roman gods and for the well-being of the emperor. The idea of an imperial authority using political means to impose religious observance had its roots in the sporadic practice of the Hellenistic Greek world (we might think of Antiochus III demanding that all the Greeks of Mesopotamia worship him), but it now became the expected norm. Within less than one hundred years' time, however, the roles had been reversed: Christianity became the normative religion, and sacrificing to "pagan" gods had become illegal. Now the image of a unified Roman Empire revolving around the powerful imperial hub was mirrored by a new kind of religious symbol: the entirety of creation revolving around a single, omnipotent god. Political centralization had effectively paved the way for theocracy.[4]

13

With Gods on Our Side

In the worlds of archaic, classical, and Hellenistic Greece, religion was never a driver of historical events. No war was ever fought for the sake of a god, no empire was expanded in the name of proselytization, no foe was crushed for believing in the wrong god. Political and military decisions were made for human reasons and analyzed in those terms. Nevertheless, whatever the mundane motives, success in war could be seen as a sign of divine support. From the *Iliad* onward, victory was interpreted by some as evidence of the gods' favor. Having gods on one's side—or, at least, being able to persuade others that they were—came to be seen as a decisive factor in a state's fate. The cult of Tykhe ("Fortune"), for example, flourished from the fourth century BC onward and expanded throughout the Hellenistic world. Nike ("Victory") appeared earlier, but again spread in Hellenistic times. Both seem to have been directly promoted by Alexander the Great, who was keen to claim (as a son of Zeus Ammon) that he had divine support. The congealing of the Greek-speaking world into imperial blocs was accompanied by a stealthy but steady amplification of propaganda promoting the idea that the world was as it was destined to be and just as the gods wanted it.

It was, however, with the Romans that the idea of a divine mandate for empire really took hold. The second-century BC Greek philosopher Panaetius, who did much to introduce Stoicism to Rome, taught that the cosmos is governed by providence, which permeates it in much the same way that the soul permeates the body (the influence of Plato's *Timaeus* is palpable). Every act and action, therefore, is the result of divine will. Panaetius, the first major philosopher to relocate to Rome, thought that little could be said about the gods themselves but did write a tract *On Providence*. Stoic philosophy, congenial as it was to an imperial ideology, gradually percolated its way into the Roman elite, albeit often translated and hybridized. Essentially, Stoicism taught that happiness is achieved not by pursuing appetites but by living according to nature: one's own nature, but also that of the universe itself. Everything that happens in the universe is directed toward the best outcome; our duty as individuals is to discern, as best we can using our rational powers, what that outcome is and to bend our lives toward facilitating it. If all the world is a play, the Stoics were fond of saying, our job is simply to play our part, whatever it is, to the best of our abilities. There was nothing in philosophical Stoicism that *required* obedience to a particular political dispensation—and there were Stoics in the later time of Nero and Vespasian who took a principled stance against the autocratic rule of emperors—but it was certainly a system that was in theory compatible with an imperialist outlook. Once the more nuanced and technical aspects of philosophical Stoicism had been whittled away, it was no giant step from a belief in universal divine providence to a belief that the Roman Empire was ordained by the gods to govern the world in the best possible way.[1]

The idea that the rise of the Roman Empire was providentially decreed was first explored by the Greek historian Polybius in the second century BC. Polybius's family had disapproved of Roman control of Macedonia, for which crime he was relegated to Rome to tutor the sons of the conquering general Lucius Aemilius Paullus. His own history of the period 264–146 BC, however, is remarkably pro-Roman. Rome's political constitution, an optimal blend of the democratic, the aristocratic, and the monarchical, has "from the beginning followed the path of nature." Polybius was not a philosopher, but he certainly could see Rome's dominion over much of the known world in providential terms: "Fortune has bowed practically all the world's interests toward one region, and forced them all to assent to one and the same aim." Polybius could on occasion be critical of Roman actions (such as Mummius's brutal sack of Corinth in 146 BC), but in general he saw the interests of the world—that is to say, those of the Greek-speaking world—as best served by obedience to their new masters. Other Rome-based Greek historians like Diodorus of Sicily and Dionysius of Halicarnassus followed suit.[2]

It was, however, in the age of Augustus (ruled 27 BC–AD 14), Rome's first emperor, that the providential vision of Rome's imperial mission reached its greatest expression. The *Aeneid*, Vergil's epic poem in twelve books of intricately crafted Latin hexameters, tells how a Trojan prince fled the smoking ruins of Troy after the Greek victory and eventually ended up in Italy, where he would found a new city. Aeneas, the prince in question, was the son of the goddess Venus; his son was Iulus, the founder of the Julian family, to whom Augustus's adoptive father Julius Caesar belonged. At one point early on in the first book, Jupiter, king of the Roman gods, addresses Venus with a grand prophecy of future glories:

> I set no limits on the Romans' achievements, nor any time-frame;
> I have given them empire without end.[3]

There is no room for chance: empire will be Rome's, because Jupiter has decreed it thus. History is written in the stars. Nor in fact is there any space for human free will. Aeneas is, in the very first sentence of the epic, driven from Troy "by fate." When he pitches up on the shores of modern Tunisia, he meets and falls in love with a beautiful widow who is founding a city, Carthage (which would later become Rome's great nemesis). Yet despite a whirlwind romance, ending in an intimate scene in a cave, Dido and Aeneas were not meant to be. Jupiter orders Mercury, messenger of the gods, "to bear his mandates through the swift breezes" and to command Aeneas to leave Carthage to found the new city in Italy. Human desires are not to stand in the way of destiny, and the Roman Empire was the culmination of destiny's great plan for the world.[4]

For Homer, Vergil's literary model, fate is a hazy and indeterminate thing. For the Roman poet, by contrast, it assumes a philosophical force. Vergil's worldview is shaped by Stoic theory. The *Aeneid* offers a vision of a city that from its very foundation was destined to rule the world, and of a royal family marked out from the start for unrivaled greatness. Augustus's victory over Antony and Cleopatra (which is prophesied in the poem) is the culmination of the gods' benevolent plan for humanity. In spite of the many-sided complexity of this poetic vision— Dido's heartrending suicide is proof enough that the poet is compassionate toward the losers too—the *Aeneid* is most fundamentally a reflection of Augustus's vision of a global empire secured for him by divine mandate.

Augustus was the gods' favorite, and his own favorite god was Apollo, whose cult he established on the Palatine Hill. Statues of Apollo sprang up all over Rome; the god's signature laurel leaf appeared on coinage. Apollo represented harmony; his opposite number was Dionysus, to whom the defeated Antony had assimilated himself. In a sense, Augustus *was* divine. "We have believed that Jupiter reigns, thundering in heaven," writes the poet Horace (a contemporary of Vergil's), "but Augustus will be treated as a god amongst us." At Rome, emperors were treated as gods once they had died. Vespasian's witty last words were "Dammit—I think I'm becoming a god." Not all made the grade: one cheeky satire on the emperor Claudius has the dead emperor refused admission to heaven and thrown down to the underworld instead. In many Greek-speaking cities of the eastern empire, however, Hellenistic practice continued, and Augustus and his successors were accorded cult worship within their own lifetimes. Many ancient historians have tended to see this process as motivated by the Greeks' own craving for a means of expressing the giddying hierarchy of Roman power within the religious "language" of their own city religion. This is true enough, but it tells only part of the story: the imperial center surely supplied resources, materials, and craftsmen for elaborate temples and statuary. But it would be misleading to think that the deification of emperors was not a straightforward fiat. The ancients were very aware that emperors were made of flesh and blood, and those who had not grasped it immediately came quickly to learn that many were (like Claudius) unworthy of adulation. As so often in political ideologies, there was an element of fuzziness here. The divinity of the emperor sat in an uncertain space between reality and metaphor.[5]

Religious propaganda played a crucial role in persuading a sizeable majority of the populace not to resist the gods' designs for Rome. Imperial ideology was extraordinarily persuasive on the whole, holding together in a single geopolitical vessel fifty million inhabitants of a vast, culturally and linguistically diverse territory. Rebellions against Rome were in fact surprisingly few (Spartacus's slave revolt was a rare anomaly). Like all ideologies, however, it was also contested. Although many aristocrats enjoyed the benefits brought by the Pax Romana in terms of power, stability, and wealth, the empire was not universally popular. It is hard now to trace a culture of resistance: history has not only been written by the victors but also been selectively preserved by them. Given that ideas of divine providence and imperial ideology were so closely intertwined, however, atheism now took on a political slant too. The atheistic literature of the period thus offers a welcome glimpse into the world of the resistance.[6]

Plato in the *Laws* identified three kinds of disbeliever: those who believed that there were no gods, those who believe the gods have no interest in human well-being, and those who think their favor can be bought by simple trades like prayers and sacrifices. In the era of the Roman principate, the first two categories were often conflated. Disbelief in providence was in effect disbelief in gods: the religious heretic was "atheistic [*atheos*], unholy, one who rejects divinity and denies providence." Part of the reason for this lies in the influence of Epicureanism, with its "thin" gods who have no influence on our world. Epicureans were often thought of as atheists precisely because they denied providence.[7]

But the Epicureans were not actively engaged in resistance to Roman hegemony. Epicureanism was fundamentally an apolitical philosophy. Its adherents disdained active engagement in civic life: that kind of questing after public recognition, they thought, led only to stress and distraction from the real aim, serene tranquility. "Live unnoticed" was one of its precepts. Political theory was thus not a mainstream concern. To locate those who rejected the providentialist view of the empire we must look elsewhere.

Shortly after Octavian's victory over Antony and Cleopatra at Actium in 31 BC, a Greek intellectual called Dionysius relocated from Halicarnassus, on what is now the west coast of Turkey, to Rome. Halicarnassus, a city steeped in Greek culture (it was, most notably, the birthplace of the great historian Herodotus), had been ravaged by war. A traditionally pro-Roman city, it had been treated savagely by Mithridates VI of Pontus in his campaigns against Rome between 88 and 63 BC. Even after Mithridates's defeat by Pompey the Great, Rome's notorious civil wars between the followers of Julius Caesar and their rivals took their toll on the region. Dionysius arrived in Rome in his thirties, full of optimism that Rome's new leader Octavian offered the best hope of ending the bloodshed that had bedeviled the eastern Mediterranean. As well as establishing himself as a masterful literary critic and teacher of rhetoric, he also wrote a history of Rome from its foundation, which partly survives.[8]

Dionysius's *Roman Antiquities* tells the early history of Rome's rise, up to the point where Polybius's work started. Although an unwearying promoter of Rome's interests, he remained a Greek and saw the world through Greek eyes; his target audience for the *Roman Antiquities* was Greek as well. His aim, rather, was to embed in the collective consciousness of his fellow Hellenes two ideas, both equally bold. The first was that the Romans are in fact ethnically Greek. The second was that Roman rule was in the best interests of the Greeks. It is no coincidence that Dionysius and Vergil were contemporaries; both paint their mythical stories about the Roman past with eminently Augustan colors, telling in their different ways of the inevitability of Roman domination of the known world.[9]

Dionysius wrote as he did not because his pro-Roman views were mainstream, but precisely because they were not. His work is powerfully polemical. He tells us a little about those who held opposing views. Dionysius protests that in his day, "almost all of the Greeks" base their views of early Rome on "false opinions" about "wandering, vagabond barbarians" who achieved their position of dominance "by chance, thanks to some fluke wrongly gifted to them." As he continues, he adds a little more detail: "The more malicious are fond of levelling open accusations against Fortune for supplying the lowliest of barbarians with the successes that are due to the Greeks. And yet why do I speak about normal people, when even some historians have set down such views in writing, indulging with their unjust, untrue accounts barbarian kings who hate the Empire, whom they ended up submitting to and sharing their lives of pleasure?"[10]

Who were these historians who wrote anti-Roman accounts, these lickspittling popinjays of foreign courts who denied the providential nature of the empire? Of the various candidates the closest fit is one man: Metrodorus of Scepsis, a sometime courtier of Rome's nemesis Mithridates VI of Pontus. Metrodorus was probably born around 140 BC and came from a humble background in Scepsis (northwestern Turkey). Having studied with Carneades in Athens, he developed a brilliant oratorical style of his own invention and a sophisticated mnemonic technique. He wowed audiences, and a wealthy woman sought him out for marriage. While Mithridates was pursuing his doomed attempt to rival Rome for dominance in Asia Minor and the eastern Mediterranean, Metrodorus moved to his court and enjoyed great favor, rising to the position of minister of justice. He was the starriest of a circle of Greek intellectuals based there, including Aesopus, Heracleides of Magnesia, and Teucrus of Cyzicus. For reasons unknown, however, he eventually turned his back on Mithridates. On an embassy he advised the Armenian king Tigranes that Mithridates's terms might not be in his best interest; Tigranes told Mithridates, and Metrodorus was apparently (details are murky) done away with. Life with a warlord was perilous.[11]

Unsurprisingly, given his allegiance to Mithridates, Metrodorus did not paint the Romans in flattering colors. Over half a century later, the poet Ovid wrote of the "man of Scepsis" who attacked Roman customs in his "bitter writings." Pliny the Elder records that he "acquired a nickname from his hatred of the very name of Rome" (what was this nickname? "Romehater"?). Is Metrodorus then one of those attacked by Dionysius? He certainly fits the bill: there is no one else we know of who could be described as a notoriously anti-Roman writer who was sponsored by a foreign king. He was not primarily a historian, but he did write a work (now lost) called *On History*.[12]

Metrodorus's attack on malicious and ignorant Greeks has two components: he argues that Romans are unworthy rulers ("wandering, vagabond barbarians") and that they see the empire as the result of chance rather than divine predestination. Metrodorus seems to have argued that Rome's rise to power in the Mediterranean was the result of fortune rather than providence. In his youth, he studied in the Academy at Athens: he was a student of Carneades's and an associate of Clitomachus's, both of whom were instrumental in the codification of philosophical atheism. Could it be that Metrodorus was prompted by the atheistic arguments circulating in the Academy to propose a new type of history of Rome's rise, one that stressed the absence of benevolent divine influence?

Whatever Metrodorus's exact role in this, it is clear that there were Greeks in the first century BC whose resistance to Rome came in the form of histories stressing the role of chance in the rise of Roman power. The opposition may well have begun in the court of Mithridates, but it spread far beyond. As so often with imperial history, we have to reconstruct the story of the losing side from hints and asides in the dominant narrative. Almost all of our sources for the Roman Empire are "butter-side up" accounts, created by the beneficiaries of empire. But with enough care and patience we can begin to tune our ears to pick up the signals when a hegemonic source is engaging with a genuine counter-hegemonic position.

The central focus for anti-providentialist history was Alexander the Great. What would have happened if he had chosen instead to turn westward and confront the nascent power of Rome? In raising such questions, anti-providential historians engaged in what is now called "what if" or "counterfactual" history (What if the Romans had invented steam power? What if the Nazis had won World War II?). Speculation on the question of who would have won in an outright war between the Macedonians and the Romans had an obvious cultural urgency, especially for Greeks still pining for their freedom. But even more than this, such meditations attacked ideas of the providential destiny of Rome. If history is to be seen as a series of chance occurrences and unintended consequences, rather than as the relentless progress of a divinely scripted drama, then Rome's grip on the world can be seen as weaker and less permanent than it might appear. Anti-Roman history was "Epicurean" in a loose, nontechnical sense, in that it stressed the role of chance and the absence of divine predestination.[13]

Alexander was a powerful figure to conjure with. Some conquering Romans liked to compare themselves to him: Julius Caesar's sometime collaborator Pompey, for example, who took the name Magnus ("the Great") in imitation of his hero, or the emperor Trajan. But the Romans could also be more ambivalent about him, treating him as the embodiment of tyrannical ambition. And the Greeks too could use him as a stick with which to beat the Romans. One of the most popular texts in all of antiquity—in fact the most widely circulated and translated text apart from the Bible—was a fantastical biography of Alexander known as the *Alexander Romance*. Although at the heart of it is the story of the campaigns against Darius II and the Persians, it is a highly inventive work of fiction: Alexander turns out to be the illegitimate son of Nectanebo, the last pharaoh of Egypt; he meets talking birds; in some versions (it was a work of great textual fluidity, which circulated in multiple different forms) he even plumbed the depths of the eastern ocean in a diving bell. All recensions, however, have a scene in which a Roman embassy approaches Alexander to pledge fealty: "We crown you," their ambassador tells him, thus ceding kingship to him. It is just about possible that the embassy really happened, but the Romans surely never acknowledged him as their king. In the inventive world of the *Alexander Romance,* the episode exists not to reflect reality but to reassure the text's readers (probably largely Greco-Egyptian) that Romans are not invincible and that their own imperial heritage is prouder.[14]

Some Greeks, however, pushed further and imagined scenarios in which the Macedonian and Roman forces engaged on the battlefield. In a digression from his history of early Rome, the Roman historian Livy (writing at the time of the emperor Augustus) takes time out to castigate "the most trivial of the Greeks" who claim the Parthians (Rome's great enemy to the east, the successors of the Persians) as superior to the Romans and argue that the Romans in Alexander's time bowed to him in submission. Livy proceeds to argue that Roman might is more impressive, in that Alexander was just one man who managed to achieve much success, whereas for generations successive Roman generals have been victorious. What is more, each Roman had to achieve what he did despite a political system that only allowed power on a temporary basis, whereas Alexander, as a sole ruler, had no obstacles. All this, he argues, tells against Alexander's likelihood of success in an imaginary battle. What is more, Alexander had fewer and less disciplined troops and less sophisticated weaponry.[15]

On the other side of the fence sat Plutarch, the eminent Greek philosopher of the late first and early second centuries. Plutarch was no anti-Roman agitator; he was in fact a Roman citizen and counted many powerful Romans among his friends. He was also well read in Latin literature, including (probably) Livy himself. On the other hand, he was a proud Hellene who tended to see the world through Hellenocentric lenses. So when he intervened, perhaps in his youth, in this controversial debate over Alexander and the Romans, he was walking a tightrope. His surviving speeches are a masterful balancing act. The question he sets himself is whether each owed success to fortune or to virtue. In the combustible context of these debates, these were highly loaded terms. Fundamentally, what was at issue was whether success was down to intrinsic superiority ("virtue"), or external circumstances ("fortune"). His solution is ingeniously diplomatic. Plutarch is insistent that Alexander prospered because of his virtue, and that if anything luck was against him. The picture of Alexander that emerges is as positive and laudatory as one could imagine. He comes across as a philosopher in action, one who spread high-minded ideals across the known world. "A few of us read Plato's *Laws,*" he opines, "but myriads of people have used and continue to use Alexander's laws." Alexander is depicted as the man who gave the civilizing power of Greek culture to the world.[16]

The Romans, by contrast, however individually virtuous, have benefited repeatedly from Fortune's favor. When the Gauls attacked the Capitol in the early fourth century BC, for instance, the sacred geese were spooked and awoke the slumbering Romans. Cases like this point to the enormous benefits that Fortune has bestowed on the city. Plutarch also points to the presence in the city of temples to Fortune: the Romans venerate her as a goddess. At first sight, then, Plutarch seems to be pretty unambiguous here. Alexander owes his success to his own qualities, the Romans owe theirs to Fortune. But here comes the twist. Fortune, Plutarch argues, means something different at Rome. The Greek word *tykhē,* like the English "fortune," has two distinct meanings: "chance" (in the sense of randomness) and "fate" (predestination). Plutarch's claim is that the advent of the Roman Empire has shifted the meaning of the word from the first to the second. "When she [Fortune] approached the Palatine and crossed the Tiber, she seems to have taken off her wings, stepped out of her sandals, and abandoned her untrustworthy and unstable globe. Thus did she enter Rome to stay, and that is how she is today." The references to wings, sandals, and the wobbly globe are all part of the iconography of *tykhē* in the first sense, of an unstable and fickle entity. *Tykhē* was now semantically transformed, Plutarch argues, from "mere chance" to "providential destiny." This is an ingenious solution contrived by a bicultural writer who could not afford to offend either side. Whereas the now lost anti-Roman, anti-providential historians seem to have argued that Rome's success was down to nothing more than a series of lucky breaks, and that it is impermanent, Plutarch claims that it was due to Fortune in the other sense: guaranteed by divine ordinance, and permanent.[17]

Plutarch is no less ingenious in his handling of the old counterfactual question: Who would have won if Alexander had confronted the Romans? Perhaps his solution is in fact too ingenious, to put the question to bed. At the end of his essay on the Romans, he ascribes Alexander's young death (he was "like a shooting star") also to the Romans' good fortune, hinting that had he lived longer that might have spelled trouble for them. But what actually would have happened (we are all clamoring to know)? "I do not think it would have been settled without the spilling of blood" is Plutarch's curt response. The speech finishes without giving any further explanation. Older classical scholars, with their characteristic instinct to resort to wooden philological method, assumed that the ending had been lost: no one could conclude like that. But it makes perfect sense once we take into account the fact that Plutarch's whole strategy had been to appease both sides. It is a mischievous ending, certainly, and one that draws attention to its own inconclusiveness. But what it discloses, ultimately, is the author's real achievement in these texts: to take one of the most controversial issues of the day, a focal point for anti-Roman sentiment, and speak on it at great length without offending Romans or Greeks.[18]

Plutarch's tour de force is best understood as an act of brinkmanship. He was well aware that there were historians of Rome who denied the role of providence in their narratives of Rome's rise; these were Livy's "most trivial of the Greeks." They will have written history without divinity so as to subvert Rome's claim to divine favor and to open up the future possibility of a different world order. Perhaps Metrodorus himself was the first to argue that Roman power would never have risen had Alexander not fortuitously (for Rome) died young. Plutarch dances on the lip of this particular precipice but pulls himself back at the last minute. It must have been seen as a wonderful display of rhetorical skill. The value of these speeches to a history of atheism, however, is that they seem to shadow the kind of arguments that truly anti-providential historians would have used.

Do the gods superintend the universe? Do they steer it on an optimal course? These are abstract, philosophical questions, but they also have a powerful political resonance in a system that was dominated by a single ruling power. The living Roman emperor, after all, was hailed as a god himself, at least in the Greek-speaking parts of the empire. Stoicism and Platonism, both of which held that there is a benign creator god who manages the world's affairs, were easily compatible with Roman imperial ideology. One of our most valuable sources for Stoic thought, indeed, is the second-century emperor Marcus Aurelius, whose self-addressed handbook can be read even now, under the title *Meditations*. A providential view of the world suggests that the current political dispensation is for the best and that it is the job of individuals to subordinate themselves to that dispensation.

An anti-providential view, on the other hand, implies that the world is run as it is thanks to happenstance rather than divine design and that the current order is not necessarily the best one, or indeed likely to be the only one. Lucian, the Greco-Syrian satirist of the second century AD, imagined a debate between the Stoic Timocles and the atheist Epicurean Damis, which culminated with a metaphor of the universe as a ship. The image is intended by Timocles to imply that there is a divine captain in charge, ordering everything and ensuring the safe passage to its ultimate destination, for the benefit of all the passengers. The Epicurean Damis, however, points out that not every ship is well run. He evokes instead a filthy, badly designed ship bobbing around purposelessly, with a wretched crew full of miscreants. That analogy is by implication as toxic for the ideology of the Roman Empire as it is for the Stoic conception of the cosmos. If there is no deity steering the universe, then there is no need to assume that the imperial system is run by skillful pilots of the ship of state. Debating the role of divine providence in the management of human lives had become a highly political act.[19]

14

Virtual Networks

When we look for atheists in classical and Hellenistic Greece, the picture we see sometimes looks to be composed of scattered dots. There were certainly isolated instances of individuals who, in their different ways, opposed mainstream ideas of religion: fifth-century BC pre-Socratics and sophists, Skeptics amassing atheist arguments, Epicureans promoting a materialist view of the world and the idea of "thin gods," even the odd disbelieving Stoic like Persaeus. There were creative writers like Euhemerus and Hermocles of Cyzicus, exploiting the theological implications of ruler deification to undermine traditional worship of the Olympians. These people were called *atheoi* by others and may perhaps have chosen the label for themselves. How do we join up these dots? Can we see atheism as a significant social force in antiquity? And, more to the point, did the ancients themselves see it that way? Did anyone ever stand back and allow a pattern to form before their eyes, as with a *pointilliste* painting?

In a sense, scattered dots are exactly what one would expect to see in a pre-Enlightenment, pre-mechanized world. There were disbelievers in Greek antiquity just as there were everywhere, but there was no obvious role for mass-movement atheism in a culture where ensuring the stability of the state—which depended on the favor of the gods—was prized above all else. Atheism has prospered in the West since the eighteenth century because society has a role for it: in an advanced capitalist economy based on technological innovation, it has been necessary to claw intellectual and moral authority away from the clergy and reallocate it to the secular specialists in science and engineering. It is this social function that has allowed athe*ism* to emerge as a movement composed of individual athe*ists*. The situation in Greece was different in two respects. First, there was no clergy monopolizing writing and learning in the first place and so no need for atheism to attack clerical authority. Priests controlled access to only one kind of knowledge: knowledge of the future, through oracles and prophecies. Second, while there was certainly plenty of technological progress—in fields as diverse as architecture, hydraulics, siege warfare, and medicine—there was no collective ideal of society moving forward through innovation. Greeks never envisaged the future as technologically different from the present. There was no Greek science fiction. When they wanted to imagine societies operating on different principles, they evoked either the deep past or distant lands (think of Euhemerus and his journey to the imaginary Panchaea). As a result there was no sense of a battle between science and religion to steer society's future.

Yet there is evidence from the pre-Christian Roman Empire, I believe, for a social movement promoting the idea that a world without gods is a preferable one—not a large-scale movement, to be sure, but one significant enough to create waves.

The reasons for the rise of atheism in the Roman Empire are in fact to be found half a millennium earlier, in classical Athens. In Hellenistic and Roman times, Greeks' sense of heritage was sharpened, refined, narrowed: while individual cities of course retained their own discrete traditions, Greekness itself was increasingly indexed to a sense of shared cultural legacy rooted in classical Athens. The most visible sign of this change was the dominance of the Attic dialect current in fifth- and fourth-century BC Athens, whether in the simplified form known as the *koinē,* or "common" tongue, or the full-blown type taught in the elite schools of the Roman Empire and promoted in handbooks of proper Greek usage that still survive. (Of words for "little pomegranate," for example, one authority writes: "The ignorant write *rhoïdion,* with the diaeresis; *we* say *rhoidion.*") This preference for Attic as "high Greek" is still with us, in the literary or "purified" (*katharevousa*) form of modern Greek. But the cult of classical Athens went well beyond language use and into the formation of literary canons promoting writers such as Thucydides, Plato, Xenophon, Demosthenes, and the tragic poets. By the time of the Roman Empire, elite Greeks re-enacted episodes from classical history in public competitions of improvised oratory: to perform the role of an Athenian father extolling his dead son's achievements in the battle of Marathon, for example, was the height of intellectual sophistication. Some chose to be associated with famous names from the past: the historian and philosopher Arrian, for example, referred to himself as "the new Xenophon," occasionally even just "Xenophon," as a tribute to his Athenian literary model. Until relatively recently, the classicizing bent of Greek culture under the Roman Empire was dismissed by many scholars as evidence of a moribund spirit, interested more in museology than in originality. Postmodernism, however, has shown that recycling the past is a form of creativity in its own right. Classicism is now seen as a tool that Greeks of the Roman period used to make sense of their own world, rather than as facile imitation.[1]

For the Athens-obsessed Greeks of the Roman period, the fact that the democratic city had seen a coterie of public intellectuals known as *atheoi* was a significant fact that required explaining. The presence of Socrates, the classical philosopher *par excellence,* on the fringes of this group was an additional prompt. Atheism was thus seen not just as an abstract philosophical position but as a part of Greece's collective history, the (Athenocentric) story it told about itself. Even though the fifth-century BC *atheoi* were subject to the comic poets' mockery, even though they were associated with theomachy by the tragic poets, even though they were sometimes subject to criminal prosecution, their presence in classical Athens gave them a legitimacy in the eyes of later Greeks. A sense of rootedness in the prestigious classical past played a pivotal role in the creation of atheism as a habitable intellectual space in the Roman era.

Atheists of this later era could sustain themselves thanks to the fantasy of connection to the great classical atheists: Diagoras, Protagoras, Critias, even Socrates himself. Such connections—let us call them "virtual networks"—required one particular invention of the Hellenistic era: doxography. Doxography (the word is in fact a nineteenth-century coinage) was one of the favored genres of late Greek literary and philosophical production. Inspired by the precedents of Aristotle and Theophrastus, and by the emergence of great libraries at Alexandria, Pergamum, Rome, and elsewhere, ancient intellectuals increasingly set about collecting, editing, and archiving the opinions (*doxai*) of those who went before. Surviving philosophical doxographies (varied in kind) include works written by Cicero, Philodemus, Arius Didymus, Alcinous, Aetius, Sextus

Empiricus, Diogenes Laertius, and others. Doxographies were not just digests for readers who could not face wading through the originals; they were creative works in their own right. Scholars have tended to look down on the doxographers and treat them simply as repositories for the views of more original (but now lost) predecessors. But it is overhasty, not to mention haughty, to despise the major literary movements of previous ages. Doxography existed not to service the needs of modern fragment hunters but to help ancient readers make sense of the chaotic patterns of earlier thought, by lending them form. In a sense the very idea of coherent philosophical "schools" in antiquity—Stoics, Epicureans, Cynics, Skeptics—is an effect of the doxographical enterprise, which tidied up the conflicting opinions of different individuals into a cogent body of knowledge. When we say "the Stoics believed that . . ." we are paying unwitting tribute to the efforts of the doxographers.[2]

The doxography of atheism is particularly significant because of the relative marginality of atheism in antiquity. To be an atheist was, for most, to be a member of a virtual rather than a face-to-face community. There were no real-world schools of atheism that allowed one disbeliever to engage in dialogue with another. It was doxography alone that offered that network, linking together disparate individuals and weaving together their disparate beliefs into a shared set of doctrines that collectively made up a philosophy of atheism.

The earliest atheist doxography is found in Plato's *Laws*. Plato's Athenian stranger refers to a body of "clever modern types" who make three different but related kinds of claim: that there are no gods, that the gods exist but have no care for mortals, and that the gods do care for mortals but can be easily bought off. Plato never names names, so this is not a doxography in the strong sense of a compendium of the views of particular thinkers, and indeed his vagueness adds to the suspicion that this is rather an attempt to caricature *the kind of thing* that *those kinds of people* believe. What Plato is offering is not an open-minded itemization of the views of the atheists but a broad-brush depiction of the kind of religious heresy that his ideal state would outlaw.[3]

Plato's vague attack on the "clever modern types" is one thing. The earliest doxography of atheism to use specific names was compiled by Epicurus. The evidence survives in Philodemus's *On Piety,* that masterpiece of modern classical detective work reconstructed from the charred papyri preserved by the eruption of Mount Vesuvius. One of the fractured columns of Philodemus's restored text reads as follows, in the translation of Dirk Obbink:[4]

> [missing text] . . . those who eliminate the divine from reality Epicurus reproached for their complete madness, as in Book 12 he reproaches Prodicus, Diagoras, and Critias among others, saying that they rave like lunatics, and he likens them to Bacchant revellers, admonishing them not to trouble or disturb us.

The reference must be to book 12 of *On Nature,* Epicurus's huge work detailing his theories of matter and the cosmos. Epicurus's objection to "those who eliminate the divine from reality" seems to have been on the grounds not that they impiously misunderstand the nature of divinity but that their "ravings" trouble and disturb the serenity of mind that he craved for his followers.[5]

Like Plato, Epicurus may well have been motivated to demonize disbelievers precisely because his own position was so perilous. As an extreme materialist whose concept of "thin" divinity was suspect in the eyes of many, he knew himself to be open to the charge of atheism. Despite this, the Epicurean school, one of the great success stories of ancient philosophy, continued to flourish until at least the third century AD—even as it continued, also, to attract charges of atheism. It is no doubt for this reason that Epicureans were always defensive on the matter of the gods and brandished their founder's atheistic doxography with great gusto.

One of the unlikeliest examples of this phenomenon has produced one of the most exciting stories of modern classical studies. Oenoanda is a smallish city in the region of southern Turkey that was known in antiquity as Lycia, perched in the northern mountainous region of the Xanthus River Valley. From the late nineteenth century onward, fragments were found of an Epicurean inscription apparently from the stoa (the portico around the central agora, or meeting place), fragments that eventually disclosed a massive, monumental summary of Epicurean doctrine. Since the late 1960s, the site has been excavated and the inscription painstakingly reconstructed. It is worth marveling at the fact that its author, one Diogenes, was permitted to set up this complex philosophical guide—the largest inscription known of from anywhere in Greco-Roman antiquity—in a public site in this tiny, remote citadel. What the inscription shows, among many other things, is that the Epicureans continued to circulate a negative doxography of atheism. The crucial passage is from the (sadly fractured) sixteenth column:[6]

> They inveigh excessively against the most holy ones [i.e., the Epicureans] as atheists. And it will become clear that it is not we who remove the gods, but others. [. . .] Diagoras of Melos, who has certain others as companions in his opinions, directly denied the existence of the gods, battling vigorously against all those who believe. In terms of underlying meaning Protagoras of Abdera had the same opinion as Diagoras, but he phrased it differently, so as to avoid the excessive brashness of the claim. For he said that he did not know whether the gods exist. This is the same as saying that he knows that the gods do not exist. For if he had said, instead of the first phrase, "I do not know that they do not exist," perhaps the roundabout way of speaking would have just about persuaded us that he was not removing the gods once and for all. But what he actually said was "that they exist," not "that they do not exist"; and so he was doing exactly the same thing as Diagoras, who spent every waking minute saying that he did not know that they exist. Therefore, as I say, in terms of underlying meaning Protagoras had the same opinion as Diagoras.

This fragment offers a tantalizing glimpse into the way that Epicureans under the Roman Empire told the story of their own awkward relationship to atheism. The first sentence shows that Epicureans ("the most holy ones") were under attack as "atheists." The following part, however, seeks to deflect that attack onto the usual suspects. It is absolutely clear, then, that the Epicurean doxography of atheism was primarily defensive in intention, a technique for parrying their enemies' thrusts at their more vulnerable point. (It is worth noting in passing, incidentally, that the Diogenes inscription gives us the earliest example of the now familiar argument that agnosticism is, philosophically speaking, the same thing as atheism.)[7]

So Plato and Epicurus, each for his own reason but both motivated by the climate of fear that followed the execution of Socrates, offered derogatory doxographies of atheism. The creation of a positive one was the innovation of the New Academy under Carneades and his successor Clitomachus, in the second century BC. Clitomachus, as we saw in chapter 11, seems to have compiled a summary list of anti-theistic arguments, the source for Sextus Empiricus's catalogue of such positions in book 9 of *Against the Mathematicians*. Carneades and Clitomachus were not interested in promoting atheism as such; rather, as Skeptics, they aimed to balance the arguments for with the arguments against, so as to produce a suspension of judgment. Nevertheless, their inventive doxography of atheistic argumentation created, for possibly the first time in human history, an intellectually coherent and substantial set of arguments against the existence of the divine.

Clitomachus's arguments left a deep mark on the world around him, albeit indirectly. His successor as head of the Academy, Philo of Larissa, was of a less skeptical bent than his predecessors, believing that certain kinds of knowledge could be securely attained. After a peaceful start in 110 BC, however, Philo's stewardship of the Academy was beset by difficulties. First, his philosophical compromise led two of his most talented students to rebel: in the 90s, Antiochus of Ascalon split off to found a school of Platonic revivalists, while on the other flank Aenesidemus left to pursue a radical skepticism. Even more unfortunate for Philo was the war that flared up between 88 and 63 BC between Rome and Mithridates VI of Pontus. Cities around the Aegean were forced to choose sides, and Athens backed the losing horse. Philo, however, relocated to Rome at the start of the war, and it was there that he met and taught one of the greatest prodigies of the age. Marcus Tullius Cicero was in his late teens at the time, and the exiled head of Plato's school made a great impression on him.

It was no doubt through Philo that Cicero came to the ideas of Clitomachus and found out about the philosophical atheists. In around 45 BC, having patched up his relationship with Julius Caesar and returned to Rome, Cicero began work on a theological study called *On the Nature of the Gods,* a dialogue divided into three books. In the first book, Velleius puts forward the Epicurean view of the gods and is rebuffed by the Academic Cotta; in the second, Balbus argues the Stoic position; in the third, Cotta again replies, putting the Academic argument. Cicero seems to have depended heavily on Clitomachus for Cotta's arguments, which are largely skeptical, arguing that the Stoics and the Epicureans make unprovable assumptions about the gods, which they cannot sustain. The crucial point for our purposes is that Cotta's attack on the Epicurean "thin gods" also contains an atheist doxography, which classical scholars now believe derives ultimately from Clitomachus, via Philo. The Epicureans' conception of the gods as incapable of intervening in our world, Cotta argues, is tantamount to atheism of the kind proposed by Diagoras, Theodorus, Protagoras, Prodicus, and Euhemerus; he briefly summarizes the positions of each. In Cicero's text the doxography is put to a specific, anti-Epicurean use, and there is a hint of hostility toward the atheist position: Cotta attacks the Epicureans by saying that they are *no better than* the atheists. Cicero, after all, was a theist; he concludes *On the Nature of the Gods* saying, in his own voice, that he sides with the Stoic Balbus, who has argued for a providentially just god. But Clitomachus and his teacher Carneades were different kinds of beasts. From their point of view, the skeptical project depended on demonstrating that the arguments against the existence of gods must be just as strong as those for. Clitomachus's writings almost certainly included a positive doxography of atheism, a distillation of all the very best arguments against divinity, going right back to classical times.[8]

Clitomachus's *On Atheism* gave atheism legitimacy and in so doing created the possibility of engagement and identification with that tradition. It is in this sense that doxography functioned as a virtual network, joining together disbelievers across time and space, in much the way that electronic media do. The written text is, after all, a technology. The postclassical Greek-speaking world, indeed, was always already a textual network. Stretching out as it did over a vast space from Sicily to Iraq, it was too disparate to be held together by real-time interaction. What is more, until Roman conquest, there was no political unity either. Religion offered only a weak coherence, since there was so much variation in regional cult, which could also be intermixed with non-Greek divinity. What united the Greek world across all of this as an "imagined community" (to use Benedict Anderson's phrase) was precisely the power of a shared sense of common texts, cultural traditions, and historical reference points clustering around Homer and classical Athens. The virtual community of ancient atheists was calqued on this process.[9]

Clitomachus's doxography does not survive, but its importance to later antiquity is crystal clear. There are two other major atheist doxographers, both from the second century AD. The first is Sextus Empiricus, the richest mine for Hellenistic philosophical atheism, whom we met in chapter 11. The other is Aëtius, a shadowy figure whose doxographical work *The Tenets* has been reconstructed by modern scholars from various sources. What he offers, however, is sensational. Sextus, as a Skeptic, is interested only in demonstrating the equal power of arguments both for and against the existence of gods; he offers the atheist arguments only as a counterweight to theist ones. Aëtius, by contrast, is interested in atheism as a free-standing intellectual position. What is more, there is not a trace of moral judgment in his account: what he offers is simply a clear-sighted compendium of arguments used by those who do not believe. By the second century AD, atheism in the full, modern sense had acquired full legitimacy as a philosophical idea.[10]

Aëtius begins by noting that "some of the philosophers" deny the existence of gods together: as examples he chooses Diagoras of Melos, Euhemerus, and the author (whom he identifies as Euripides) of the Sisyphus fragment. This catalogue of names is of a familiar type, which suggests that it derives ultimately from Clitomachus. But this is not just a tired rehash. Aëtius uses forceful, mocking language to describe traditional views of the gods: the poets talk "nonsense" about divine omnipotence; Plato is full of "archaic, lunatic nonsense" when he claims that a god created the universe in his own image, pointing out the implication that this would mean that the god in question is spherical. "Nonsense," *lēros,* is a word drawn from the savage satire of comedy. This ridicule is designed to perform a particular function: it is group-building rhetoric, designed to get the reader on the speaker's side and giggling at the absurdity of traditional theism. As we read this, we are supposed to be reinforced in our skepticism.

Aëtius draws up three different types of argument. The first attacks the idea of omnipotence. If the god is omnipotent, can he make snow black, fire cold, and so forth? Surely not, Aëtius implies; so he cannot be omnipotent. This is an early version of now-familiar omnipotence paradoxes ("Can God make a stone so heavy he cannot lift it?" "Can God eat himself?"). The second is cosmological. Certain thinkers argue that the cosmos is created by a divine force. But creation is necessarily an event in time. If there was creation, there was a time before creation. What happened then? Did the god not exist during that time? That is unacceptable for any view of gods as eternal. Was he asleep? That too is unthinkable, for sleep suggests weariness, which is impossible for an omnipotent being. If he was awake, however, he was not yet fulfilled, since he had not completed his plan, and that too suggests that he has not always been complete in his blessedness. The final argument is one that goes back to Euripides's *Bellerophon:* if the gods are in charge of moral punishment and reward, how do we explain wrongdoing in the world? With more than a tinge of misogyny (the crimes of women are always worse), Aëtius adduces the mythical instances of Clytemnestra murdering the "excellent" Agamemnon and Deianeira destroying Heracles.

To ask what Aëtius himself thought of such arguments would be to miss the point. His fundamental doxographic aim was not to evaluate or judge the ideas of others but to capture the kind of argumentation and rhetoric characteristic of this particular community. What is striking in this precious testimony, along with the argumentation, is the use of the language of mockery, which implies an attempt to reinforce group cohesion by stigmatizing those outside. This is exactly how communities sustain themselves, especially virtual ones that depend on texts rather than face-to-face communication. There are strong parallels, for example, with the letters attributed to the apostle Paul: there too we find the same combination of group-affirming arguments, appeal to tradition, and derision leveled at those poor, benighted fools who do not belong.

In his own his atheist doxography, Sextus Empiricus refers at one point to "the company [*tagma*] of the atheists." Sextus uses the phrase metaphorically, to refer to the virtual community of disbelievers he himself has constructed by linking together different thinkers from different periods in time and space. The doxographic gaze, surveying Greek thought throughout the ages, sees patterns where others see mere arbitrary dots. What Aëtius suggests, however, is the possibility of a real community. Was there actually a movement toward atheism in the early Roman Empire? That is the question to which we now turn.[11]

15

Imagine

By the second century AD, a long period of stability and opportunity had funneled power and resource upward into the hands of an elite keen to compete with one another for prestige. This was an "age of ambition," to quote one eminent scholar. Behind this culture of aristocratic self-promotion was the concept of the Roman peace, Pax Romana. The Latin word *"pax"* means something subtly different from its English equivalent: not the absolute absence of war but its successful prosecution, so as to subjugate malcontents. "Pacification" is a better translation. The emperor Vespasian's Temple of Peace was a monument to his crushing of Jerusalem and the destruction of the Second Temple in AD 70. "They make a desert and call it *pax*," says an astute Scottish resistance leader in Tacitus's account of the conquest of Britain.[1]

The Roman Empire was a highly integrated system, a masterpiece of hegemonic design. Practical decisions were made locally by centrally appointed governors and city councils formed of co-opted local elites; difficult decisions and questions of principle were referred to the imperial bureaucracy at the center. The provinces retained their autonomy in religious and cultural matters (although there was also in the Greek-speaking parts a tacit expectation that worship should be offered to the emperor). The illusion that Rome's provincial subjects retained the autonomy and self-determination that they had enjoyed in the ancient city-state was offset by the ever-present awareness that Rome held the real power. One sage philosopher advised a young Greek with aspirations to political power in his city to keep reminding himself that "you rule, but you are also ruled . . . watch the boots above your head."[2]

The equilibrium of the empire was maintained by the tension of two opposing forces. On the one hand, Rome, the hub of empire, drew the gaze of all: much of the known world was now subject to one imperial master, the ultimate authority in matters to do with politics, the law, and the military. This centralization, however, was balanced by an amplification of individual local, religious, and philosophical identities. In every part of the empire, international deities established themselves alongside traditional ones, among them the Egyptian goddess Isis, the Iranian fire god Mithras, the Syrian fish deity Atargatis, another Syrian Jupiter Dolichenus, and of course Yahweh in both his Jewish and his newer Christian guises. Ancient Greek philosophies such as Pythagoreanism and Platonism re-emerged in new, mystical guises alongside Stoicism and Epicureanism. Globalization was accompanied by what cultural theorists call "glocalization," a retrenchment of regional, nonstandard, and subcultural identities as a response to the interconnectedness of the new world and the perceived threat of being subsumed into a homogeneous whole. Yet this multiplication of religious forms was itself a product of empire, and in particular of Rome's status as a multicultural hub. "Throughout all the empires, provinces and cities," observes a Christian writer of the second century AD, "we see people with their own individual rites (the Eleusinians worship Ceres, the Phrygians the Mother, the Epidaurians Asclepius, the Chaldaeans Baal, the Syrians Astarte, the Taurians Diana, the Gauls Mercury)—but the Romans worship the whole lot." The imperial capital was the marketplace of the world, and in that marketplace anything could be acquired—including religious beliefs. Empire-wide networks facilitated the spread of new cults far and wide: the army was particularly important in this respect. Thus it was that, for example, sanctuaries of Jupiter Dolichenus, Mithras, and Isis ended up in Britain, in the distant northeast of the empire.[3]

But what of atheists? Now that it was a named and philosophically established position, and "virtual networks" had been created via doxographies, did atheism similarly spread across the known world? The evidence is more difficult to track than with religious cults, since disbelievers were not concerned to leave physical traces of their absence of belief. There are no shrines, statues, inscriptions, coins, or graffiti indicating their presence. Yet it seems clear that atheism did indeed flourish alongside the many cults of the empire, even if we must instead tease their traces delicately out of literary sources.

Lucius Apuleius of Madaura was one of the most colorful figures who trod the stage of the second-century AD Roman Empire (a stage, indeed, that was well set for polychromatic personalities). A number of his philosophical and rhetorical works survive, although he is remembered primarily for his riotous novel *The Golden Ass* or *Metamorphoses*. This tells of one Lucius, whose voracious curiosity sees him get mixed up in magic and transformed into a donkey; after a long string of ordeals, he is returned to human form and thereupon converts to the cult of Isis. Many have seen in his namesake Lucius more than a touch of Apuleius himself, who shared the same blend of adventurousness, mischief, and religiosity. (Augustine notoriously took *The Golden Ass* as an autobiography.) And indeed the author seems to have had adventures of his own with religion and magic. At some point in the 150s, on his way home to Madaura (the modern town of M'Daourouch in Algeria), he stopped off at Oea, now the Libyan capital Tripoli. There he fell sick, but his misfortune turned to advantage when he met, befriended, and eventually married a wealthy widow several years his senior called Aemilia Pudentilla. All went well until two parties with designs on Pudentilla's fortune, Aemilianus and Rufinus, started stirring up trouble. Their plan was to win her children over to their side (which they did) and then prosecute Apuleius in court on the grounds that he had captured her heart by magic.

But they had reckoned without one of the greatest orators of the age. The trial was a high-profile affair, taking place in AD 158 or 159 before the proconsul of North Africa, Claudius Maximus, at Sabrata (modern Zowara). We have his masterful defense speech: modeled loosely on Socrates's own defense at Athens in 399 BC, it patiently skewers all of the opposition's arguments, ridiculing their claims and painting Apuleius as the model of philosophical bookishness and integrity. Apuleius also artfully turns the tables on the prosecution, arguing for their own moral failings. In particular, he paints himself as a paragon of religious observance and his prosecutor Aemilianus as constitutionally averse to ritual worship. The supposed magical objects he has been hoarding are in fact talismans associated with mystery cults and testify to his immersion in conventional religion. As for Aemilianus:

> I know that there are some people, among them this Aemilianus,
> who enjoy mocking all things divine. I understand from several peo-

ple at Oea who know him that to this very day he has never prayed to any god or visited any temple, while if he passes any shrine he considers it a wrong to raise his hand to his lips in reverence. He has never given a first-fruit offering of crops, vines or animals to any of the agricultural gods who supply his food and clothes. His farm has no shrine, holy place or grove. But why do I speak of groves or shrines? Those who have visited his estate say they have never seen there any stone where an oil offering has been made, or one branch where a wreath has been hung. That is why he has two nicknames. He is called Charon, as I have said, since he is grumpy in personality and appearance. But he is also called Mezentius, because he holds the gods in contempt.[4]

Apuleius presents his opponent as an out-and-out atheist, someone with no concern for worshipping the gods. Associating him with Mezentius was a rhetorical masterstroke: the latter appears in Vergil's *Aeneid* as a *contemptor deorum* (despiser of the gods), a theomachic barbarian whom "pious Aeneas" must defeat to found Rome. Apuleius was implying that his accuser's religious stance made him the embodiment of religious, moral, and social disorder and an enemy of Roman values.[5]

Was Aemilianus really an atheist? The obvious difficulty is that it is hard to know how much adjustment to make for Apuleius's rhetoric. Exaggerated invective was a familiar feature of the ancient courtroom: listeners would have known that they should take such accusations with fistfuls of salt, much as they would the standard charges of adultery, poisoning, and a penchant for oral sex. But this will not quite explain Apuleius's attack, since he suggests that Aemilianus is part of a community of like-minded individuals. "I know that there are some people," he opines, "among them this Aemilianus ... " Aemilianus is (according to Apuleius) one of a number of such people. The phrasing in fact recalls the doxographers' descriptions of the atheists as a virtual network: "There are some of the philosophers, such as Diagoras of Melos and Theodorus of Cyrene and Euhemerus of Tegea, who say that the gods do not exist at all." Do we have in Apuleius evidence for a comparable network in North Africa, but this time a network of real-life atheists?[6]

Those who have considered the case of Aemilianus and his community have sometimes concluded that he was not an atheist in our sense, but a Christian. But there were very few Christians in North Africa in the mid-second century AD, and it is hard not to conclude that those who would count Apuleius's prosecutor among their number have been prompted to do so by an ideologically based desire to swell their ranks.[7]

Atheism does not seem to have been especially controversial in the early Roman Empire. Those like Aemilianus no doubt lived relatively unmolested, so long as they participated in the civic lives of their communities (which may have included the bare minimum of religious observance). There were no restrictions on the articulation of atheistic beliefs or prosecutions. Even so mainstream a figure as Pliny—this is Pliny the Elder, the Roman military and naval commander and victim of the eruption of Vesuvius in AD 79—on occasion expressed himself a religious skeptic. The second book of his encyclopedia the *Natural History* promotes a naturalist view of the world as united by a single, all-pervasive cosmic power (not unlike that of the early pre-Socratics). This theory has little room for any conception of deity. "I think of it as a sign of human imbecility to try to find out the shape and form of a god," he writes. "Whoever 'god' is—if in fact he exists at all—he consists in pure sense, sight, sound, soul, mind: he is purely himself." Pliny goes on to poke fun at the multiplicity of gods found in different houses, cities, and countries: "From this we can infer that there are more deities than humans!" Illogicalities are also mocked: gods marry without producing children; some of them are always old, others always young; all sorts of odd, implausible, and immoral stories are told about them. Like Prodicus and Euhemerus, he argues that religious belief originated in the celebration of human achievements: the names of the gods, and even the stars themselves, were born (he claims) from the "merits of men." It is ludicrous to think that any divinity that might exist would pay any attention to humanity. The idea that Fortune, in the sense of mere chance, is a deity is also absurd, but no more credible is the notion that everything is predetermined. The conception of divinity, he asserts, derives from a human need for a belief in justified rewards and punishment for moral and immoral behavior. As a whole, Pliny's disquisition suggests that the idea of deity is a human construction. "God," he says at one point, "is one mortal helping another." We make our own divinity through our behavior toward others.[8]

Pliny was no radical; he was simply a reflective, intelligent, well-read individual who had no reason to suppress these skeptical thoughts. Certainly, atheism could still be imagined as countercultural. Demonax of Cyprus was a second-century AD philosopher given to speaking his mind whatever the consequences. The satirist Lucian of Samosata, in his biography of him, suggests that he saw himself as an atheist in the classical mode. His accusers at Athens, Lucian writes, "brought against him the same charges as Anytus and Melytus brought against Socrates, claiming that he had never been seen sacrificing, and that he alone of all had never been initiated into the Eleusinian Mysteries." His response to the first accusation was that the gods have no need of sacrificial offerings; to the second he replied that he was worried about joining the cult since if the rites were unimpressive he would not be able to stop himself from turning the uninitiated away from the mysteries, and if they were he would feel that he had to tell everyone. In other words, by not allowing himself to be initiated he has stopped himself from profaning the Mysteries—as Diagoras of Melos, classical Athens's atheist *par excellence,* had famously done (or been accused of doing) in 415 BC. Demonax was implicitly acknowledging his own atheism but taking steps to avoid causing the kind of ruckus that his predecessors created. The Athenians were amused at his answer and dropped the stones they were about to hurl at him.

Among the many philosophical jokes Lucian records, there are a few that suggest mockery of conventional religion. One of his friends asked him to go to the sanctuary of the healing god Asclepius to pray for his son. "You obviously think Asclepius is pretty deaf," Demonax replied, "if he cannot hear us praying here." Someone asked him if he thought that the soul was immortal, and he replied, "Oh yes, immortal in the way that everything is." When he met a seer making public prophecies for money, he told him he could not justify the fee: "If you think you can change destiny, then whatever you ask for you're charging too little; but if the future turns out as the god has decreed it, what use is prophecy?" Demonax seems to have been a philosopher in the Cynic mode ("He seemed to follow the man of Sinope in his dress"): aggressively satirical, an enemy of dogma rather than a doctrinaire adherent to any particular philosophical code. This made him more of an assailant of existing ideas about religion than an active evangelist for atheism.[9]

If Demonax remains an obscure figure, his biographer, Lucian (ca. AD 120–180), is one of the most influential ancient Greek writers of all. Born in Mesopotamian Samosata (near Adıyaman in modern Turkey), he attained literary fame across the empire. His squibs and fantasies have often earned him the label of atheist. One tenth-century Byzantine encyclopedia tells us about his nickname: " 'Blasphemer' or 'slanderer'— better, in fact, to call him 'atheist,' because in his dialogues he went so far as to ridicule religious discourse . . . The story goes that he was killed by dogs, because of his rabid attacks on the truth, for in his *Life of Peregrinus* he inveighs against Christianity, and (accursed man!) blasphemes against Christ himself. For that reason he paid the penalty befitting his rabidity in this world, and in the life to come he will share the eternal fire with Satan." No more temperate was the sixteenth-century Catholic Inquisition, which placed his work on their list of proscribed books. Conversely, however, he was also championed by the early modern humanists, who saw him as a fearless mocker of religious flummery. Thomas More and Erasmus were both keen translators and literary imitators; later on he would inspire Voltaire and Swift.[10]

Lucian won his reputation as an atheist, and as Satan's eternal companion, primarily because he satirized Christians. He was in fact the earliest non-Christian writer of Greek to mention the new cult of Christ, whom he cheerfully mocked as "the impaled sophist" (assimilating the Roman practice of crucifixion to the Greek *anaskolopisis,* or "impaling," used for the most degraded criminals). But Christians, who were few in number at this time, are not in fact his primary target. He is much more concerned with exposing the logical fallacies of mainstream Greek ideas about the gods and the ludicrous ritual practices of the pious.[11]

Was Lucian actually an atheist, as the Byzantine encyclopedia claimed? This is a question that has divided scholars. It is, in fact, probably the wrong question to ask. Most of his writings are dramatic dialogues and fictions, texts that do not reveal their author's opinion. He revels in the play of multiple literary identities, weaving in references to "Lukinos" (a play on his own Greek name, Loukianos), "the Syrian," "Tykhiades"

("Child of Fate"), and similar. Lucian never sits his readers down and confesses his innermost thoughts. Nor does he feel any strong obligation to be consistent: he can quite happily mock religion in one text while attacking someone for impiety in another. Like his biographical subject Demonax, he was not so much a dogmatic atheist as a merciless mocker of pretentiousness and folly, and it just so happened that religion offered a number of highly visible targets.[12]

When Lucian trains his sights on religion it is usually religion of a very traditional variety. Like other intellectuals of the day, he was saturated with the ancient literature of archaic Greece and democratic Athens. His was a learned, refined form of humor, targeted at those who knew their Thucydides, Euripides, and Plato. His *Dialogues of the Gods,* for example, pokes fun at the deities of Homer and mythology and places them in comically prosaic situations. Pan tries to get Hermes to recognize him as his father, which will mean addressing the awkward issue of why he (the son) is half goat . . . who, then, is the mother? Hermes (the messenger god) protests to his mother that it is not fair that the younger gods have to do all of the errand jobs. Hera reveals to Zeus that that nice young man Ixion, who has been coming around to dinner, has been making passes at her. The fun here lies in the clash of literary registers: the Olympian gods are supposed to manifest themselves solemn and dignified in sublime poetry, not whine about practicalities in knockabout farce. There is nothing intrinsically atheistic about these dialogues, but they are hardly flattering either.

More trenchant are his mockeries of religious institutions. One essay deals with animal sacrifice, the climax of any Greek or Roman ritual. "What the numbskulls do at their sacrifices, festivals and processions in honour of the gods," he begins, "what they pray for and vow that they will do, what they think about them—well, I doubt anyone is so downcast or depressed as not to roar with laughter at the daftness of their actions." This was a potentially scandalous stance to take, from the perspective of mainstream religion. Lucian's attack, indeed, goes to the heart of the underlying principles of Greek ritual. Sacrifice, in ancient religion, was a form of exchange. It depended upon a contract of reciprocity between gods and humans: if we do well by the gods in our devotional acts, the logic ran, they will do right by us. Lucian quickly pinpoints the logical fallacy and skewers the rationale. "So, it seems that none of their actions is done without some kind of payment. They sell us the good things in life. You can buy your health in exchange for a calf, say. Four bulls will get you wealth, a hundred a kingdom." But (Lucian reasons) this makes no sense: if the gods really are gods, and as powerful and mighty as we say they are, what need do they have of human offerings? And why are they so greedy that they wreak horrible vengeance on humans who fail to sacrifice? Does a bit of sacrificial smoke matter that much to them?[13]

Lucian deals with religion with the kind of uncompromisingly rationalist literalism that makes myth seem ludicrous. Humor is a weapon: it creates an us-against-them scenario and co-opts the reader in its aggressive mockery of the other side's intellectual failings. (The same tactics are adopted in modern anti-religious polemic: think, for example, of Bertrand Russell's miniature celestial teapot orbiting around the sun.) This tactic implies not just an individual stance against organized religion but also an attempt, quite possibly successful, to identify with a network, however virtual, of like-minded individuals.[14]

Another squib deals with funerals, in a similar vein: it is ludicrous, he mocks, to think that weeping and wailing about the dead make any difference. Heavily influenced here by the Cynics, Lucian sees death as proof that vanity and pretension are temporary and insubstantial. Cynics thought that the world of human culture is an illusion—*tuphos*, "delusion," was their word, and a favorite Lucianic word too—and that death returns us to our true, organic role in the natural world. Diogenes the Cynic was said to have left instructions for his body to be tossed outside the city walls for the animals to feed upon. In one of Lucian's dialogues, Charon, the underworld's ferryman, visits the upper world with Hermes and cackles at the baubles that attract the living. "Is that gold, that bright, shiny substance? Pale yellow, with a tinge of red? I am always hearing of it, but this is the first time that I have seen it." Hermes confirms that it is, and that it is the reason for all sorts of wars, crimes, and abuses. "People are incredibly stupid, from what you say," responds Charon; "imagine conceiving such a passion for something pale and heavy." The *Dialogues of the Dead,* meanwhile, stages a series of encounters in the afterlife in which various historical and mythical individuals bemoan or mock the ludicrous behavior of the living.[15]

From this perspective, organized religion is just another form of *tuphos,* "delusion." The idea of powerful, anthropomorphic deities whose favor can be bought by ritual action and pious attitudes is one of the ridiculous absurdities of human culture: "These rites and beliefs on the part of the masses seem to me to call not for someone to criticise them, but for some Heraclitus or Democritus: the one to ridicule their daftness, the other to bewail their dumbness." Democritus was known as "the laughing philosopher," Heraclitus as "the weeping philosopher." In English idiom, Lucian is saying that it is hard to know whether to laugh at organized religion or to cry.[16]

Satirists are not bound to be consistent: there are certainly other works of Lucian's that feature the Olympian gods in a fairly conventional guise, sitting on Olympus and pulling mortal strings as they do in Homeric epic. But his Olympians always seem nervous and unsure of their position, as if their status were precarious and likely to be snatched away at any moment. One of his flights of fancy has Timon, the legendary misanthrope of classical Athens (who would later be the subject of one of Shakespeare's plays), inveighing against Zeus for his failure to punish wrongdoers. "Where now is your 'roaring flash,'" he appeals, "where is your 'thumping thunder,' your 'blazing, flashing, crashing bolt'? All that has turned out to be nonsense and poetic vapidity—nothing more than the clatter of language." No wonder, he continues, Salmoneus thought he could get away with imitating your thunder. "You are getting the reward for your laziness: no one sacrifices to you or garlands you, except thoughtlessly at the Olympic Games (and even then not because he thinks it necessary, but out of support for traditional practice). Little by little, O most noble of the gods, they are treating you like Cronus, forcing you out of your position of esteem." Zeus, Timon protests, has grown old and ineffectual—and as a consequence traditional religion has lost its appeal to the masses. Now, in Lucian's little plot, all this abuse from this "grimy, squalid, disheveled man . . . mouthy and overbold (no doubt one of the philosophers)" causes Zeus to sit up and take note. Zeus sends riches to Timon as recompense for his virtuous life and the many sacrifices he had performed, thus re-establishing the correlation between human action and divine reward that had fallen into abeyance. But the twist in the tale is that Timon rejects the offer of wealth, on the grounds that money only brings trouble. Timon—personifying Lucian's own aggressively cynical stance—is interested only in vengeance on malefactors, which he then proceeds to enact gleefully, beating up the parasites who have mistreated him over the years. Even though Zeus is represented as a real figure, and capable of rewarding mortals, it would be hard to extract a positive theistic message from the dialogue. The implication is rather that if you feel frustrated about the way the world is treating you, it is better to take matters into your own hands than to wait for gods to sort things out.[17]

As king of the gods, Zeus stands, by metonymy, for traditional theology as a whole. To defeat Zeus is to defeat religion as conventionally understood. And indeed Lucian takes great pleasure in pitching an overconfident Zeus into discussion with clever intellectuals who show the incoherence of his reasoning. In one dialogue, *Zeus Refuted,* the king of the gods is confronted by one Cyniscus ("Little Cynic"), who quizzes him about predestination, including an old chestnut that has puzzled all readers of Homer's *Iliad* (where Zeus admits himself powerless to save his own son Sarpedon): Are gods subject to fate, or can they change it? And then again, if our lives are predestined, how can we be held morally responsible for our actions? Zeus has no answers. The dialogue simply closes with the god expressing frustration: "You are an overbold sophist. I'm not going to put up with this anymore."[18]

Yet another dialogue, *Zeus the Tragedian,* opens with Zeus lamenting in tragic style. When interrogated by the other gods, he reveals that the source of his woes is a debate that has been going on in Athens, between a Stoic Timocles and an Epicurean Damis, on the question of whether the gods intervene in human affairs, and even whether they exist or not. At first, Timocles carried the audience with him, but after a while he tired and the audience began to shift toward Damis's side. Zeus was so aghast that he brought night in. The following day, the gods eavesdrop on the conversation and are distressed to find the disbeliever, Damis, entirely dominant.

Damis's compendium of different atheistic arguments reduces Timocles to aphasia. It is, in effect, a dramatization of the kind of doxography we find in Sextus Empiricus and Aëtius, a neat example of how we might expect a real atheist to argue when faced by a committed theist. The debate turns on two related questions: whether the gods intervene in our world and whether they exist at all. Damis initially argues that they cannot intervene, since they have never punished him for denying their role—nor, indeed, have they punished Timocles for his many (unspecified) crimes. Surely any gods that exist have no time to watch over every single instance of justice and injustice. Timocles responds with an argument that goes back to Plato's *Laws* (and has often been repeated ever since): he points to the regularity of nature and the cycles of organic creation, which suggest to him a providential ordering. Damis counters that the regularity of nature proves only that it is now regular, not that it was intentionally created that way. Discussion now turns to Homer, whom they both agree to be the best poet, but Damis has no difficulty in showing that his poetic skill is not dependent on his theology, which is inventive and self-contradictory. The tragic poets are no more trustworthy. At this point, Timocles changes tack, arguing that religion is culturally universal: Are all the nations on the planet therefore wrong? This is one of the theist arguments that Sextus Empiricus puts forward, and Damis comes up with exactly the same counterargument, which is that the fact that many people believe something to be the case does not prove that it is true. And in fact, he proceeds, many peoples believe things about the gods that others find ludicrous: that they enjoy all kinds of exotic sacrifice (including human sacrifice), or that (in the case of the Egyptians) they take the form of animals. Timocles now turns to the predictive power of oracles; Damis points out that oracles tend to be produced in highly ambiguous language that can be taken either way (he uses the famous example from Herodotus: the priestess at Delphi told Croesus of Lydia that if he attacked Cyrus he would "destroy a great empire"). Damis's critique of the efficacy of oracles perhaps reflects the similar views of Oenomaus of Gadara, a Cynic who wrote in the early second century AD (remembered, as it happens, by the Jewish tradition as an interlocutor of rabbis and the greatest of the Greek philosophers). "Can't you hear Zeus when he thunders?" asks Timocles, accusing Damis of being a *theomakhos*. Damis replies that he hears thunder, but there is no proof that Zeus is behind it—and he takes the opportunity to remind Timocles that the Cretans have a tomb of Zeus, which suggests that they think he was a mortal. Timocles's penultimate argument is an analogy from sea voyaging. To sail a ship you need a captain, who will order all the different groups to do their jobs. Damis, however, turns the example on its head, and points out that many ships are run incompetently; who is to say that the universe is not the same? Finally, Timocles comes up with a philosophical syllogism: "If there are altars, then there are gods; there are altars, therefore there are gods." The logic is, of course, inadequate, and it takes Damis no time at all to dismiss it. But what is interesting is that it is an (intentionally, on Lucian's part) garbled version of the syllogistic argument for the existence of gods of Zeno, the founder of Stoicism: "It would be reasonable for someone to honour the gods; it is not reasonable to honour beings that do not exist; therefore gods exist." The gods, in conclusion, acknowledge the force of Damis's arguments but console themselves that only the Greek intellectual elite have realized all of this; the run of humanity will continue as before.[19]

Lucian's dramatization of the debate between Damis and Timocles is, of course, comically exaggerated, but it does show in broad outline how a debate between an atheist and a theist might have proceeded. There are realistic touches: in this elite culture obsessed with the public display of intellectual brio, it is highly likely that public dialogues such as this occurred, with people (and, in Lucian's fantasy, gods too) gathering around to watch the intellectual fireworks. The satire even hints at the idea that atheism might expand and spread throughout the Greek world, when Zeus worries that "if people are persuaded that there are no gods at all, or that we have no thought for humans, we shall go without sacrifices, presents and honours on earth, and will sit idly in heaven beset by famine." Echoing Aristophanes's *Birds,* where the citizens of Cloudcuckooland try to starve the gods out of heaven by usurping their sacrifices, Zeus imagines a time when respect for the gods has died. The implications of this are immense: through his fictional characters, Lucian explores the possibility that arguments against the existence of gods could ultimately persuade everyone not to practice religion.[20]

There is one last piece of evidence suggesting that atheists were recognizable figures in the communities of Roman Greece and that their ideas were taken seriously. Plutarch (ca. AD 45–120) was a prodigious writer of histories, a moralist, a theological philosopher in the Platonic tradition, a Roman citizen, a priest at Delphi, and a proud Boeotian who boasted that he had turned down career advancement to stay in his home town of Chaeronea (where Philip of Macedon confirmed his subjugation of Greece). He was, however, a far more interesting character than that description suggests: a sometime vegetarian who believed that animals are rational beings, the author of a daring love story in which an older woman abducts a younger man (he was, within the narrow confines of ancient moralism, something of a feminist), the only ancient source to preserve the mythical romance of the Egyptian gods Isis and Osiris, and the writer of a tract *On the Face That Appears on the Moon*. He also composed one of the most moving pieces of classical literature, a philosophical consolation addressed to his wife after the death of their daughter. Though bookish and pious, he was a rounded personality; though orthodox in many respects, he was thrilled by arcane knowledge and oblique perspectives.[21]

It was this fascination with the out of the way, coupled with a nigh-obsessive religiosity, that led him to address the question of atheism. He did not, however, confront it directly. One of his many surviving tracts is called *On Superstition,* and it deals with what he saw as a false, bastardized form of religion: *deisidaimonia,* literally "fear of the demonic." *Deisidaimonia* had long inspired condescension in aristocrats of Plutarch's kind. Already in the late fourth century BC, Aristotle's pupil Theophrastus had included the *deisidaimōn* in his comic gallery of *Characters:* the type of person who is constantly worrying about ritual purity, about chance incidents such as animals crossing his path, always seeing visions and demanding their interpretation. Plutarch takes over Theophrastus's characterization and amplifies it, using a range of supercilious stereotypes: superstition is associated with defilement ("He sits outside his house with sackcloth on and wearing filthy rags; and often he rolls naked in the mire as he confesses his multiple sins and wrongdoings") and seen as characteristic of old women (always an easy target for stereotypers) and Jews. Plutarch was writing in the aftermath of the sack of Jerusalem in AD 70 (which at one point he seems to blame on Jewish superstitious scruples: he claims they were unwilling to fight on the Shabbat), when a wave of anti-Jewish sentiment was rippling through the empire. The caricatured nature of his attack suggests that this may not be his real target.[22]

In fact, despite its ostensible target of the *deisidaimones, On Supersti-*

tion is really an oblique attack on atheism. Plutarch's strategy through-out is to compare the superstitious man to the atheist. "The atheist," he writes, "thinks there are no gods; the superstitious man wishes there were none, but believes in them against his will; for he is afraid not to believe." His argument is that both superstition and atheism share a common ignorance, for both misunderstand the nature of the divine, which is thoroughly benevolent. (Plutarch's argumentation in this tract is thoroughly perverse: everything that is good in your life you should attribute to the gods, everything that is bad you should blame on other causes!) For Plutarch, the gods are always benevolent; any attribution to them of hostile intent is necessarily a misunderstanding of their nature. Faced with the traditional poetic idea that the gods visit terrible suffer-ings on mortals, it is—Plutarch concedes—entirely rational to disbelieve in the gods. So atheism is a more intellectually respectable response than belief in the idea of malign divinity. But atheism and superstition alike are based on the same erroneous assumption that gods can do wrong.[23]

Who were the *atheoi* thus targeted? A clue comes in the form of the title. An ancient list of Plutarch's works (the Lamprias catalogue) gives number 155 as "*On Superstition,* against Epicurus." Modern editors have tended to assume that this is a slip, based on the fact that on the first page Plutarch mentions those who think the universe is created from "atoms and void," which is an unambiguous reference to the Epicure-ans. The essay as a whole, however, makes perfect sense as a critique of Epicurean arguments against the existence of gods as conventionally understood. What Plutarch is doing, fundamentally, is attacking the kind of argument rooted in myth used by the Epicureans Lucretius and (in Lucian's *Zeus the Tragedian*) Damis. Lucretius's famous line "Such is the terrible evil that religion was able to urge" was motivated by an analysis of King Agamemnon's sacrifice of his own daughter to Artemis, when his fleet was becalmed at Aulis: this, Lucretius argued, sprang from a false, and religiously inspired, belief that the winds are the work of gods rather than natural forces. Plutarch eviscerates this line of attack, not by refuting but by redirecting it: what it shows, he says, is not that religion is wrong, but that that myth fundamentally misrepresents divinity. It is a case of superstition to believe, for example, that when the mythical Niobe boasted of her children's beauty Artemis shot them down, just as it is atheistic to disbelieve in gods on that basis. Only the pious understand the essentially benevolent nature of divinity.[24]

Atheism was a widespread and well understood phenomenon in the early Roman Empire. This was partly thanks to the popularity of Epicureanism, a philosophical system that considered gods at best remote and uninterested in human affairs. But atheism was also larger than Epicureanism: now understood as a respectable philosophical position, it presented itself as an alternative to traditional theism, a legitimate option available in the newly globalized marketplace of religions and philosophies. It was now possible to imagine the possibility of a world that had left religions behind: the Olympians would be, as Lucian envisaged it, starving for want of sacrificial smoke. Within two centuries of Plutarch and Lucian, however, that dream was dead: the religious landscape of the Roman Empire had been entirely reshaped, and there was no room in it for disbelievers.

16

Christians, Heretics, and Other Atheists

In AD 293, the emperor Diocletian partitioned the empire between four rulers, a division of power known to modern scholars as the tetrarchy ("empire of the four"). There were now four imperial offices: a senior "Augustus" and a junior "Caesar" for both the eastern and the western halves of the empire. Equally radical was the reform of succession: each Augustus was to be replaced not by a biological or adopted son but by the Caesar (who would in turn be replaced centrally). The dynastic principle of family inheritance was gone.

When Diocletian resigned in 305, following his own twenty-year rule, he must have thought that he had found a permanent solution to the instability that had bedeviled imperial succession of the previous fifty years (a half century that had seen twenty-six different men lay claim to the title of emperor, sometimes simultaneously and in conflict with one another). Instead, with a depressing predictability, the co-regents began warring among themselves. When Constantius I, the western Augustus, died in York in 306, his son Constantine was immediately proclaimed Augustus in his stead. In the same year, Maxentius, himself the son of a former western Augustus, had himself proclaimed emperor in Rome. Constantine and Maxentius were set on collision course. The issue was resolved finally when Constantine marched on Rome and defeated him at the battle of the Milvian Bridge on October 28, 312.

The challenge facing Constantine was the same one that Diocletian had sought to address: how to hold together an enormous empire that had in recent memory come perilously close to irreparable fragmentation. Constantine chose a different set of solutions, which were even more far-reaching than Diocletian's. He reformed the coinage, introducing the 24-karat gold solidus that in the eastern empire remained the standard currency for six hundred years: now all could trade with confidence, knowing that they could trust the money in their pocket. Like other tetrarchs before him he founded a new capital, but his was the most successful: he orchestrated the shift of the center of empire to Byzantium, at the mouth of the Black Sea, which he refounded as Constantinople ("the *polis* of Constantine"). This fortress city remained the hub of the eastern empire until 1453, when the Ottomans conquered it and made it their own capital. (Its modern name, Istanbul, reflects its historic uniqueness to its Greek inhabitants: when they visited it they simply went "to the city," *eis tēn polin.*) Though the tetrarchic system endured vestigially, Constantine re-established the principle of dynastic succession. Most significant of all, he paved the way for the adoption of Christianity as a state religion. It is unclear when he became a Christian and what was the extent of his commitment. The story that he converted before the battle of the Milvian Bridge on seeing a Christogram or a flaming cross in the sky beforehand (with the convenient label *In hoc signo vinces:* "In this sign you will conquer!") was a propagandistic fiction. He certainly did not stop supporting non-Christian practices, but he did facilitate the spread of the new religion. His Edict of Milan in 313 permitted all citizens to worship whichever god they chose (in sharp contrast with Diocletian's policy of Christian persecution). He encouraged the association of the imperial hierarchy with the new religion with financial support, building programs and promoting Christians to high office. He also arbitrated in theological disputes. In AD 315 he rejected the cause of the Donatists, a sect of North African puritans who rejected those who had renounced Christianity during Diocletian's persecution. In 325 came the Council of Nicaea, which amongst other things decided in favor of the proposition that Christ's divine nature was essentially identical to that of the father. Opponents of this belief, the followers of Arius (who claimed that the son was subordinate and lesser), were now heretics. The profession of faith established at this council, the Nicene Creed ("I believe in one God . . ."), is still used today by Catholics and others. Christianity was still only one religion among many in the empire, but Constantine had placed it at the heart of his imperial program and expressed a strong personal commitment to it. It was under Constantine that the crucifix emerged as the iconic symbol of Christianity, and the Chi-Rho Christogram (☧) was adopted on the imperial military standard. Political and theological authority had become closely interlinked.[1]

It is important to be clear that the Christianization of the empire emerges out of Roman history, rather than being something superimposed on it from without. Many of us have grown up with a conventional, confessionally influenced portrait of a persecuted but resilient network of devotees fired by the word of their god and evangelizing across the empire, despite brutal persecution, sweeping away the tired old ritualized practices until the popular support was so powerful that the emperor himself could not withstand it. In fact, ancient Christians were not an especially distinctive sect, however much they liked to claim that they were (Clement of Alexandria, for example, speaks of a "third race," alongside the Greeks and barbarians). It is easy to be seduced by ancient stories of brutal torture and martyrdom, which imply an ongoing war between virtuous Christians and the thuggish emissaries of the Roman state, but many of these stories are creations of the post-Constantinian era, heavily embroidered, born of a time when such persecution as there had been was a distant (and burnished) memory. Christianity in fact never seems to have been outlawed by the Romans. The only systematic persecutor was Diocletian, founder of the tetrarchy, who followed up his decrees against the Manichaeans (AD 299–302) with a short-lived edict against the Christians in 303 ordering the destruction of scriptures and buildings and the prohibition of Christian assembly for worship. There were assuredly other instances of intense anti-Christian hostility, and some Christians were indeed treated brutally, but these were isolated incidents rather than a broader pattern. The Christian idealization of martyrdom, and the polishing of martyr myths, began in earnest in the fourth century, paradoxically when there was nothing to fear from the state: rather, the myth of collective victimhood was projected as a means of galvanizing the international community in celebration of the heroic sacrifice of their predecessors.[2]

Most normal Christians were not separated from their non-Christian neighbors by a huge gulf: they wore the same clothes, bore the same names, ate the same food, lived in the same towns. Early Christians, like other inhabitants of the Roman Empire, were more concerned with getting by than with histrionic assertions of their difference from others.

Nor did becoming Christian necessarily mean rejecting other forms of religious practice. Some Christians were borderline Jews. Even after Christianity became Rome's state religion in the fourth century AD, many still clung to the old ways: even as late as the sixth century, there were those who acknowledged the Olympian gods. Polytheism and Christianity could exist side by side without any obvious friction. On the marvelous silver Projecta casket of the late fourth century (now in the British Museum) a Christian inscription accompanies a relief depiction of Venus. A fourth-century Roman called Firmicus Maternus wrote both an astrological work that treated the planets as traditional Roman deities and an anti-pagan tract *On the Error of Profane Religions*. Did he convert in the interim, as scholars tend to assume? Maybe, but maybe he simply saw no great contradiction. In the fifth century, the brilliant epic poet Nonnus of Panopolis wrote a versification of the Gospel of John and an account of the adventures of the "pagan" god Dionysus (in forty-eight books!). It was, as one scholar has put it, "easy to be a Christian and something else."[3]

Christians certainly expanded in numbers with astonishing speed, but not until the third century. One scholar has "guesstimated" that in AD 200, a mere 0.35 percent of the Roman Empire—perhaps two hundred thousand people—were Christians. Most Greeks and Romans had at this stage little awareness or understanding of the cult of Jesus. For example, Herodian's historical account of the Roman Empire, written in the mid-third century, contains not a single reference to Christianity. The same guesstimating scholar, however, has also reckoned that the numbers grew by around one million in the first half of the third century and by around five million in the second. By AD 300, they accounted for 10 percent of the population. Christianity could no longer be overlooked by Greco-Roman polytheists. This massive expansion raises the question not just of why Christianity grew so rapidly but also—more difficult to explain in confessional terms—why it grew rapidly *then*. Perhaps amid all the political instability of the third century, the promise that each individual, regardless of sex or social station, could be saved in the afterlife by turning to Jesus acquired a greater appeal to citizens of the empire. We shall never know the motivations of those millions of ordinary people who have left no written trace behind them.[4]

Whatever the explanation for the third-century explosion, Constantine's own promotion of Christianity was not the result of weight of numbers alone. Ten percent of the population was still a small minority. His calculation was surely a political one instead: claiming for himself the authority of the all-powerful, universal Christian god (without dispensing with the others) was a shrewd exercise in branding for an emperor concerned to hold together a worryingly fissile realm. Nor had he been the first Roman ruler to try to co-opt divine power in the service of empire. Even before Augustus had become the first *princeps*, Rome's imperial mission had been associated with divine providence. Stoic philosophy, which imagined a universe governed for the good by a single divine force, had proven congenial to a Roman imperial mentality from earliest times. Emperors had presented themselves as conduits for divine power, assuming the office of *pontifex maximus*, chief priest of all the cults at Rome; propagandistic art repeatedly depicted them as sacrificers in chief on behalf of the state. (Even after the adoption of Christianity as the imperial religion, emperors continued to hold this title until the end of the fourth century; in the fifth century it began to be used, as it still is today, for the head of the Catholic Church.) Emperors were worshipped as gods, during their lifetimes in the Greek-speaking parts of the empire and after their deaths (if they gained favor) in the west. Crucially, other experiments with religious unification had been essayed before Constantine adopted Christianity: Septimius Severus and Julia Domna had sought to promote the Syrian god Elagabal ("El of the Mountain"); Aurelian (AD 270–275) had tried again with Sol Invictus ("the Unconquered Sun," a god favored also by Constantine himself). The Roman Empire had always had theocratic elements to it, even if they had not always been consistently activated. It was, in fact, a general assumption throughout Greco-Roman antiquity that ruling vast, centralized empires was best done by co-opting the will of gods.[5]

The primary political challenge that presented itself throughout Greco-Roman antiquity was always a variant on the same theme: how to create unity out of diversity in a world without the armature of modern nationalism. Religion had always been part of the answer to that challenge. In archaic Greece, polytheism had been an appropriate expression of the sameness-but-difference of hundreds of autonomous or semi-autonomous city-states. In the later Roman period, monotheistic, centralized religion conveyed the desire for political unity in an empire that had come dangerously close to collapse.

Constantine's adoption of Christianity may not have seemed revolutionary to most observers at the time: the Roman pantheon was roomy, and there was nothing at all remarkable about an emperor adding another god to it. The effects over the course of the fourth century, however, were seismic. The brief reign of Julian (AD 361–363) aside, all subsequent emperors were Christians. In AD 380 Theodosius I (ruled AD 379–395) issued a decree from Thessalonica that pronounced Christianity the official religion of the empire and ordered all subjects to follow it. This was the making of Catholicism, Christianity in its orthodox form approved by the emperor. According to the edict, those who submitted to this particular theological orthodoxy, treating the Trinity as a single deity according to the findings of the Council of Nicaea, were entitled to call themselves "Catholics." All the rest—no distinction is drawn between polytheists, atheists, Jews, and theologically unsound Christians—were judged *dementes vesanosque* ("demented lunatics"), branded heretics, and threatened with punishment both divine and imperial. The subtle alignment of imperial and divine authority is telling. The omnipotent Christian god and the emperor stand in a relationship of exact analogy. A year later, Theodosius came up with another edict insisting that those who did not profess the Nicene version of the faith should be branded and driven from all cities. As one scholar has noted, Theodosius redefined the very nature of religion, which was "no longer merely normative *practice*: it has become a defined set of *beliefs* authorised by descent from the apostles and from Nicaea, and now issuing out of the mouth of the Roman ruler." For the first time in the history of the Greco-Roman world, political authority was systematically boring down into the hearts and minds of individual subjects, assessing their beliefs against decreed standards of orthodoxy and rewarding or punishing them appropriately.[6]

This was the real ideological revolution engendered by the Christianization of the empire: the alliance between absolute power and religious absolutism. Christianity had always produced theological dissent and schism. That tendency had now been turned into a tool of imperial power. Theodosian law enforced the idea that the health and prosperity of everyone in the empire depended fundamentally upon the adoption of not just the right religion but the right theological position on the right religion. Like all successful techniques of social control, this new focus on religious identity also involved identifying and stigmatizing outsiders. The *Codex Theodosianus,* a massive compilation of imperial law from the time of Theodosius II—the grandson of Theodosius I who ruled between AD 408 and 450—devotes the last of its sixteen books first to defining the model of Catholic Christianity that the empire sought to promote and then to various forms of legislation against all of those who do not fit the model. There are laws of course against heretics (the word derives from the Greek *hairesis,* "sect" or "cult"), mostly other types of Christians (Montanists, Eunomians, Priscillianists, Donatists, Apollinarians, Arians and so forth), who are prohibited from congregating or using any kind of ecclesiastical language to describe what they do; in many cases they are to be banished from the cities of the empire. Heresy should be treated as a crime against the state, since "any crime committed against divine religion is treated as an aggression against everyone." There is even legislation against *remembering* heretics: "No one shall recall to memory a Manichaean or a Donatist . . . There shall be one Catholic worship, one salvation." Apostates—those who renounce Christianity—are to be isolated from the rest of the community and forbidden to pass on property to their heirs. There are laws protecting Jews, but Jews are also forbidden from trying to convert Christians or owning Christian slaves. "Superstition"—traditional Greco-Roman polytheism—is to cease, temples to be closed, sacrifices to be abolished. Those who sacrifice or worship cult images shall be fined or put to death. Even public debate about religion is banned. The extent to which these policies were put into practice has been debated, but at the very least they provide a powerful rhetorical case for the exclusion of everything but Nicene Christianity.[7]

The Theodosian Code defines Catholic Christianity in opposition to a series of religious "others," execrated as manifestations of madness and deviancy and threatened with state violence. This was a massive change, for Greco-Roman polytheism had seen itself not as a unified system that excluded others but as an infinitely extensible network of local cults. The elasticity of polytheism meant that it had no external borders: if new deities were uncovered, they could simply be added to the list. Monotheism, by contrast, carried with it the idea of right and wrong belief. In earlier periods, that different people worshipped different gods had been viewed as an empirical fact about the world; now it was a problem that required correction, using the full power of the state and the law. Earlier Greeks and Romans had not even had a word for the acceptance that there were many gods, since this was seen as a self-evident ethnographic reality rather than a theological worldview. The word "polytheist," like "pagan," is a Christian coinage and implicitly suggests its inferiority to its polar opposite, "monotheist." (Personally I prefer to describe those who cleaved to the old ways as "polytheists" rather than the more obviously pejorative "pagans" [*pagani*, "rustics"], but it is important at all times to recognize that when considering late antiquity we are forced to adopt a set of religious distinctions and categories that would have been alien to an earlier era, and that stack the deck in favor of a Christian worldview.)

One religious crime, however, is missing from the Theodosian catalogue. Nowhere does this statute book mention atheism. It is, apparently, unimaginable in this world that anyone could be without religion. There are only two possibilities: true *religio* or false *superstitio*. The assumption underlying this position seems to be the belief that all humans are born with a natural sense of the divine but that some people have been led into misunderstanding by false teaching, a common belief among Christians of the time. This doctrine created a cultural blind spot: with no role to play in this binary construction of the world, with no place to occupy on the scale between true religion and false superstition, atheism now became effectively invisible.

The Christianization of the Roman Empire put an end to serious philosophical atheism for over a millennium. The word itself, indeed, acquired an additional meaning, which was wholly negative: rather than the rational critique of theism as a whole, it came to mean simply the absence of belief in the *Christian* god. For Christians in late antiquity, there was no contradiction at all in referring, for example, to "atheist polytheists": polytheism was a misunderstanding of the true nature of the one god, which led its benighted practitioners into the "atheistic" position of rejecting the Christian message. Christian heretics too could be called *atheoi*: in such cases the issue was not even that they did not believe in the Christian god, but rather that they did not believe in him in the right way. The earliest instance of this usage comes in the writings of Philo of Alexandria, a Greco-Jewish intellectual who died around AD 50. "Those who are dead in their soul are truly atheists," he writes, "while those arrayed alongside the true god live an eternal life." Or: "Atheism is the source of all crimes." Or most strikingly: "The atheists are waging a war against the lovers of God, a war that admits of no treaty or diplomacy." (This is, incidentally, the earliest instance I know of the "militant atheism" trope so beloved of present-day theists.) Perhaps Philo can be excused this paranoia, given the prevalence of anti-Semitism and pogroms in first-century Alexandria. But it was also a paranoia rooted in the Hebrew Bible's vision of the Israelites as a people set apart from others, fundamentally and irreconcilably alien. That distinctively monotheistic sense that there can only be one true religion has a tendency to foster sharp divisions between communities, and indeed a sense of the inevitability of violence between them. In Christian writings from the fourth century onward too we find time and again the idea of *atheoi* as mortal enemies that need to be joined in battle: the atheists are "universal enemies"! Catholic Christians have "drawn up the battle lines against the innumerable atheist heretics"! This figurative war could be quickly literalized, too: religious-sectarian hostility, which had been rare in the polytheist world, became a regular feature of life. A recent study of sacred violence between Catholics and Donatists in North Africa alone runs to over eight hundred pages. The baneful idea of holy war against unbelievers had put in its first appearance. Religious difference, for just about the first time in Mediterranean antiquity, had become the driver of conflict.[8]

But were Christians not themselves called "atheists" by Greeks and Romans? This is often asserted, but in fact the evidence for it comes almost entirely from Christian sources themselves. The fourth-century Christian bishop Eusebius of Caesarea, for example, depicts Constantine's rival Licinius as himself conducting his own "holy war" on behalf of traditional polytheism. While offering sacrifice in a grove, he is said to have inveighed against Constantine for "betraying his ancestral inheritance and taking up an atheistic belief . . . let us set out to war against the atheists!" Eusebius of course had no way of knowing what Licinius actually said at the time. The idea of a holy war waged against Christian "atheists" is his own construction, projected onto Licinius; it serves merely to legitimize Constantine's response, which is to reverse the terms and attack the polytheist "atheists" himself. The reversibility of the accusation of atheism is in fact a recurrent feature of Christian discourse. The story of the martyrdom of Polycarp of Smyrna, set at some point between AD 155 and 167, offers a wonderful example. The hero of the story, a virtuous old Christian, is arraigned before the governor and a bloodthirsty crowd in the arena. "Swear to Caesar's good fortune!" commands the governor. "Repent! Say the words: 'Away with the atheists!'" Polycarp turns to address the crowd, waving his fist at them, crying, "Away with the atheists!" thus redirecting the charge of atheism at the polytheists. This act of defiance earns him a fiery martyrdom at the stake. But although Polycarp's impressive response to persecution makes for a neat, punchy climax to the story, that story is itself surely historically inaccurate. No non-Christian would have uttered the words attributed to the governor. The idea of "repentance" (*metanoia*) is a Judeo-Christian one, and the phrase "away with" (*aire*) directly echoes language used in the Gospels to condemn Jesus. It seems unlikely that a Roman governor, apparently hostile to Christianity, should have borrowed Christian phraseology so explicitly. The story of Polycarp's martyrdom may have been invented entirely or (perhaps more likely) embellished with motifs designed to appeal to a Christian audience, and indeed to draw out the parallels with the execution of Jesus.[9]

The conclusion seems inevitable that the violent "othering" as atheists of those who hold different religious views was overwhelmingly a Judeo-Christian creation, which was then projected back onto the polytheists. There were, to be sure, some subtler uses of this device. In about AD 150, a Syrian called Justin wrote a work in defense of Christianity that invoked the figure of Socrates, who (he claimed) tried to lead humanity away from these demons by using "true reason and critical examination"—but was condemned to death as an impious (*asebē*) atheist (*atheon*) and for introducing a new type of divinity. Socrates has been reimagined as a Christian martyr! "That is why we [i.e., the Christians] are called atheists," Justin continues. "And we confess that we are athe-ists . . . at least as far as these kinds of imagined gods are concerned. But not with respect to the truest god, the father of justice and self-control and the other virtues, who is free from all impurity." Christians, then, are indeed atheists! Or, rather, atheists of a kind. Instead of simply reversing the supposed accusation of atheism, like other Christian writ-ers of the era, Justin accepts and embraces it: like Socrates, he turns his back on the gods of polytheism.[10]

Indeed, while there were those early Christians who decried the ear-lier classical *atheoi* as the worst kind of disbelievers, there were others who took them as allies in their war on polytheism. In the second cen-tury, Clement of Alexandria wrote of the paradox that "the label 'athe-ist' has been applied to Euhemerus of Acragas [*sic*], Nicanor of Cyprus [otherwise unknown], the Melians Diagoras and Hippo, and in addition Theodorus of Cyrene, and many others beside, who lived chaste lives and perceived religious error somewhat more sharply than others did." In Clement's view, it was not the virtuous Diagoras and his peers who deserved to be called atheists but the polytheists they criticized. Euhe-merus's *Sacred History,* indeed, was a particular favorite of the early Christians: that even some of the ancients themselves had seen that their gods were just deified mortals was taken as firm proof that belief in the Olympian gods was fundamentally misplaced.[11]

It is at first sight a curiosity that the classical *atheoi* were welcomed so enthusiastically in this new era. Their Christian readers, however, were interested only in the rhetorical leverage that they could exert on recalcitrant polytheists, and indeed on wavering Christians. There was no serious engagement with their ideas at the philosophical level—and certainly no sense that Christianity itself could be interrogated by athe-istic reasoning. For Christian apologists, philosophical atheism was nec-essarily consigned to the pre-Christian past, its critique directed not at theism in general but at polytheism in particular. Atheism, now viewed as the debunking of false superstition rather than the interrogation of supernatural belief, could serve no purpose now that the true Christian message had been revealed.

The arrival of Catholic Christianity—Christianity conjoined with imperial power—meant the end of ancient atheism in the West. Once it had been established that the paradigm of true versus false religion was the only one that mattered, there was nowhere to place atheism on the mental map. Cosmological and philosophical debate remained intense, of course, but it was unthinkable outside of the framework of Christian monotheism. Individuals surely experienced doubt and disbelief, just as they always have in all cultures, but they were invisible to dominant society and so have left no trace in the historical record. It is this blind spot that has sustained the illusion that disbelief outside of the post-Enlightenment West is unthinkable. The apparent rise of atheism in the last two centuries, however, is not a historical anomaly; viewed from the longer perspective of ancient history, what is anomalous is the global dominance of monotheistic religions and the resultant inability to acknowledge the existence of disbelievers.

Acknowledgments

I am hugely grateful to the British Academy, which awarded me a grant that absolved me of my university duties during 2012–2013. I am grateful, too, to my former students and colleagues at Corpus Christi College, Oxford, who tolerated my absence during that period with good humor. Teaching extraordinary students is a wonderful privilege, and not one that I take for granted. A number of specialist academic colleagues have read drafts and steered me through dangerous waters: David Sedley, James Warren, John Ma, Edith Hall, Robert Parker, Robin Osborne, Neil McLynn, Christopher Kelly. My children, India and Soli; my partner, Emily; and my parents, Judy and Guy, have been rocks. Judy and Emily also read large parts of the manuscript for me. Many thanks, too, to my agents Catherine Clarke and George Lucas, to my editors, George Andreou at Knopf and Neil Belton, Walter Donohue, and Julian Loose at Faber and Faber, and to my excellent copy editor, Amy Ryan.

Notes

A Dialogue

1. Quotation: Plato, *Laws* 888b. I have written this book for a broad readership. It has some of the trappings of academia, in the form of endnotes, bibliographical references, and (no doubt) a certain obsessiveness. On the other hand, it deals with a millennium of history in a small compass and cannot be comprehensive. Modern scholarship is cited primarily in the latest anglophone discussions, with a weighting toward works that will be accessible and affordable to a wide readership.

2. A good, skeptical account of neurotheology is M. Blume, "God in the brain: how much can neurotheology explain?," in P. Becker and U. Diewald (eds.), *Zukunftsperspektiven im theologisch-naturwissenschaftlichen Dialog* (Göttingen: Vandenhoeck and Ruprecht, 2011), 306–14. *Homo religiosus:* K. Armstrong, *The Case for God: What Religion Really Means* (London: Vintage, 2010), 13–34.

3. E. E. Evans-Pritchard, *Witchcraft, Oracles and Magic Among the Azande,* abb. ed. (Oxford: Clarendon Press, 1973), 106–7 (note especially that "faith and skepticism are alike traditional").

4. J. Arnold, *Belief and Unbelief in Medieval Europe* (London and New York: Bloomsbury, 2011), 230 (quotation), 2–3 (Thomas Tailour).

5. On the emergence of Israelite monotheism see especially M. Smith, *The Early History of God: Yahweh and Other Deities in Ancient Israel,* 2nd ed. (Grand Rapids, MI: Eerdmans, 2002). I owe my understanding of these issues, such as it is, to discussions with Professor Francesca Stavrakopoulou of the University of Exeter.

6. Other histories of ancient atheism include P. Decharme, *La critique des traditions religieuses chez les Grecs des origines au temps de Plutarque* (Paris: Picard, 1904); A. Drachmann, *Atheism in Pagan Antiquity* (London: Gyldendal, 1922), useful but methodologically outdated; H. Ley, *Geschichte der Aufklärung und des Atheismus,* vol. 1 (Berlin: Deutscher Verlag der Wissenschaften, 1966), vitiated by its schematically Marxist stance. For more recent discussions see G. Dorival and D. Pralon (eds.), *Nier les dieux, nier dieu* (Aix-en-Provence: Publications de l'Université de Provence, 2002); H. Cancik-Lindemaier, "Gottlosigkeit im Altertum: Materialismus, Pantheismus, Religionskritik, Atheismus," in R. Faber and S. Lanwerd (eds.), *Atheismus: Ideologie, Philosophie oder Mentalität?* (Würzberg: Königshausen and Neumann, 2006), 15–33; J. Bremmer, "Atheism in Antiquity," in M. Martin (ed.), *The Cambridge Com-*

panion to Atheism (Cambridge: Cambridge University Press, 2007), 11–26; U. Berner and I. Tanaseanu-Döbler (eds.), *Religion und Kritik in der Antike* (Münster: LIT Verlag, 2009); D. Sedley, "The Pre-Socratics to the Hellenistic Age" in S. Bullivant and M. Ruse (eds.), *The Oxford Handbook of Atheism* (Oxford: Oxford University Press, 2013), 139–51.

7. Quotation from P. O'Sullivan, "Sophistic Ethics, Old Atheism, and 'Critias' on Religion," *Classical World* 105 (2012): 174, with n. 36. For a recent contrast between Christianity and Greek religion see R. Parker, *On Greek Religion* (Ithaca, NY: Cornell University Press, 2011), the first two chapters of which are called, respectively, "Why Believe Without Revelation?" and "Religion Without a Church." For a critique of the concept of embedded religion see B. Nongbri, "Dislodging 'Embedded' Religion: A Brief Note on a Scholarly Trope," *Numen* 55 (2008), 440–60.

8. Inscription: no. 120 in P. J. Rhodes and R. Osborne, *Greek Historical Inscriptions, 404–323 BC* (Oxford: Oxford University Press, 2004), 534–35 = *Inscriptiones Graecae* 42 1.121. The Diogenes story is told at Diogenes Laertius, *Lives of the Eminent Philosophers* 6.59 (where the bon mot is said to be otherwise attributed to Diagoras of Melos).

Part One: Archaic Greece
1. Polytheistic Greece

1. For a "historical ecology" of the ancient Mediterranean see P. Horden and N. Purcell, *The Corrupting Sea: A Study of Mediterranean History* (Oxford and Malden, MA: Blackwell, 2000), and for the prehistoric period C. Broodbank, *The Making of the Middle Sea: A History of the Mediterranean from the Beginning to the Emergence of the Classical World* (London: Thames and Hudson, 2013). More generally on early Greece see O. Murray, *Early Greece,* 2nd ed. (London: Fontana, 1993); J. Hall, *A History of the Archaic Greek World, ca. 1200–479 BCE* (Oxford and Malden, MA: Blackwell, 2007); R. Osborne, *Greece in the Making, 1200–479 BC,* 2nd ed. (Abingdon, UK, and New York: Routledge, 2009). For a more general survey of Greek history see J. Boardman, J. Griffin, and O. Murray, *The Oxford History of Greece and the Hellenistic World,* 2nd ed. (Oxford: Oxford University Press, 2001); and for a spritely survey of ancient Mediterranean cultures generally, R. Miles, *Ancient Worlds: The Search for the Origins of Western Civilization* (London: Allen Lane, 2010).

2. Shipping: L. Casson, *Ships and Seamanship in the Ancient World,* rev. ed. (Baltimore: Johns Hopkins University Press, 1995). J. Lesley Fitton, *Minoans* (London: British Museum Press, 2002) offers an accessible introduction to Minoan culture. On the Mycenaeans see R. Castleden, *The Mycenaeans* (London: Routledge, 1995). The warlord or "big man" in Greece: J. Whitley, "Social Diversity in Dark Age Greece," *The Annual of the British School at Athens* 86 (1991): 341–65.

3. Intermarriage at Pithecusae is argued for on the basis of archaeological evidence by J. N. Coldstream, "Mixed Marriages at the Frontiers of the Early Greek World," *Oxford Journal of Archaeology* 12 (1993): 89–107. Not all have been convinced (e.g., D. Ogden, *Greek Bastardy* [Oxford: Oxford University Press, 1996]: 322–23), but whether we call it "marriage" or not, cohabitation

and miscegenation in early Italy seems likely (Hall, *History,* 257). I base my account of Greece's expansion in the archaic period and beyond on I. Morris, "Economic Growth in Ancient Greece," *Journal of Institutional and Theoretical Economics* 160 (2004): 709–42. The measurement of the Greek economy remains a controversial area, but the overall pattern of rapid growth is hard to deny.

4. The emergence of the *polis* is one of the most widely studied phenomena in all of ancient history. The most important studies are those of the Copenhagen Polis Centre: see especially M. H. Hansen, "95 Theses About the Greek 'Polis' in the Archaic and Classical Periods: A Report on the Results Obtained by the Copenhagen Polis Centre in the Period 1993–2003," *Historia: Zeitschrift für Alte Geschichte* 52 (2003): 257–82; M. H. Hansen and T. H. Nielsen (eds.), *An Inventory of Archaic and Classical Poleis* (Oxford: Oxford University Press, 2004), with an overview online at http://www.teachtext.net/bn/cpc/. For orientation see Hall, *History,* 67–92 (with useful bibliography); and Osborne, *Greece in the Making,* 128–30 and 220–30.

5. On these developments see Broodbank, *The Middle Sea,* 460–95. Tin Islands: Strabo 3.5.11 (claiming there are ten of them).

6. Carthage: see R. Miles, *Carthage Must Be Destroyed* (London: Allen Lane, 2010), with 58–95 on the early period.

7. Number of *poleis:* Hansen, "95 Theses," 263–64.

8. Herodotus 8.144.1–3. J. M. Hall, *Ethnic Identity in Greek Antiquity* (Cambridge: Cambridge University Press, 1997); J. M. Hall, *Hellenicity: Between Ethnicity and Culture* (Chicago: University of Chicago Press, 2002). Specifically on Macedonian ethnicity, see Hall's "Contested Ethnicities: Perceptions of Macedonia Within Evolving Definitions of Greek Identity," in I. Malkin (ed.), *Ancient Perceptions of Greek Ethnicity* (Washington, DC: Center for Hellenic Studies, 2001).

9. On the regionalized nature of archaic and classical Greece see C. Dougherty and L. Kurke (eds.), *The Cultures Within Greek Culture* (Cambridge: Cambridge University Press, 2003). J. Ober, *Athenian Legacies: Essays on the Politics of Going on Together* (Princeton: Princeton University Press, 2005), 69–91 has influentially introduced the anthropological concept of "thin coherence," although he is speaking of the individual Greek state rather than Greek culture as a whole.

10. Introductions to Greek religion include W. Burkert, *Greek Religion,* trans. J. Raffan (Oxford: Blackwell, 1985); J. Bremmer, *Greek Religion* (Oxford: Oxford University Press, 1994); Price, *Religions;* D. Ogden (ed.), *A Companion to Greek Religion* (Oxford: Blackwell, 2007); R. Parker, *On Greek Religion* (Ithaca: Cornell University Press, 2011).

11. "How shall I sing of you?": *Homeric Hymn to Apollo* 19. For discussion of the tension between singularity and multiplicity of individual Greek gods, see H. S. Versnel, *Coping with the Gods: Wayward Readings in Greek Theology* (Leiden: Brill, 2011), 40–87; also Parker, *On Greek Religion,* 65–73.

12. 120 festival days in Athens: e.g., L. B. Zaidman and P. S. Pantel, *Religion in the Ancient Greek City,* trans. Paul Cartledge (Cambridge: Cambridge University Press, 1992), 102–4. Priests: see especially (mostly on Athens) R. Garland, "Priests and Power in Classical Athens," in M. Beard and J. North (eds.), *Pagan Priests: Religion and Power in the Ancient World* (London: Duckworth, 1990), 75–91. Biographical details on Sophocles's career are recorded in the ancient

Life of Sophocles, although they are not uncontroversial (e.g., M. Lefkowitz, *Lives of the Greek Poets,* 2nd ed. [Baltimore: Johns Hopkins University Press, 2012], 82).

13. Council agenda: Aristotle, *Constitution of Athens,* 43.4. More generally on the Greek distinction between sacred and profane, see W. R. Connor, "Sacred and Secular," *Ancient Society* 19 (1988): 161–88, with the important modifications of S. Scullion, " 'Pilgrimage' and Greek Religion: Sacred and Secular in the Pagan Polis," in J. Elsner and I. Rutherford (eds.), *Pilgrimage in Greco-Roman and Early Christian Antiquity* (Cambridge: Cambridge University Press, 2005), 111–19. Scullion modifies the older view that "it is difficult to locate a 'secular' realm of any significance in the fifth-century Greek polis" (L. J. Samons II, *Empire of the Owl: Imperial Athenian Finance* (Stuttgart: Franz Steiner, 2000), 327). Sacred and profane buildings: Isocrates 7.66; finance: Demosthenes 24.9. More generally on the interpermeation of sacred and nonsacred finance, see Samons, *Empire of the Owl.* Quotation: Price, *Religions of the Ancient Greeks,* 3.

14. On the law courts see especially A. Lanni, *Law and Justice in the Courts of Classical Athens* (Cambridge: Cambridge University Press, 2006). G. Martin discusses the orators' religious strategies in *Divine Talk: Religious Argumentation in Demosthenes* (Oxford: Oxford University Press, 2009). See his p. 205 on the vagueness of references to divine intervention.

15. Mystery cults: W. Burkert, *Ancient Mystery Cults* (Cambridge, MA: Harvard University Press, 1987). Orphic texts: F. Graf and S. I. Johnston, *Ritual Texts for the Afterlife: Orpheus and the Bacchic Gold Tablets* (London and New York: Routledge, 2007); R. G. Edmonds III (ed.), *The "Orphic" Gold Tablets and Greek Religion: Further Along the Path* (Cambridge: Cambridge University Press, 2010). On the idea of personal religion see Versnel, *Coping with the Gods,* 119–37.

16. On the phenomenon of "divine translation" across the ancient Near Eastern and eastern Mediterranean worlds, see M. Smith, *God in Translation: Deities in Cross-Cultural Discourse in the Biblical World* (Tübingen: Mohr Siebeck, 2008). Herodotus 1.131.1. For expansion and qualification of this point see T. Harrison, *Divinity and History: The Religion of Herodotus* (Oxford: Oxford University Press, 2000), 208–22. On the "Mosaic distinction" and its consequences for cultural conflict see J. Assmann, *Moses the Egyptian: The Memory of Egypt in Western Monotheism* (Cambridge, MA: Harvard University Press, 1998) and *The Price of Monotheism* (Palo Alto, CA: Stanford University Press, 2010).

2. Good Books

1. Setne Khaemwas: see, for example, G. Maspero, *Popular Stories of Ancient Egypt,* edited with an introduction by Hasan El-Shamy (Oxford: Oxford University Press, 2002), 95–118. For the general idea see J. Sawyer, *Sacred Languages and Sacred Texts* (London: Routledge, 1999), which sets the emergence of the Christian idea of the sacred text against a Near Eastern background. Torah scrolls: S. Sabar, "Torah and Magic: the Torah Scroll and Its Appurtenances as Magical Objects in Traditional Jewish Culture," *European Journal of Jewish Studies* 3 (2009): 135–70. On the sacralization of the Hebrew Bible

see S. A. Nigosian, *From Ancient Writings to Sacred Texts: The Old Testament and Apocrypha* (Baltimore: Johns Hopkins University Press). Justinian: *Codex Justinianus* 3.1.14.1; and more generally on the sanctity of the Christian Bible in antiquity see C. Rapp, "Holy Texts, Holy Books, Holy Scribes: Aspects of Scriptural Holiness in Late Antiquity," in W. Klingshirn and L. Safran (eds.), *The Early Christian Book* (Washington, DC: Catholic University Press, 2006), 194–222.

2. For good discussion of Greece's lack of sacred scripture see "Sacred Texts and Canonicity," in S. I. Johnston (ed.), *Religions of the Ancient World: A Guide* (Cambridge, MA: Harvard University Press, 2004), 633–35. W. V. Harris, *Ancient Literacy* (Cambridge, MA: Harvard University Press, 1989) offers a sober analysis of likely literacy levels.

3. A variety of interesting and up-to-date approaches to Homer can be sampled in R. Rutherford, *Homer* (Oxford: Oxford University Press, 1996; revised Cambridge University Press, 2013); I. Morris and B. Powell (eds.), *A New Companion to Homer* (Leiden: Brill, 1997); D. Cairns (ed.), *Oxford Readings in Homer's Iliad* (Oxford: Oxford University Press, 2001); and R. Fowler (ed.), *The Cambridge Companion to Homer* (Cambridge: Cambridge University Press, 2004). There are many introductions to Greek literature: see for example T. Whitmarsh, *Ancient Greek Literature* (Cambridge: Polity Press, 2004). School texts of Homer: see T. Morgan, *Literate Education in the Hellenistic and Roman Worlds* (Cambridge: Cambridge University Press, 1998), 313 (I have rounded the figures: the exact numbers are fifty-eight papyri of Homer, twenty of Euripides, and seven of Menander).

4. Herodotus 2.53.

5. Homer, *Iliad* 1.5; *Cypria* fragment 1 in M. L. West, *Greek Epic Fragments* (Cambridge, MA: Harvard University Press, 2003). A coherent Homeric and Hesiodic theology is argued for (wrongly, in my view) by W. Allan, "Divine Justice and Cosmic Order in Early Greek Epic," *The Journal of Hellenic Studies* 126 (2006): 1–35. Insignificant mortals: Homer, *Iliad* 21.461–67.

6. Ares and Aphrodite: Homer, *Odyssey* 8.266–366. Deception of Zeus: *Iliad* 14.154–377.

7. Homer, *Iliad* 2.484–86.

8. Xenophanes fragment 19 in D. W. Graham (ed.), *The Texts of Early Greek Philosophy: The Complete Fragments and Selected Testimonies of the Major Presocratics* (Cambridge: Cambridge University Press, 2010). Plato: *Republic* 377d–378e, 379c–380c.

9. Quotation: Heraclitus, *Homeric Problems* 1, translated by D. Russell and D. Konstan, *Heraclitus: Homeric Problems* (Atlanta: Society of Biblical Literature, 2005). Theagenes of Rhegium: H. Diels and W. Kranz, *Die Fragmente der Vorsokratiker,* vol. 1, 6th ed. (Berlin: Weidmann, 1951), 8A2. Metrodorus of Lampsacus: Diogenes Laertius 2.11. Derveni papyrus: G. Betegh, *The Derveni Papyrus: Cosmology, Theology and Interpretation* (Cambridge: Cambridge University Press, 2004). On the origins of ancient allegory see D. Obbink, "Early Greek Allegory," in R. Copeland and P. Struck (eds.), *The Cambridge Companion to Allegory* (Cambridge: Cambridge University Press, 2010), 15–25. This useful volume contains chapters on allegory throughout antiquity. On the religious-allegorical interpretation of Homer see especially R. Lamberton, *Homer the Theologian: Neoplatonist Allegorical Reading and the Growth of the Epic Tradition* (Berkeley: University of California Press, 1989). Greek and

Jewish allegoresis: M. Niehoff, *Jewish Exegesis and Homeric Scholarship in Alexandria* (Cambridge: Cambridge University Press, 2011).

10. Cave of the Nymphs: Homer, *Odyssey* 13.102–12. On Porphyry see R. Lamberton, *Homer the Theologian*, 121–32; and *Porphyry, On the Cave of the Nymphs: Translation and Introductory Essay* (Barrytown, NY: Station Hill Press, 1983).

11. There is little evidence for the performance of Homer. My sketch of the rhapsode is derived from Plato's *Ion*.

12. "Stories told to Alcinous": e.g., Diogenianus, *Proverbs* 2.86 (in F. G. Schneidewin and E. L. von Leutsch, *Corpus paroemiographorum Graecorum*, vol. 1 [Göttingen: Vandenhoeck & Ruprecht, 1839; reprinted Hildesheim: Olms, 1965]).

13. Xenophanes, fragment 9.21–22 in Graham, *The Texts of Early Greek Philosophy;* Herodotus 2.113–20 (different versions in Euripides, *Helen,* and (supposedly) Stesichorus's now lost *Palinode*). Homer and Odysseus: Philostratus, *On Heroes* 43.12–16. Troy never captured: Dio Chrysostom, *Oration* 11. Eyewitness diary: Dictys of Crete, *Journal.* Generally on the accusations of fiction leveled at Homeric and Hesiodic gods see D. Feeney, *The Gods in Epic: Poets and Critics of the Classical Tradition* (Oxford: Oxford University Press, 1991); and L. Kim, *Homer Between History and Fiction in Imperial Greek Literature* (Cambridge: Cambridge University Press, 2010).

14. Hecataeus, author 1 fragments 1 and 19 in F. Jacoby, *Die Fragmente der griechischen Historiker* (Leiden: Brill, 1923–).

15. Palaephatus is translated by J. Stern, *Palaephatus: On Unbelievable Tales* (Wauconda, IL: Bolchazy-Carducci, 1996), whose rendering I adapt below. On the confused biographical tradition surrounding him see pp. 1–4.

16. Palaephatus 1.

17. B. J. Sivertsen, *The Parting of the Sea: How Volcanoes, Earthquakes, and Plagues Shaped the Story of Exodus* (Princeton: Princeton University Press, 2009).

18. Actaeon: chapter 6. Europa: chapter 15. The gods figure more heavily in the last seven chapters (46–52), but these are usually thought to be a later addition to the Palaephatean text (this hypothesis is probably right: they are very different in feel). See Stern, *Palaephatus,* 5, and 9–10, on his handling of the gods, an interpretation that I follow here. See also K. Brodersen, "'Das aber ist eine Lüge!': zur rationalistischen Mythenkritik des Palaiphatos," in R. von Haeling (ed.), *Griechische Mythologie und frühes Christentum* (Darmstadt: Wissenschaftliche Gesellschaft, 2005), 44–57; and G. Hawes, *Rationalizing Myth in Antiquity* (Oxford: Oxford University Press, 2014), 37–91.

3. Battling the Gods

1. This account of the various functions of myth is necessarily brief. For a full account of the manifold ways in which it has been conceptualized see E. Csapo, *Theories of Mythology* (Oxford: Blackwell, 2005).

2. Prometheus: Hesiod, *Theogony* 514–616.

3. Menoetius: Ibid.

4. Zeus's overthrow: *Prometheus Bound* 755–70. For a similar prophecy see Hesiod, *Theogony* 886–90.

5. Pliny: *Natural History* 2.5.27. On the omnipotence paradox see for example P. Grim, "Impossibility Arguments," in M. Martin (ed.), *The Cambridge Companion to Atheism* (Cambridge: Cambridge University Press, 2007), 200–204. *Bia* and *kratos*: Hesiod, *Theogony* 385–87, and Aeschylus, *Prometheus Bound* 1–87.

6. *Iliad* 1.565–69.

7. On the centrality of debate and competition to early Greek society see especially E. Barker, *Entering the Agōn: Dissent and Authority in Homer, Historiography and Tragedy* (Oxford: Oxford University Press, 2009).

8. Cult of the war dead in historical times: B. Currie, *Pindar and the Cult of Heroes* (Oxford: Oxford University Press, 2005), 89–119. Divinization of rulers: Versnel, *Coping with the Gods: Wayward Readings in Greek Theology* (Leiden: Brill, 2011), 439–92, and below, chapter 10.

9. Pisistratus: Herodotus 1.60, with W. R. Connor, "Tribes, Festivals and Processions; Civic Ceremonial and Political Manipulation in Archaic Greece," *Journal of Hellenic Studies* 107 (1987): 40–50.

10. Homer, *Iliad* 5.311–430, 850–909; 21.211–97.

11. This is the version found in Pherecydes (*Fragmente der griechischen Historiker* 3 F 119 = schol. *Iliad* 6.153). The reason for supposing this to be the *Catalogue*'s story is that Apollodorus (who tends to follow the *Catalogue*) recounts the first part about Aesopus and Aegina (*Library* 1.9.3). Contrary to what is sometimes said, this version is compatible with Theognis 698–715 and Alcaeus fr. 38a, which have Sisyphus escaping from the underworld: this may just be the later part of the story recounted in Pherecydes. Folkloric tales of the tricking of death are type 332 in A. Aarne and S. Thompson, *The Types of the Folk-Tale: A Classification and Bibliography*, 2nd ed. (Helsinki: Academia Scientarum Fennica, 1981).

12. Fragment 10(d) in R. Merkelbach and M. L. West, *Fragmenta Hesiodea* (Oxford: Clarendon Press, 1967) = *P. Michigan inv.* 1447 ii 14–19; see also Apollodorus, *Library* 1.53. For the addition see *Etymologicum Genuinum* under "Alcyone"; the Greek, which is ambiguous at this point, could also mean that he "wanted to be thought of as a god."

13. Apollodorus, *Library* 1.9.7.

14. Imitation: Diodorus of Sicily 6.6.4–5; Vergil, *Aeneid* 6.585–95; Galen, *On the Method of Healing* 14.10.18; pseudo-Hyginus, *Stories* 61, 239.

15. S. Trzaskoma and R. Scott Smith, "Apollodorus 1.9.7: Salmoneus' Thunder Machine," *Philologus* 149 (2005): 328–46. For the *bronteion* and the *keraunoskopeion* see Pollux 4.19.130.

4. The Material Cosmos

1. For accessible introductions to the pre-Socratics see A. A. Long (ed.), *The Cambridge Companion to Early Greek Philosophy* (Cambridge: Cambridge University Press, 1999); and J. Warren, *Presocratics* (Stocksfield, UK: Acumen, 2007). They are cited from D. W. Graham, *The Texts of Early Greek Philosophy: The Complete Fragments and Selected Testimonies of the Major Presocratics*, 2 vols. (Cambridge: Cambridge University Press, 2010). T. S. Kuhn, *The Structure of Scientific Revolutions*, 3rd ed. (Chicago: Chicago University Press, 1996; 1st ed. 1962).

2. "Intelligent design" and the pre-Socratics (and other philosophers), D. Sedley, *Creationism and Its Critics in Antiquity* (Berkeley: University of California Press, 2007). For naturalism see for example M. Ruse, "Naturalism and the Scientific Method," in S. Bullivant and M. Ruse (eds.), *The Oxford Handbook of Atheism* (Oxford: Oxford University Press, 2013), 383–96.

3. G. Lloyd, *The Revolutions of Wisdom: Studies in the Claims and Practice of Ancient Greek Science* (Berkeley: University of California Press, 1989), 83–103; Hesiod, *Works and Days* 650–62.

4. Kostas Vlassopoulos in particular has challenged the Greek/Near Eastern distinction: see his *Unthinking the Greek Polis: Ancient Greek History Beyond Eurocentrism* (Cambridge: Cambridge University Press, 2007); and *Greeks and Barbarians* (Cambridge: Cambridge University Press, 2013).

5. On Near Eastern influences on the pre-Socratics see M. L. West, *Early Greek Philosophy and the Orient* (Oxford: Oxford University Press, 1971)—not universally accepted, but certainly suggestive.

6. Thales fell down a well: Plato, *Theaetetus* 174a. Eclipse: Herodotus 1.74.2, Pliny *Natural History* 2.53. Phoenician: Herodotus 1.170.3, Diogenes Laertius 1.22. Studied in Egypt: Diogenes Laertius 1.24, pseudo-Plutarch *Opinions* 1.3.1, Proclus *On Euclid* 65.3–11.

7. The theological aspects of the pre-Socratic *arkhē* are discussed from a different perspective by A. Drozdek, *Greek Philosophers as Theologians: The Divine Arkhe* (Aldershot: Ashgate, 2007); see also S. Broadie, "Rational Theology," in Long, *The Cambridge Companion to Early Greek Philosophy*, 205–24. Thales and *thal*: A. Feldman, "Thoughts on Thales," *Classical Journal* 41 (1945): 4–6.

8. Thales on god as creator and designer: fragments 35–37 in Graham, *The Texts of Early Greek Philosophy*. Anaximander on thunder: fragments 30–31. Anaximenes: fragments 12, 27–28. Anaximenes on seasonal change: fragments 30–31; rainbows 32–33; earthquakes 34. Anaximander on heavenly bodies: fragment 20; Anaximenes fragment 12. Life emerged from the sea: Anaximander fragments 19–20.

9. God: Anaximander fragment 19, Anaximenes fragments 36–38. Quotation: Anaximander fragment 19. Anaximander also identifies gods with "innumerable worlds" at fragment 41 and with "countless heavens" in 42: whatever underlies these opaque claims, there is certainly a strikingly recurrent association of the idea of divinity with the infinite.

10. Xenophanes fragments 29, 31, 32, 33 in Graham, *The Texts of Early Greek Philosophy*. Anthropomorphism in religion: S. Guthrie, *Faces in the Clouds: A New Theory of Religion* (New York: Oxford University Press, 1993).

11. Fictions: fragment 9.21–22. Prophecy: fragments 43, 44; heating of the earth: fragment 56; caves: fragment 57; rain: fragment 53; solar systems, salination, fossils: fragment 59; sun and moon: fragments 60, 67; lightning: fragment 71; rainbows: fragment 72; comets, shooting stars, meteors: fragment 70; Saint Elmo's fire: fragment 73.

12. One god: fragment 35; unmoving, unchanging: fragments 38, 42; uncreated and eternal: fragments 41, 42; causing movement through his mind: fragment 37. On Xenophanes's wavering between monotheism and polytheism see Versnel, *Coping with the Gods: Wayward Readings in Greek Theology* (Leiden: Brill, 2011), 244–68.

13. Zeno fragment 15 in Graham, *The Texts of Early Greek Philosophy*.

14. Some of the testimonies say that Hippo came from southern Italy; perhaps he

relocated there from Samos at some point (there was much to-ing and fro-ing between the two during the period). Evidence for activity in Athens comes in the form of a parody by the Athenian comic poet Cratinus: see Hippo testimonium 2 in H. Diels and W. Kranz, *Die Fragmente der Vorsokratiker,* vol. 1, 6th ed. (Berlin: Weidmann, 1951), 385–87. The soul is the brain: testimonium 3. An "atheist": testimonia 4, 8. More generally see S. Shapiro, "Hippon the Atheist: The Surprisingly Intelligent Views of Hippon of Samos," *Journal of Ancient Civilizations* 14 (1999): 111–23). No soul in Homer and Hesiod: J.-P. Vernant, "Psuche: Simulacrum of the Body or Image of the Divine?," in F. I. Zeitlin (ed.), *Mortals and Immortals: Collected Essays* (Princeton: Princeton University Press, 1991), 186–94. On mystery cults see in general W. Burkert, *Ancient Mystery Cults* (Cambridge, MA: Harvard University Press, 1987).

15. Hippo fragment 2 in Diels and Kranz, *Die Fragmente der Vorsokratiker.* For Michael Hendry's alternative reading see http://www.curculio.org/Ioci /november.pdf (accessed April 2014).

16. Mind: fragments 30–34 in Graham, *The Texts of Early Greek Philosophy.* I follow the reconstruction of Anaxagoras's thought in Sedley, *Creationism,* 1–30.

17. Reputation as an atheist: Plato, *Apology of Socrates* 26c–d. For more on the trial of Anaxagoras see chapter 8. Plato's criticism: *Phaedo* 98c, with Sedley, *Creationism,* 87. Mind as creator: fragment 33.

18. Athens: Leucippus and Democritus fragment 4 in Graham, *The Texts of Early Greek Philosophy.*

19. Multiple worlds with varying degrees of life: fragment 53. Big bang: R. Collins, cited at W. J. Wood, *God* (Durham, UK: Acumen, 2011), 21.

20. Material soul: fragments 113–15. Gods as misperceptions of natural phenomena: fragment 183. Gods as nocturnal visions: 186–88.

Part Two: Classical Athens

1. Number of *poleis:* M. H. Hansen, "95 Theses about the Greek 'Polis' in the Archaic and Classical Periods: A Report on the Results Obtained by the Copenhagen Polis Centre in the Period 1993–2003," *Historia: Zeitschrift für Alte Geschichte* 52 (2003): 257–82, at 263–64. For orientation on Athenian democracy see, for example, J. Ober, *Mass and Elite in Democratic Athens: Rhetoric, Ideology, and the Power of the People* (Princeton: Princeton University Press, 1989); R. Osborne, *Greece in the Making, 1200–479 BC,* 2nd ed. (Abingdon, UK, and New York: Routledge, 2009): 276–97 and *Athens and Athenian Democracy* (Cambridge: Cambridge University Press, 2010); P. J. Rhodes (ed.), *Athenian Democracy* (Oxford: Oxford University Press, 2004). More generally: S. Hornblower, *The Greek World, 479–323 BC,* 3rd ed. (London: Routledge, 2002).

2. For a lively account of the rise of Persia and the conflict with Greece, see T. Holland, *Persian Fire: The First World Empire and the Battle for the West* (London: Little, Brown, 2005).

3. On the Delian League see especially A. Powell, *Athens and Sparta: Constructing Greek Political and Social History from 478 BC,* 2nd ed. (London: Routledge, 2001); and the essays in P. Low (ed.), *The Athenian Empire* (Edinburgh: Edinburgh University Press, 2008).

4. On the Peloponnesian War see G. Cawkwell, *Thucydides and the Pelopon-nesian War* (London: Routledge, 1997); D. Kagan, *The Peloponnesian War* (New York: Viking, 2003).

5. Laurion: quotation from Diodorus of Sicily 3.13.3, who perhaps relies on earlier testimony. Possible numbers of slaves are canvassed by R. Osborne, *Athens and Athenian Democracy* (Cambridge: Cambridge University Press, 2010), 86–88. For a brief survey of issues around Athenian slavery see also T. E. Rihll, "Classical Athens," in K. Bradley and P. Cartledge (eds.), *The Cambridge World History of Slavery,* vol. 1, *The Ancient Mediterranean World* (Cambridge: Cambridge University Press, 2011), 48–73. Aelian, *Varied History* 2.1.9 offers a catalogue of the imperialist cruelties of the classical Athenians.

5. Cause and Effect

1. Euripides, *Trojan Women* 988–90.

2. On the law courts see especially A. Lanni, *Law and Justice in the Courts of Classical Athens* (Cambridge: Cambridge University Press, 2006).

3. Sacred olive tree: Lysias 7. Generally on the representation of religion in Greek oratory see G. Martin, *Divine Talk: Religious Argumentation in Demosthenes* (Oxford: Oxford University Press, 2009), 1–216. See his p. 205 on the vagueness of references to divine intervention. Aristophanes parodies the blaming of gods (*Clouds* 85), and Plato overtly disapproves of it (*Republic* 379c–380c; also pseudo-Plato, *Alcibiades* II 142d). This idea has its roots in Homer, however (see *Odyssey* 1.32–34).

4. For this kind of explanation of intellectual change on the basis of political change the work of G. E. R. Lloyd has been pivotal: see *Magic, Reason and Experience: Studies in the Origins and Development of Greek Science* (Cambridge: Cambridge University Press, 1979), *Science, Folklore and Ideology* (Cambridge: Cambridge University Press, 1983), *The Revolutions of Wisdom: Studies in the Claims and Practice of Ancient Greek Science* (Berkeley: University of California Press, 1989), *Demystifying Mentalities* (Cambridge: Cambridge University Press, 1990).

5. Lloyd, *Magic, Reason and Experience,* 38–49.

6. All quotations from Hippocrates, *On the Sacred Disease* 1–2. See more generally Lloyd, *Magic, Reason and Experience,* 15–27.

7. On the rhetorical denigration of opponents in Greek science see Lloyd, *Science, Folklore and Ideology,* 119–35. The one area where the early medical writers do acknowledge divine influence is in dreams (see the Hippocratic *On Dreams*).

8. The contrast between Greek and biblical approaches to the recording of the past is drawn in characteristically forthright terms by R. Lane Fox, *The Unauthorized Version: Truth and Fiction in the Bible* (London: Penguin, 2006). Herodotus invokes the now-fragmentary Hecataeus of Miletus as a partial precedent. There has been some skepticism over Herodotus's claims about his travels: see especially D. Fehling, *Herodotus and His Sources: Citation, Invention and Narrative Art,* trans. J. G. Howie (Leeds: F. Cairns, 1989).

9. On Herodotus's relationship to contemporary Athenian intellectual life see R. Thomas, *Herodotus in Context: Ethnography, Science and the Art of Persuasion* (Cambridge: Cambridge University Press, 2002). Quotations: Herodotus, preface; 1.5–6.

10. Phye: 1.60; Thales: 1.75; Nile: 2.22.

11. Herodotus as rationalist: see for example D. Lateiner, *The Historical Method of Herodotus* (Toronto: Toronto University Press, 1989); as religious thinker: T. Harrison, *Divinity and History: The Religion of Herodotus* (Oxford: Oxford University Press, 2000); and J. D. Mikalson, *Herodotus and Religion in the Persian Wars* (Chapel Hill: University of North Carolina Press, 2003). For a recent assessment see S. Scullion, "Herodotus and Greek Religion," in C. Dewald and J. Marincola (eds.), *The Cambridge Companion to Herodotus* (Cambridge: Cambridge University Press, 2006), 192–208; Scullion discusses the rare references to specific gods and the commoner language of abstract divinity at 194–97; see also Harrison, *Divinity and History,* 158–81. Quotation about human prosperity: Herodotus 1.5. Herodotus's preoccupation with *tisis* is a central theme of J. Gould, *Herodotus* (London: Weidenfeld and Nicolson, 1989). It is true that there are occasions when gods seem to intervene, notably 1.87 (Croesus prays; rain falls), 6.105 (the epiphany of Pan to Phidippides), and 8.36–39 (local Delphic heroes appear to the invading Persians). In these instances, certainly, Herodotus comes closer to conventional religiosity, but note that Herodotus always keeps the idea of divine intervention at arm's length: in the first case he leaves open the possibility of coincidence, and the second and third are reported by characters within the narrative rather than in his own voice.

12. Herodotus quotation: 7.46 (Artabanus reflecting with Xerxes on the brevity of life).

13. Marcellinus, *Life of Thucydides* 22; a late-antique biography, but Marcellinus explicitly attributes this observation to his source Antyllus (a grammarian of unknown date). Marcellinus writes that "he was thought *ērema* an atheist": unlike most commentators I take the adverb with the verb rather than the noun (i.e., "he was whispered to be an atheist," rather than "he was thought to be something of an atheist"). W. Furley, "Thucydides and Religion," in A. Rengakos and A. Tsakmakis (eds.), *Brill's Companion to Thucydides* (Leiden: Brill, 2006), 415–38 offers an excellent survey of Thucydidean attitudes to religion and the gods.

14. Thucydides 2.54; more generally on his treatment of oracles see Furley, "Thucydides and Religion," 418–21. On religion as human practice see B. Jordan, "Religion in Thucydides," *Transactions of the American Philological Association* 116 (1986): 119–47.

15. Thucydides 3.36–50 (quotation from 3.39).

16. Melian debate: 5.84–116 (quotation from 5.105).

17. Thucydides 7.87.

18. Nicias quotation: Thucydides 7.86.

19. Thucydides 7.50.

20. Mutilation of the herms: Thucydides 6.27–8.

6. "Concerning the Gods, I Cannot Know"

1. On the sophists see W. K. C. Guthrie, *A History of Greek Philosophy,* vol. 3, *The Fifth Century Enlightenment. Part 1: The Sophists* (Cambridge: Cambridge University Press, 1969), with pp. 226–47 on the criticism of traditional religion; G. B. Kerferd, *The Sophistic Movement* (Cambridge: Cambridge University

Press, 1981); S. Broadie, "Socrates and the Sophists," in D. N. Sedley (ed.), *The Cambridge Companion to Greek and Roman Philosophy* (Cambridge: Cambridge University Press, 2003), 73–97. The texts are gathered in D. W. Graham, *The Texts of Early Greek Philosophy: The Complete Fragments and Selected Testimonies of the Major Presocratics,* part 2 (Cambridge: Cambridge University Press, 2010). The quotation from *On the Gods* is fragment 29.

2. Dating of the visit: J. Walsh, "The Dramatic Dates of Plato's *Protagoras* and the Lesson of *Arete,*" *The Classical Quarterly* 34 (1984): 101–6, arguing that Plato also blended in details relating to an earlier visit.

3. Plato, *Protagoras* 310a–b.

4. Protagoras, fragment 21 in Graham, *The Texts of Early Greek Philosophy.*

5. Xenophanes, fragment 33 in Graham, *The Texts of Early Greek Philosophy* (vol. 1).

6. Exile and book-burning: fragment 31 (Cicero, *On the Nature of the Gods* 1.24.63). Reputation for atheism: M. Winiarczyk, "Wer galt im Altertum als Atheist?," *Philologus* 128 (1984): 177–78. Humanistic religion: L. Lampert, *How Philosophy Became Socratic: A Study of Plato's Protagoras, Charmides, and Republic* (Chicago: Chicago University Press, 2010), 60; see, more fully, E. Schiappa, *Protagoras and Logos: A Study in Greek Philosophy and Rhetoric* (Columbia: University of South Carolina Press, 1991), 141–53. Lampert rests heavily on a book by the notoriously conservative ideologue Werner Jaeger, *The Theology of the Early Greek Philosophers* (Oxford: Oxford University Press, 1947), 189–90. The myth: Plato, *Protagoras* 320c–322d = Protagoras fragment 45.

7. Prodicus's reputation for atheism: Winiarczy, "Wer galt," 177. For the papyrus see D. Obbink, *Philodemus on Piety Part 1* (Oxford: Clarendon Press, 1996); see also A. Henrichs, "Two Doxographical Notes: Democritus and Prodicus on Religion," *Harvard Studies in Classical Philology* 79 (1975): 93–123.

8. For more on Democritus see chapter 5. For the argument (predating the reexamination of Philodemus) that Democritus underlies the anthropological account in Diodorus of Sicily 1.8 see T. Cole, *Democritus and the Sources of Greek Anthropology* (Cleveland: Western Reserve University 1967). Democritus on the origins of religion: see Sextus Empiricus, *Against the Mathematicians* 9.24 = fragment 183 in Graham, *The Texts of Early Greek Philosophy.* Herculaneum fragment: *Herculaneum Papyrus* 1428, fragment 19. See Henrichs, "Two Doxographical Notes," 96–106.

9. *Herculaneum Papyrus* 1428, fragment 19, which is fragment 72 in R. Mayhew, *Prodicus the Sophist: Texts, Translations, and Commentary* (Oxford: Oxford University Press, 2011). I follow Henrichs in translating "thought of [*nomizomenous*] as gods" as "the gods of popular belief" on the grounds that *nomizein* has a distinctive semantic field when it comes to religion: see below, p. 119. Henrichs has a fuller account of Prodicus on atheism in "The Atheism of Prodicus," *Cronache Ercolanesi* 6 (1976): 15–21.

10. Prodicus and the deification of natural bounty: Cicero, *On the Nature of the Gods* 1.42.118; Sextus Empiricus, *Against the Mathematicians* 9.18, 9.52. These appear as Prodicus, fragments 29–30 in Graham, *The Texts of Early Greek Philosophy* and 73–75 in Mayhew, *Prodicus the Sophist.* Two-stage process: Henrichs, "Two Doxographical Notes," 111, 113–15, and Mayhew, *Prodicus the Sophist,* xvii–xiii. Castor and Pollux ("the Dioscuri") are mentioned in fragment 71 Mayhew, but a gap follows immediately, and their invention is not

specified; they are often associated with sailing, but horsemanship is another possibility. "Changing letters": Philodemus, *On Piety* 19 Obbink = fragment 70 in Mayhew. E. R. Dodds thought that Prodicus underlay Euripides, *Bacchae* 274–85 (see his *Euripides, Bacchae,* 2nd ed. (Oxford: Oxford University Press, 1960), 104–5.

11. For the alternative translation see Mayhew, *Prodicus the Sophist,* 47.

12. On the Sisyphus fragment see, among others, M. Davies, "Sisyphus and the Invention of Religion ('Critias' *TrGF* 1 [43] F 19 = B 25 DK)," *Bulletin of the Institute of Classical Studies* 36 (1989): 16–32; N. Pechstein, *Euripides Satyrographos: ein Kommentar zu den euripideischen Satyrspielfragmenten* (Stuttgart and Leipzig: Teubner, 1998); P. O'Sullivan, "Sophistic Ethics, Old Atheism, and 'Critias' on Religion," *Classical World* 105 (2012): 167–85; D. N. Sedley, "The Atheist Underground," in V. Harte and M. Lane (eds.), *Politeia in Greek and Roman Philosophy* (Cambridge: Cambridge University Press, 2013), 329–48; T. Whitmarsh, "Atheist Aesthetics: The Sisyphus Fragment, Poetics, and the Creativity of Drama," *Cambridge Classical Journal* 60 (2014): 109–24.

13. M. Foucault, *Discipline and Punish: The Birth of the Prison,* tr. by Alan Sheridan (London: Allen Lane, 1977).

14. Odysseus in the underworld: Homer, *Odyssey* 11.593–94.

7. Playing the Gods

1. Generally on Athenian theater see A. W. Pickard-Cambridge, *The Dramatic Festivals of Athens,* rev. 2nd ed. by J. Gould and D. M. Lewis (Oxford: Oxford University Press, 1988). For orientation on the role of the theater in Athenian society see J. Winkler and F. Zeitlin (eds.), *Nothing to Do with Dionysus? Athenian Drama in Its Social Context* (Princeton, NJ: Princeton University Press, 1990); E. Csapo and W. J. Slater, *The Context of Ancient Drama* (Ann Arbor: University of Michigan Press, 1994); C. Pelling (ed.), *Greek Tragedy and the Historian* (Oxford: Clarendon Press, 1997); D. Wiles, *Tragedy in Athens: Performance Space and Theatrical Meaning* (Cambridge: Cambridge University Press, 1997); E. Csapo and M. Miller (eds.), *The Origins of Theater in Ancient Greece and Beyond* (Cambridge: Cambridge University Press, 2007).

2. Aristotle, *Poetics* 1449a. On the weakness of the ritual case see S. Scullion, "Nothing to Do with Dionysus: Tragedy Misconceived as Ritual," *Classical Quarterly* 52 (2002): 102–37. For "ritualist" approaches to Greek drama see W. Burkert, "Greek Tragedy and Sacrificial Ritual," *Greek Roman and Byzantine Studies* 7 (1966): 88–121; R. Seaford, *Reciprocity and Ritual: Homer and Tragedy in the Developing City-State* (Oxford: Oxford University Press, 1994); C. Sourvinou-Inwood, *Tragedy and Athenian Religion* (Lanham, MD: Lexington, 2003); A. Bierl, *Ritual and Performativity: The Chorus in Greek Comedy* (Washington, DC: Center for Hellenic Studies, 2009).

3. Euripides, *Trojan Women* 67–68. Generally on the representation of gods in tragedy see R. Parker, "Gods Cruel and Kind: Tragic and Civic Theology," in C. Pelling (ed.), *Greek Tragedy and the Ancient Historian* (Oxford: Oxford University Press, 1997), 143–60. For the contrary view that tragedy did teach Athenians a form of civic piety, see C. Sourvinou-Inwood, "Tragedy and Religion," in Pelling, *Greek Tragedy,* 161–86.

4. Aristophanes, *Knights* 30–35.

5. Euripides: Aristophanes, *Thesmophoriazusae* 451. *Clouds* quotations: 818–19, 365–84 (quotation from 365–67).

6. On the date and contemporary resonance of *Oedipus the King* see especially B. M. W. Knox, "The Date of the *Oedipus Tyrannus* of Sophocles," *American Journal of Philology* 77 (1956): 133–47; reprinted in *Word and Action: Essays on the Ancient Theatre* (Baltimore: Johns Hopkins University Press, 1979), 112–24. Knox argues that the play should be dated to after the second outbreak of plague in Athens, specifically to 425 (but this seems to push the evidence too far). It should be said that an alternative interpretation of Sophocles's choice to begin with a plague could be to explain it as an echo of the *Iliad*. Discussion of Sophocles and religion in R. Parker, "Through a Glass Darkly: Sophocles and the Divine," in J. Griffin (ed.), *Sophocles Revisited: Essays Presented to Sir Hugh Lloyd-Jones* (Oxford: Oxford University Press, 1999), 11–30.

7. Diopeithes decree: Plutarch, *Pericles* 32.1 (see also Diodorus of Sicily 12.39.2); more details in the following chapter. Apollo and Diopeithes: Xenophon, *History of Greece* 3.3.3 (if this is the same Diopeithes; see M. A. Flower, *The Seer in Ancient Greece* [Berkeley: University of California Press, 2008], 123–24). The connection with Apollo may also be implied at Aristophanes, *Knights* 1086 (if Apollo is distancing himself from his own prophet). Descriptions of Tiresias: *Oedipus the King* 387–88. On the overlap of terminology with itinerant prophets of the new gods see H. S. Versnel, *Ter Unus: Isis, Dionysos, Hermes; Three Studies in Greek Henotheism* (Leiden: Brill, 1990), 116–18 (although it should be conceded that Aeschylus's Cassandra is also called a vagabond prophetess: *Agamemnon* 1273–74). Diopeithes the madman: Amipsias, fragment 10, Teleclides fragment 7, scholion on Aristophanes, *Wasps* 380a, 380c, 988c. Drums: Phrynichus fragment 9 (also Aelian fragments 22–23). All references to comic fragments are to the edition of R. Kassel and C. Austin, Poetae Comici Graeci (Berlin: de Gruyter, 1983-2001). Aristophanes: *Birds* 980–89.

8. Sophocles, *Oedipus the King* 857–58.

9. Ibid., 906–10.

10. Naming gods in prayers: Aeschylus, *Agamemnon* 160–61: "Zeus, whoever he is, if this name is pleasing to him." Denying prophecy: Xenophanes, fragment 43 in D. W. Graham, *The Texts of Early Greek Philosophy: The Complete Fragments and Selected Testimonies of the Major Presocratics,* part I (Cambridge: Cambridge University Press, 2010); Euripides, *Helen* 744–57.

11. Sophocles, *Oedipus the King* 1080; Democritus, fragments 231, 236, 239, 240 in Graham, *The Texts of Early Greek Philosophy.*

12. Oedipus the *atheos*: Sophocles, *Oedipus the King* 1360.

13. Aristophanes, *Women at the Thesmophoria* 450–51. Similarly, at *Frogs* 836 he is accused by Aeschylus of being an "enemy of the gods." Satyrus, *Life of Euripides* F6 fr. 39 col. 10, in S. Schorn (ed.), *Satyros aus Kallatis: Sammlung der Fragmente mit Kommentar* (Basel: Schwabe, 2004). M. Winiarczyk, "Wer galt im Altertum als Atheist?," *Philologus* 128 (1984): 171–72 lists seven ancient instances where he is associated with atheism. Many of the "impious" passages from his plays (but not, strangely, the *Bellerophon* fragment) are collected and discussed by M. R. Lefkowitz, "'Impiety' and 'Atheism' in Euripides' Dramas," *Classical Quarterly* 39 (1989): 70–82 (reprinted in J. Mossman [ed.], *Euripides* [Oxford: Oxford University Press, 2003], 102–21). Lefkowitz seeks to

limit the impact of such passages by discussing what happens to their speakers rather than the philosophical implications of the words. See also C. Sourvinou-Inwood, *Tragedy and Athenian Religion*, 291–458 (especially 294–97 on atheism); A. Rubel, *Fear and Loathing in Ancient Athens: Religion and Politics During the Peloponnesian War* (Abingdon, UK: Routledge, 2014), 167–79.

14. Euripides, *Trojan Women* 884–88. The ancient commentator on this passage notes that these words "derive from the sayings of Anaxagoras."

15. Euripides, *Heracles* 342–47, 1262–65, 1341–46; Xenophanes fragment in Graham, *The Texts of Early Greek Philosophy;* Pindar, *Olympian Ode* 1.28–35; *Olympian Ode* 9.35–41. On the theological issues raised by *Heracles* see H. Yunis, *A New Creed: Fundamental Religious Beliefs in the Athenian Polis and Euripidean Drama* (Göttingen: Vandenhoeck and Ruprecht, 1988), 139–71. Sourvinou-Inwood, *Tragedy and Athenian Religion*, 361–77, is more conservative.

16. *Bellerophon* fragment 1. On the problem of evil and its consequences for religious thought see M. L. Peterson, "The Problem of Evil," in S. Bullivant and M. Ruse (eds.), *The Oxford Handbook of Atheism* (Oxford: Oxford University Press, 2013), 71–86. For a recent attempt to reconstruct the plot of *Bellerophon* (arguing, implausibly to my mind, that the "atheistic" fragment is spoken by Stheneboea) see D. W. Dixon, "Reconsidering Euripides' *Bellerophon*," *Classical Quarterly* 64 (2014): 493–506.

17. Homer, *Iliad* 6.200–201; 6.199. Pindar, *Isthmian Ode* 7.44–48 (and implicitly at *Olympian Ode* 13.91–93).

18. On the correspondences between *Peace* and *Bellerophon* see M. Telò, "Embodying the Tragic Father(s), Autobiography and Intertextuality in Aristophanes," *Classical Antiquity* 29 (2010): 308–17, with further bibliography. In-depth discussion of the Bellerophon fragment in C. Riedweg, "The 'Atheistic' Fragment from Euripides' *Bellerophontes* (286 N2)," *Illinois Classical Studies* 15 (1990): 39–53.

19. Pollux 4.127–32.

20. On the parallel titles see for example R. Janko, "The Derveni Papyrus ('Diagoras of Melos, *Apopyrgizontes Logoi?*'), A New Translation," *Classical Philology* 96 (2001): 1–32, especially 7. Although *apopyrgizein* is unattested elsewhere in Greek, there is a similar word, *apoteikhizein*, from *teikhos*, "a wall"; the ancient writers on siege craft use it to mean "knock down a city wall." Connection with Diagoras: T. Bergk, *Griechische Literaturgeschichte* vol. 3, ed. G. Hinrichs (Berlin: Weidmann, 1884), 473. For more on Diagoras see the following chapter.

21. Aristophanes's *Birds* and Diagoras: see lines 1072–78. "Melian famine": 186, with F. E. Romer, "Atheism, Impiety and the *Limos Melios* in Aristophanes' *Birds*," *American Journal of Philology* 115 (1994): 351–65.

8. Atheism on Trial

1. For text, translation, and details see G. Betegh, *The Derveni Papyrus: Cosmology, Theology and Interpretation* (Cambridge: Cambridge University Press, 2004). For more discussion see A. Laks and G. Most (eds.), *Studies on the Derveni Papyrus* (Oxford: Oxford University Press, 1997). Orphism: Betegh, *Derveni Papyrus,* 68–73 (cautiously). The Orphic texts were certainly not scripture

in the Abrahamic sense: see R. G. Edmonds III, *Redefining Ancient Orphism: A Study in Greek Religion* (Cambridge: Cambridge University Press, 2013), 95–138. Note also that the so-called Getty Hexameters, an "Orphic" poem from late fifth-century BC Selinous (in Sicily), have a reference to "lawless houses" (22), which may denote those outwith the religious group. For text, translation, and essays see C. A. Faraone and D. Obbink (eds.), *The Getty Hexameters: Poetry, Magic, and Mystery in Ancient Selinous* (Oxford: Oxford University Press, 2013).

2. My translation follows the text of Betegh, *The Derveni Papyrus.*

3. Homer does know the expression "This did not happen without a god [*atheei*]" (*Odyssey* 18.353), but otherwise the earliest usages I can find are in the fifth-century BC authors Aeschylus (*Eumenides* 540, *Bacchylides* 11.109) and Pindar (*Pythian Odes* 4.162), where it means in effect "accursed." Crescendo: Gorgias, *Palamedes* 36; Euripides, *Bacchae* 995, 1015, *Andromache* 491, *Helen* 1148 (compare *The Madness of Hercules* 433). The adverb is always used in conjunction with another negative in early Greek: see Antiphon, *Against the Stepmother* 21, 23, *Tetralogy* 1; Plato, *Gorgias* 481a, 523b. Socrates: Plato, *Apology* 26c. Cyclopes: Homer, *Odyssey* 9.106–8. "Surnamed" (*epiklētheis* or similar) the *atheos*: Hippo *testimonia* 8, 9 in H. Diels and W. Kranz, *Die Fragmente der Vorsokratiker*, 6th ed. (Berlin: Weidmann, 1951); Diagoras: testimonia 6A, 9B, 17, 53, etc., in M. Winiarczyk, *Diagorae Melii et Theodori Cyrenaei reliquiae* (Leipzig: Teubner, 1981); Theodorus: 1A, B, C, 17, 26B in Winiarczyk.

4. I follow here the developmental account of *asebeia* given by M. Ostwald, *From Popular Sovereignty to the Sovereignty of Law: Law, Society and Politics in Fifth-Century Athens* (Berkeley: University of California Press, 1986), 528–36, although there is much that remains uncertain. The idea that Diopeithes's decree transformed the meaning of the terms also underlies E. Derenne, *Les procès d'impiété intentés aux philosophes à Athènes au Vme et au IVme siècles avant J.-C.* (Liège: Vaillant-Carmanne; Paris: Champion, 1930). For temple inscriptions relating to *asebeia* see A. Delli Pizzi, "Impiety in Epigraphic Evidence," *Kernos* 24 (2011): 59–76. For what we know of Diopeithes see M. Flower, *The Seer in Ancient Greece* (Berkeley: University of California Press, 2008), 124–25. *Asebeia* is first mentioned, to my knowledge, in the sixth century (Theognis 1180; Xenophanes fr. A14 in M. L. West, *Iambi et elegi Graeci*, vol. 2. (Oxford: Clarendon Press, 1972).

5. Decree: Plutarch, *Pericles* 32.1. There are arguments against historicity in K. J. Dover, "The Freedom of the Intellectual in Greek Society," *Talanta* 7 (1976): 24–54; reprinted in *The Greeks and Their Legacy: Collected Papers*, vol. 2: *Prose Literature, History, Society, Transmission, Influence* (Oxford: Blackwell, 1988), 135–58, 138–41, but the evidence for both decree and trial is exhaustively sifted by J. Mansfeld, "The Chronology of Anaxagoras' Athenian Period and the Date of His Trial. Part II. The Plot Against Pericles and His Associates," *Mnemosyne* 33 (1980): 17–95, who accepts both as historical (and dates the former to 438/7 BC and the latter to 437/6—rather earlier than most would). On *eisangelia* I follow M. H. Hansen, *Eisangelia: The Sovereignty of the People's Court in Athens in the Fourth Century B.C. and the Impeachment of Generals and Politicians* (Odense: Odense University Press, 1975).

6. On Plutarch's use of Craterus of Macedon as a source see P. A. Stadter, *A Commentary on Plutarch's Pericles* (Chapel Hill: University of North Carolina

Press, 1989), lxix–lxx; and C. Higbie, "Craterus and the Use of Inscriptions in Ancient Scholarship," *Transactions of the American Philological Association* 129 (1999): 43–83.

7. That *nomizein* the gods always (up until Plato) means "to venerate through ritual" is argued by M. Giordano-Zecharya, "As Socrates Shows, the Athenians Did Not Believe in Gods," *Numen* 52 (2005): 325–55; see, however, the criticisms of H. Versnel, *Coping with the Gods: Wayward Readings in Greek Theology* (Leiden: Brill, 2011), 554–59. The full range of meanings for classical times is surveyed by W. Fahr, *ΘΕΟΥΣ NOMIZEIN: Zum Problem der Anfänge des Atheismus bei den Griechen* (Hildesheim: Olms, 1969). See p. 166 for the evidence that the meaning "believing in the gods" goes back at least to the 420s. D. Cohen, *Law, Sexuality and Society: The Enforcement of Morals in Classical Athens* (Cambridge: Cambridge University Press, 1991), 211–13 argues that correct belief in the gods was a central part of Athenian conceptions of piety (but all of his evidence postdates the Diopeithes decree—in which, however, he does not believe).

8. On the politicization of the courts, see R. Bauman, *Political Trials in Ancient Greece* (London: Routledge, 1990), who gives an instrumental role to the trials of Pericles and his circle (pp. 35–49). Bauman accepts as historical more of the later story tradition than many would.

9. Aristotle, *Virtues and Vices* 1251a. In my interpretation of the elasticity of *asebeia* I follow Cohen, *Law, Sexuality and Society,* 203–217. For sensible, cautious, and succinct discussion see R. Parker, "Law and Religion," in M. Gagarin and D. Cohen (eds.), *The Cambridge Companion to Ancient Greek Law* (Cambridge: Cambridge University Press, 2005), 65–68. Impious man accuses his father: Plato, *Euthyphro.* Demosthenes: *Against Meidias* 51, 55.

10. Delli Pizzi, "Impiety": 4 notes the absence of mention of *asebeia* in relation to the Diopeithes decree. On the widespread political uses of *asebeia* see Bauman, *Political Trials* (index under *"asebeia"* and "impiety"), with the caveat I have mentioned. On drama see the previous chapter.

11. Diogenes of Apollonia: see Diogenes Laertius, *Lives of the Eminent Philosophers* 9.57, and Aelian, *Varied History* 2.31 (testimonia 1 and 3 in H. Diels and W. Kranz, *Die Fragmente der Vorsokratiker,* 6th ed. [Berlin: Weidmann, 1952]). Protagoras: Aristotle fragment 67 Rose (prosecution), Timon of Phlius fragment 5 Diels and Diogenes Laertius 9.52 (book burning), Sextus Empiricus, *Against the Mathematicians* 9.56 (prosecuted and escaped). Fourth-century trials: L.-L. O'Sullivan, "Athenian Impiety Trials in the Late Fourth Century B.C.," *Classical Quarterly* 47 (1997): 136–52. Derenne, *Les procès d'impiété* covers all of this material, albeit uncritically. R. Parker, *Athenian Religion: A History* (Oxford: Oxford University Press, 1997), 207–10, gives a levelheaded assessment of the evidence, on which I rest here. Further studies are cited by Delli Pizzi, "Impiety," n. 3.

12. Anaxagoras tried for *asebeia*: Diodorus of Sicily 12.39.2 (paraphrasing his fourth-century BC source, Ephorus), Diogenes Laertius 2.12 (prosecuted by Cleon, not Diopeithes), etc. Mansfeld, "Chronology," 82–3, convincingly undermines arguments against the historicity of the trial and observes the Platonic allusion to it at *Apology* 26d. Evidence for Diagoras of Melos: F. Jacoby, *Diagoras ὁ ἄθεος* (Berlin: Akademie Verlag, 1959), 3–8; and especially M. Winiarczyk, *Diagorae Melii et Theodori Cyrenaei reliquiae.* Jacoby believes that Diagoras was exiled for his beliefs; Winiarczyk by contrast argues that he

gained his reputation for atheism solely on the basis of the profanation of the mysteries ("Diagoras von Melos: Wahrheit und Legende [Fortsetzung]," *Eos* 68 [1980]: 51–75). Atheism: testimonia 38–68 Winiarczyk. Aristoxenus: testimonium 69, with the interpretation of Decharme, *Les procès d'impiété*, 61–62. An atheistic *Phrygian Discourse* is also attributed to Diagoras by a Christian writer, Tatian, but this is likely to have been in fact a Hellenistic text in the euhemerist tradition (J. Rives, "Phrygian tales," *Greek Roman and Byzantine Studies* 45 [2005]: 230–32). Conversion to atheism: testimonium 9B, 26; statue of Heracles: testimonia 6A and 27–33, 63; storm: testimonia 34–35B.

13. On the events of 415 BC see W. D. Furley, *Andocides and the Herms: A Study of Crisis in Fifth-Century Athenian Religion* (London: Institute of Classical Studies, 1996). Names and number of those accused of impiety: Ostwald, *Popular Sovereignty,* 537–50. Thucydides: 6.27–28, and see above, chapter 6. The *eisangelia* against Alcibiades is preserved at Plutarch, *Alcibiades* 22 (no doubt via Craterus of Macedon or a similar source).

14. Diogenes Laertius, *Lives of the Eminent Philosophers* 2.97, 100. Trial of Theodorus: O'Sullivan, "Athenian Impiety Trials," 142–46 (arguing, amongst other things, that there is some evidence for political manipulation here as well).

15. On "reappropriation" of labels, connotative reassignment, and group formation see A. Galinsky et al., "The Reappropriation of Stigmatizing Labels: The Reciprocal Relationship Between Power and Self-Labeling," *Psychological Science* 24 no. 10 (2013): 2020–29. I wonder whether the (potentially) positive term *amakhos*, "impossible to fight against," may have provided an implicit model for the positive, theomachic sense of *atheos*. "Atheist underground": D. Sedley, "The Atheist Underground," in V. Harte and M. Lane (eds.), *Politeia in Greek and Roman Philosophy* (Cambridge: Cambridge University Press, 2013), 329–48.

9. Plato and the Atheists

1. For a history of the period, see for example P. Rhodes, *A History of the Classical Greek World, 478–323 BC* (Oxford: Blackwell, 2006), 257–72.

2. Amnesty: C. Joyce, "The Athenian Amnesty and Scrutiny of 403," *Classical Quarterly* 58 (2008): 507–18. Leon of Salamis: Plato, *Apology* 32c–d; *Letter* 7 324d–325a. Association with the tyrants: Xenophon, *Memorabilia* 1.2.12; Aeschines, *Against Timarchus* 173 (and see T. Brickhouse and N. Smith, *Socrates on Trial* [Princeton: Princeton University Press, 1989], 71–73). It has been long debated whether the title figure of Plato's *Critias* is to be identified with the tyrant Critias, but nothing in the text rules out the association. On the details of the trial see Brickhouse and Smith, *Socrates on Trial;* R. Parker, *Athenian Religion* (Oxford: Oxford University Press, 1996), 199–216. For a readable account of the death of Socrates and its significance see E. Wilson, *The Death of Socrates: Hero, Villain, Chatterbox, Saint* (Cambridge, MA: Harvard University Press, 2007). Another entertaining account of Socrates is B. Hughes, *The Hemlock Cup: Socrates, Athens and the Search for the Good Life* (New York: Knopf, 2011). More generally, see S. Ahbel-Rappe and R. Kamtekar (eds.), *A Companion to Socrates* (Malden, MA: Blackwell, 2006); and D. R. Morrison (ed.), *The Cambridge Companion to Socrates* (Cambridge: Cambridge University Press, 2010).

3. Formal charge: most fully at Diogenes Laertius 2.40; shorter versions at Plato, *Apology* 24b and Xenophon, *Memorabilia of Socrates* 1.1. Impiety: Plato, *Euthyphro* 5c, *Apology* 35d; Xenophon, *Apology* 22, etc. Brickhouse and Smith, *Socrates on Trial,* 33 misleadingly claim that the Diopeithes decree "was annulled . . . by the general amnesty of 403/2." This confuses two things: the general amnesty issued to those involved with the Thirty (see previous note) and a separate attempt to streamline and rationalize the laws into a systematic code. As a result of the latter, "decrees" like those of Diopeithes were still recognized but seen as not necessarily eternal. See Rhodes, *History of the Classical Greek World,* 260–62. Little is known, however, about this streamlining attempt, and its effects were impermanent (see, for example, A. Lanni, *Law and Justice in the Courts of Classical Athens* [Cambridge: Cambridge University Press, 2006], 142–47). "Corrupting the young" is understood as "persuading them to obey yourself rather than the fathers who bore them" at Xenophon, *Apology* 39.

4. *Daimonion* as voice: Plato, *Apology* 31d, *Phaedrus* 242c; as sign: Plato, *Apology* 40b, *Phaedrus* 242b. Philosophers have debated whether the *daimonion* compromised Socrates's commitment to rationality: see P. Destrée and N. D. Smith (eds.), *Socrates' Divine Sign: Religion, Practice, and Value in Socratic Philosophy* (Kelowna, BC: Academic Printing and Publishing, 2005).

5. For an attempt to reconstruct Socrates's religious views see M. L. McPherran, *The Religion of Socrates* (University Park: Pennsylvania State University Press, 1996).

6. For a general, if now rather dated introduction to Xenophon see J. Anderson, *Xenophon* (London: Duckworth, 1974).

7. On what can be known about Plato's life see for example J. Annas, *Plato: A Brief Insight* (New York: Sterling, 2003; ill. ed. 2009), 17–38. The ancient biographical tradition is analyzed (and found wanting) by A. Riginos, *Platonica: The Anecdotes Concerning the Life and Writings of Plato* (Leiden: Brill, 1976). Lucian: *True Stories* 2.17.

8. Xenophon, *Apology* 1 argues that "others" have given grandiose versions of the speech, without communicating the substance. More generally on the instrumental power of stories of Socrates's death see Wilson, *The Death of Socrates.* Evidence for Socrates's thought also comes in the fragments of Aeschines the Socratic, but these are sparse.

9. Doughnut: Bettany Hughes, personal conversation. Aristophanes in Plato's *Apology,* 19b–c. On the impossibility of recapturing the historical Socrates see A. Dorion, "The Rise and Fall of the Socratic Problem," in Morrison, *The Cambridge Companion to Socrates,* 1–23.

10. For the view of the historical Socrates as an ethical philosopher see especially G. Vlastos, *Socrates: Ironist and Moral Philosopher* (Ithaca, NY: Cornell University Press, 1991) and *Socratic Studies* (Cambridge: Cambridge University Press, 1994). Xenophon: *Memorabilia* 1.1–4, also discussed in chapter 9.

11. Plato, *Apology* 26b–26e.

12. M. F. Burnyeat, "The Impiety of Socrates," *Ancient Philosophy* 17 (1997): 1–12, reprinted in *Explorations in Ancient and Modern Philosophy,* vol. 2 (Cambridge: Cambridge University Press, 2012), 224–37. Oracle: Plato, *Apology* 21a; quotation: 29d; mythological gods: Plato, *Euthyphro* 6a–c.

13. In general on Plato's "theology" see L. Gerson, *God and Greek Philosophy: Studies in the Early History of Natural Theology* (London and New York: Routledge, 1990), 33–81. More generally on Plato: Annas, *Plato* and A. Mason,

Plato (Durham: Acumen, 2010), who has lucid discussions of all of the Platonic ideas of forms, the soul, and the god. Plato's dialogues do not present his ideas systematically; any "theory" has to be reconstructed from multiple sources. As a result, I refer at this point to secondary discussions, rather than to the original Platonic text.

14. Second best, in contrast to *The Republic: Laws* 739d–e. Generally on the *Laws* see C. Bobonich (ed.), *Plato's Laws: A Critical Guide* (Cambridge: Cambridge University Press, 2010). On the religious aspects see R. Mayhew "The Theology of the *Laws*," in Bobobich, *Plato's Laws,* 197–216. Mayhew's translation and commentary upon *Laws* 10 (*Plato, Laws 10* [Oxford: Oxford University Press, 2008]) is also valuable.

15. Three types of religious criminal: *Laws* 885b. Atheist underground: D. Sedley, "The Atheist Underground," in V. Harte and M. Lane (eds.), *Politeia in Greek and Roman Philosophy* (Cambridge: Cambridge University Press, 2013), 329–48.

16. Punishments for insulting the gods: *Laws* 885a–b; 907d–908a; 909d.

Part Three: The Hellenistic Era

1. On Macedon's ambiguous position within Greek ethnicity, see Hall's "Contested Ethnicities: Perceptions of Macedonia Within Evolving Definitions of Greek Identity," in I. Malkin (ed.), *Ancient Perceptions of Greek Ethnicity* (Washington, DC: Center for Hellenic Studies, 2001), 159–86. Alexander I: Herodotus 5.22. For a comprehensive historical account of Macedonia see the three volumes of N. G. L. Hammond's *A History of Macedonia* (Oxford: Oxford University Press, 1972–1988; vol. 2 jointly with G. T. Griffith), and more recently J. Roisman and I. Worthington (eds.), *A Companion to Ancient Macedonia* (Oxford: Wiley-Blackwell, 2010); R. Lane Fox (ed.), *Brill's Companion to Ancient Macedon: Studies in the Archaeology and History of Ancient Macedon, 650 B.C.—300 A.D.* (Leiden: Brill, 2011).

2. Euripides's visit to Macedonia is recorded in the ancient *Life of Euripides,* the fragmentary dialogue of Satyrus, and the letters. For a highly skeptical reading of the tradition see M. R. Lefkowitz, *Lives of the Greek Poets,* 2nd ed. (Baltimore: Johns Hopkins University Press, 2012), 98–100. There is certainly a lively inventiveness in these various sources about Euripides and Macedonia (see for example J. Hanink, "The *Life* of the Author in the Letters of 'Euripides,'" *Greek, Roman and Byzantine Studies* 50 (2010): 537–64). On the date of 408–407 BC for Euripides's *Archelaus* see A. Harder, *Euripides' Kresphontes and Archelaus: Introduction, Text and Commentary* (Leiden: Brill, 1985), 125–26, although the argument admittedly rests on crediting the Macedonian visit (see however her further arguments at 125 n.1).

3. R. Lane Fox, *Alexander the Great* (Harmondsworth, UK: Penguin, 1973) remains an excellent overview of Alexander's career.

4. On the Hellenistic world in general see F. W. Walbank, *The Hellenistic World,* rev. ed. (Cambridge, MA: Harvard University Press, 1993); G. Shipley, *The Greek World After Alexander* (London and New York: Routledge, 2000); A. Erskine, *A Companion to the Hellenistic World* (Malden, MA: Wiley, 2005); G. R. Bugh, *The Cambridge Companion to the Hellenistic World* (Cambridge: Cambridge University Press, 2006).

10. Gods and Kings

1. On the iconography of Alexander see A. Stewart, *Faces of Power: Alexander's Image and Hellenistic Politics* (Berkeley: University of California Press).
2. *Iliad:* Plutarch, *Alexander* 8. Visit to Troy: Arrian, *Anabasis* 1.11–12, Plutarch, *Alexander* 15. Anecdote: *Alexander Romance* 1.42.11–13.
3. On Alexander's insistence on *proskynēsis* and introduction of foreign dress see Arrian, *Anabasis* 4.11 and especially Plutarch, *Alexander* 45 (where he suggests this may have been a strategy to win over "the barbarians").
4. Sophocles: *Oedipus the King* 48, 31; Aristophanes, *Birds* 1706–19. Lysander: Plutarch, *Lysander* 18. Samian cult: P. Cartledge, *Agesilaus and the Crisis of Sparta* (London: Duckworth, 1987), 83–96. Possible precedents for ruler cult in Greece: see R. Mondi, "ΣΚΗΠΤΟΥΧΟΙ ΒΑΣΙΛΕΙΣ: An Argument for Divine Kingship in Early Greece," *Arethusa* 13 (1980): 203–16.
5. Dionysius and the Olympics: Dionysius of Halicarnassus, *Lysias* 28. Great King: Lysias 33 Dionysus: Favorinus, *Corinthiaca* (= "Dio Chrysostom" 37) 21, and for all the evidence for divinization L. J. Sanders. "Dionysius I of Syracuse and the Origins of the Ruler Cult in the Greek World," *Historia: Zeitschrift für Alte Geschichte* 40 (1991): 275–87. It has sometimes been claimed that Philip II, Alexander's father, received cult at Macedon, but there is no firm proof: see M. Mari, "The Ruler Cult in Macedonia," *Studi Ellenistici* 20 (2008): 219–68.
6. On the details of Alexander's campaigns see R. Lane Fox, *Alexander the Great* (Harmondsworth, UK: Penguin, 1973).
7. "Two-horned one": Qur'an 18:83–99. On artistic depictions of Alexander as a god during his lifetime see Stewart, *Faces of Power,* 95–102.
8. On *isotheoi timai,* and specifically on a decree of Teos relating to Antiochus III and his wife, Laodike, see A. Chaniotis, "La divinité mortelle d'Antiochos III à Téos," *Kernos* 20 (2007): 153–71. The ambiguity of the term *"isotheoi timai"* is discussed on pp. 158–59.
9. The examples here are drawn from A. Chaniotis, "The Divinity of Hellenistic Rulers," in A. Esrkine, *A Companion to the Hellenistic World* (Malden, MA: Wiley, 2005), 436–37. Interpretations of ruler cult: C. Habicht, *Gottmenschentum und griechische Städte,* 2nd ed. (Munich: Beck, 1970); S. R. F. Price, *Rituals and Power: The Roman Imperial Cult in Asia Minor* (Cambridge: Cambridge University Press, 1984); P. P. Iossif, A. N. Chankowski, and C. C. Iorber (eds.), *More Than Men, Less Than Gods: Studies in Ruler Cult and Emperor Worship* (Louvain: Peeters, 2011).
10. Impiety: Philippides in R. Kassel and C. Austin (eds.), *Poetae Comici Graeci* vol. 7 (Berlin: de Gruyter, 2010), 347.
11. On the contradictions of ruler cult see especially H. S. Versnel, *Coping with the Gods: Wayward Readings in Greek Theology* (Leiden: Brill, 2011), 439–92. The quotation is from an orally delivered paper by Richard Gordon, and it is recorded by Versnel on p. 471.
12. Theocritus 17.1–19.
13. Entry of Demetrius: Versnel, *Coping with the Gods,* 444–45.
14. Hermocles of Cyzicus, in J. U. Powell, *Collectanea Alexandrina* (Oxford: Clarendon Press, 1925; reprint 1970), 173–74.
15. The three types of divine absence correspond to the three types of disbelief listed at Plato, *Laws* 885b.
16. The Greek texts of Euhemerus are collected by M. Winiarczyk, *Euhemerus*

Messenius, Reliquiae (Stuttgart and Leipzig: Teubner, 1981). The authoritative, book-length discussion is M. Winiarczyk, *The Sacred History of Euhemerus of Messene* (Berlin: de Gruyter, 2013). I discuss Euhemerus in *Beyond the Second Sophistic: Adventures in Greek Postclassicism* (Berkeley: University of California Press, 2013), 49–62.

17. Euhemerus is summarized by Diodorus of Sicily, *Library* 5.41–46 and 6.1.

18. Diodorus does tell us that Euhemerus says that "the ancients" envisaged two types of god: as well as the Olympians, i.e., the divinized humans, there were the natural elements (sun, moon, stars, winds, and so forth) (fragment 25 Winiarczyk (in *Euhemerus Messenius, Reliquiae).* But there is no reason to believe that Euhemerus thought these were really divine, rather than the fantasies of the ancients. In other words, it is probable that Euhemerus was atheistic in the modern sense, i.e., that he denied all divinity.

19. *Iambus* 1.9–11. Callimachus's poem probably dates to the 270s.

20. Biography of Persaeus and list of his book titles: Diogenes Laertius 7.6, 7.36 = H. von Arnim, *Stoicorum Veterum Fragmenta* (Munich: K. G. Saur, 2004), vol. 1, nos. 439 and 435 (henceforth *SVF*). On the background of the court of Antigonus Gonatas see A. Erskine, *The Hellenistic Stoa* (London: Duckworth, 1989), 87–88. Cicero: *On the Nature of the Gods* 1.38. The papyrus is *Herculaneum Papyrus* 1428, from Philodemus's *On Piety;* Persaeus is discussed at ii.28–iii.13 (printed, along with the Cicero passage, at *SVF* 448). For the two-stage interpretation I follow the analysis of Philodemus by A. Henrichs, "Two Doxographical Notes: Democritus and Prodicus," *Harvard Studies in Classical Philology* 79 (1975): 115–23. The first attempt to argue away Persaeus's atheism appears at A. Dyck, *Cicero De Natura Deorum Book I* (Cambridge: Cambridge University Press, 2003), 110; the second at K. Algra, "Stoic Theology," in B. Inwood (ed.), *The Cambridge Companion to Stoicism* (Cambridge: Cambridge University Press, 2003), 158.

11. Philosophical Atheism

1. For good introductions to Hellenistic philosophy see A. A. Long, *Hellenistic Philosophy: Stoics, Epicureans, Skeptics,* 2nd ed. (Berkeley: University of California Press, 1986); K. Algra, J. Barns, J. Mansfeld, and M. Schofield (eds.), *The Cambridge History of Hellenistic Philosophy* (Cambridge: Cambridge University Press, 1999). The major sources are available in A. A. Long and D. N. Sedley, *The Hellenistic Philosophers,* vol. 1, *Translations of the Principal Sources with Philosophical Commentary* (Cambridge: Cambridge University Press, 1987). Volume 2 has the original Greek and Latin texts.

2. For introductions to the Stoics see B. Inwood, *The Cambridge Companion to the Stoics* (Cambridge: Cambridge University Press, 2003); J. Sellars, *Stoicism* (Berkeley: University of California Press, 2006). Stoic theology is discussed (with ancient sources) by Long and Sedley, *The Hellenistic Philosophers,* 274–79, 323–33.

3. Epictetus's leg: Origen, *Against Celsus* 7.53. On Epictetus's philosophy see especially A. A. Long, *Epictetus: A Stoic and Socratic Guide to Life* (Oxford: Clarendon Press, 2002). Stockdale: J. B. Stockdale, *Courage Under Fire: Testing Epictetus's Doctrines in a Laboratory of Human Behavior* (Hoover Institution, 1990: http://media.hoover.org/sites/default/files/documents/StockdaleCourage .pdf); "world of technology" quotation on p. 7.

4. Zeus, Athena, Hera, and so forth: Diogenes Laertius, *Lives of the Eminent Philosophers* 7.147 = Long and Sedley, *The Hellenistic Philosophers*, 323. On the influence of Stoic cosmic ideas on Christianity see T. Rasimus, T. Engberg-Pedersen, and I. Dunderberg (eds.), *Stoicism in Early Christianity* (Grand Rapids, MI: Baker, 2010).

5. For a succinct history of Cynicism, see W. Desmond, *Cynics* (Stocksfield, UK: Acumen, 2008); interesting, provocative essays in R. B. Branham and M.-O. Goulet-Cazé, *The Cynics: The Cynic Movement in Antiquity and Its Legacy* (Berkeley: University of California Press, 2000). The jokes are found at Diogenes Laertius 6.22–69; on these see R. B. Branham, "Defacing the Currency: Diogenes' Rhetoric and the Invention of Rhetoric," in Branham and Goulet-Cazé, *The Cynics*, 81–104.

6. Brisk survey of early Cynic views of religion in M.-O. Goulet-Cazé, "Religion and the Early Cynics," in Branham and Goulet-Cazé, *The Cynics*, 47–80; also Desmond, *Cynics*, 115–22, who focuses on later material. Mockery of sacrifice and dedications: Diogenes Laertius 6.63, 6.59. Diogenes on the nonexistence of gods: Cicero, *On the Nature of the Gods* 3.34–35; Lysias the pharmacist: Diogenes Laertius 6.42. Cercidas: fragment 4.44–48 in J. U. Powell (ed.), *Collectanea Alexandrina* (Oxford: Clarendon Press, 1925).

7. For introductions see R. J. Hankinson, *The Skeptics* (London: Routledge, 1988); H. Thorsrud, *Ancient Skepticism* (Stocksfield, UK: Acumen, 2009).

8. Rhetoricians, hair, and nails: Diogenes Laertius, *Lives of the Eminent Philosophers* 4.62. Embassy to Rome: Plutarch, *Life of Cato the Elder* 22.2, 23.2. Speeches on justice: Cicero, *Republic* 3.12.21. Expulsion: Athenaeus, *Sophists at Supper* 12.547a; Aelian, *Varied History* 9.12. For discussion of the historical circumstances around the embassy see E. Gruen, *Studies in Greek Culture and Roman Policy* (Berkeley: University of California Press, 1990), 174–77.

9. Contradictory views of the gods: Sextus Empiricus, *Outlines of Pyrrhonism* 3.2–4. Carneades's argument from sensation: Sextus Empiricus, *Against the Mathematicians* 9.139–41. Skepticism toward religion: see A. A. Long, "Skepticism About Gods in Hellenistic Philosophy," in M. Griffith and D. J. Mastronarde (eds.), *Cabinet of the Muses: Essays on Classical and Comparative Literature in Honor of Thomas J. Rosenmeyer* (Atlanta: Scholars Press, 1990), 279–91; Long and Sedley, *The Hellenistic Philosophers*, 462–63; P. A. Meijer, *Stoic Theology: Proofs for the Existence of the Cosmic God and the Traditional Gods* (Delft: Eburon, 2007), 149–206.

10. Cicero, *On the Nature of the Gods* 3.38; Sextus Empiricus, *Against the Mathematicians* 9.152–77.

11. Sextus Empiricus, *Against the Mathematicians* 9.182–84 = Long and Sedley, *The Hellenistic Philosophers*, 463. Also Cicero, *On the Nature of the Gods* 3.43–44. See M. E. Burnyeat, "Gods and Heaps," in M. Schofield and M. Nussbaum (eds.), *Language and Logos: Studies in Ancient Greek Philosophy Presented to G. E. L. Owen* (Cambridge: Cambridge University Press, 1982), 315–38.

12. Carneades not an atheist: e.g., Long, "Skepticism About Gods," 280–81; A. Drozdek, "Skeptics and a Religious Instinct," *Minerva* 18 (2005): 93–108. Cicero: *On the Nature of the Gods* 3.44.

13. This paragraph and the previous rest heavily on the interpretation of D. Sedley, "From the Pre-Socratics to the Hellenistic Age," in S. Bullivant and M. Ruse (eds.), *The Oxford Handbook of Atheism* (Oxford: Oxford University Press, 2013), 139–51.

14. Biography of Clitomachus: Diogenes Laertius, *Lives of the Eminent Philosophers* 4.67. Atheist catalogue: M. Winiarczyk, "Der erste Atheistenkatalog des Kleitomachus," *Philologus* 120 (1976): 32–46. The title *On Atheism* is recorded at Theophilus, *To Autolycus* 3.7. The lists appear at Cicero, *On the Nature of the Gods* 1.117–19, and Sextus Empiricus, *Against the Mathematicians* 9.50–58. On Epicurus see the following chapter.

15. Sextus's teacher and student: Diogenes Laertius, *Lives of the Eminent Philosophers* 9.116. Doctor: Sextus Empiricus, *Against the Mathematicians* 1.260; *Outlines of Pyrrhonism* 2.238. On Sextus see more generally Thorsrud, *Ancient Skepticism,* 123–46; P. Pellegrin, "Sextus Empiricus," in R. Bett (ed.), *The Cambridge Companion to Ancient Scepticism* (Cambridge: Cambridge University Press, 2010): 120–41.

16. Arguments against the gods: *Against the Mathematicians* 9.14–194; also H. W. Attridge, "The Philosophical Critique of Religion Under the Early Empire," in W. Haase (ed.), *Aufstieg und Niedergang der römischen Welt* 2.16.1 (Berlin and New York: de Gruyter, 1978), 46–51. Arguments equally strong on both sides: 9.59; Skeptic practices but does not believe: 9.49.

17. *Against the Mathematicians* 9.14–47.

18. Ibid., 9.49–59.

19. Ibid., 9.60–74.

20. Ibid., 9.75–122.

21. Ibid., 9.123–32.

22. Ibid., 9.133–36. This tactic of using *parabolē* (comparison) argumentation to refute Zeno's syllogisms may derive from Alexinus: see M. Schofield, "The Syllogisms of Zeno of Citium," *Phronesis* 28 (1983): 31–57. Skeptics take part in ritual but do not believe: 9.49.

23. *Against the Mathematicians* 9.136–75.

24. Ibid., 9.176–77.

12. Epicurus *Theomakhos*

1. For introductions to Epicurus and Epicureanism see J. M. Rist, *Epicurus: An Introduction* (Cambridge: Cambridge University Press, 1971); J. Warren (ed.), *The Cambridge Companion to Epicureanism* (Cambridge: Cambridge University Press, 2009). On Epicurus's life and the history of the garden see D. Clay, "The Athenian Garden," in Warren, *The Cambridge Companion,* 9–28.

2. The atoms of the soul: Epicurus, *Letter to Herodotus* 63. Death is nothing to us: Epicurus, *Authoritative Opinions* 2. On the Epicurean view of death (and its differences from the Democritean) see J. Warren, *Facing Death: Epicurus and His Critics* (Oxford: Clarendon Press, 2005); and "Removing Fear," in Warren, *Cambridge Companion,* 242–48.

3. Critical of atheists: Philodemus, *On Piety* column 19 lines 519–48. Existence of the gods: Epicurus, *Letter to Menoeceus* 123. Personal responsibility: Ibid., 133 (arguing against the presocratic *anagkē* or "compulsion" rather than traditional piety, but the point surely has wider relevance). For the Epicurean view of religion see A. A. Long and D. N. Sedley, *The Hellenistic Philosophers,* vol. 1, *Translations of the Principal Sources with Philosophical Commentary* (Cambridge: Cambridge University Press, 1987), 139–49; D. Obbink, "The Atheism of Epicurus," *Greek, Roman and Byzantine Studies* 30 (1989): 187–223 (who

also collects the accusations of atheism); *Philodemus, On Piety Part 1* (Oxford: Oxford University Press, 1996), 1–23; J. Mansfeld, "Aspects of Epicurean Theology," *Mnemosyne* 46 (1993): 172–210; Warren, "Removing Fear," 238–42; and D. Konstan, "Epicurus on the Gods," in J. Fish and K. Sanders (eds.), *Epicurus and the Epicurean Tradition* (Cambridge: Cambridge University Press, 2011), 53–71.

4. All perceptions are true: sources and discussion at Long and Sedley, *The Hellenistic Philosophers,* 78–86. Waking and dreaming perceptions of gods: Cicero, *On the Nature of the Gods* 1.46–49; Lucretius, *On the Nature of Things* 5.1169–71. Philodemus, *On Piety* column 8 lines 224–41 does not mention dreams, *pace* Obbink, *Philodemus On Piety* 6.

5. Incorporeal gods perceptible only to the mind: Cicero, *On the Nature of the Gods,* 1.49.

6. Epicurus on conventional misapprehension of the divine: Obbink, "The Atheism of Epicurus," 194–202. Religious experience and psychosis: R. Dawkins, *The God Delusion* (London: Random House, 2006), 112–17.

7. Gaps: Lucretius, *On the Nature of Things* 5.146–54. The earliest reference to the "gaps between universes" theory comes at Cicero, *On the Nature of the Gods,* 1.18.

8. Theodorus and others tried in the late fourth century: see L.-L. O'Sullivan, "Athenian Impiety Trials in the Late Fourth Century B.C.," *Classical Quarterly* 47 (1997): 136–52.

9. For this interpretation see Obbink, "The Atheism of Epicurus," and D. Sedley, "Epicurus' Theological Innatism," in Fish and Sanders, *Epicurus and the Epicurean Tradition,* 29–52; against this reading see Mansfield, "Aspects of Epicurean Theology," and Konstan, "Epicurus on the Gods." *Enagismata* and celebrations: Diogenes Laertius 10.18. In general on the "divinization" of Epicurus see Clay, "The Athenian Garden," 20–26.

10. Epicurus's reputation as an atheist: M. Winiarczyk, "Wer galt im Altertum als Atheist?," *Philologus* 128 (1984): 168–70.

11. On Lucretius and his reception see especially S. Gillespie and P. Hardie (eds.), *The Cambridge Companion to Lucretius* (Cambridge: Cambridge University Press, 2007); S. Greenblatt, *The Swerve: How the World Became Modern* (New York: Norton, 2011). On the nineteenth and twentieth centuries: F. Turner, "Lucretius Among the Victorians," *Victorian Studies* 16 (1973): 329–48; S. Gillespie and D. Mackenzie, "Lucretius and the Moderns," in Gillespie and Hardie, *The Cambridge Companion to Lucretius,* 306–24.

12. Lucretius, *On the Nature of Things* 1.62–79. On Lucretius's portrait of Epicurus see in general M. Gale, *Myth and Poetry in Lucretius* (Cambridge: Cambridge University Press, 1994), 190–207.

13. Knots of religion: 1.931–932, repeated at 4.7.

14. Iphianassa: 80–101. Voltaire: R. Barbour, "Moral and Political Philosophy," in Gillespie and Hardie, *The Cambridge Companion to Lucretius,* 164.

15. Lucretius, *On the Nature of Things* 1.102–9.

16. Ibid., 5.7–12.

17. Ibid., 5.14–21 (quotation from 19).

18. Lucretius, *On the Nature of Things* 5.1161–1240 (quotation from 1194–1203).

19. Ibid., 1.1–49; 3.18–30; 5.146–55.

Part Four: Rome

1. On Rome and the Hellenistic kingdoms see especially E. Gruen, *The Hellenistic World and the Coming of Rome* (Berkeley: University of California Press, 1986). For a readable biography of Mithridates (using an alternative spelling) see A. Mayor, *The Poison King: The Life and Legend of Mithradates, Rome's Deadliest Enemy* (Princeton, NJ: Princeton University Press, 2010). Generally on the rise of Rome see M. Beard and M. Crawford, *Rome in the Late Republic: Problems and Interpretations,* 2nd ed. (London: Duckworth, 1999); H. I. Flower (ed.), *The Cambridge Companion to the Roman Republic* (Cambridge: Cambridge University Press, 2004); N. S. Rosenstein and R. Morstein-Marx (eds.), *A Companion to the Roman Republic* (Oxford: Blackwell, 2006).
2. Parade of Syracusan loot: Polybius 9.10.
3. Aelius Aristides 26.97. On the techniques whereby the empire was symbolically united see C. Ando, *Imperial Ideology and Provincial Loyalty in the Roman Empire* (Berkeley: University of California Press, 2000). Generally on the rise of the principate see M. Goodman, *The Roman World, 44 BC–AD 180* (London and New York: Routledge, 1997); C. Kelly, *The Roman Empire: A Very Short Introduction* (Oxford: Oxford University Press, 2006); D. S. Potter, *A Companion to the Roman Empire* (Malden, MA: Blackwell, 2006).
4. Jewish refusal to sacrifice: Josephus, *Jewish War* 2.409. On Decius's decree see J. B. Rives, "The Decree of Decius and the Religion of Empire," *The Journal of Roman Studies* 89 (1999): 135–54.

13. With Gods on Our Side

1. Panaetius, *On Providence:* Cicero, *Letters to Atticus* 13.8. In general on the development of ideas of imperial providence see M. Dragona-Monachou, "Divine Providence in the Philosophy of Empire," in *Aufstieg und Niedergang der römischen Welt* 2.36.7 (1994): 4417–90. The multifaceted relationship between Stoicism and Rome is surveyed by P. A. Brunt, "Stoicism and the Principate," *Papers of the British School at Rome* 43 (1975): 7–35, reprinted in his *Studies in Stoicism* (Oxford: Oxford University Press, 2013), 275–309.
2. Polybius quotations: 6.4, 1.4. On his "weakly Stoic" conception of providence see R. Brouwer, "Polybius and Stoic *Tyche,*" *Greek, Roman, and Byzantine Studies* 51 (2011): 111–32; and more generally on his pro-Roman providentialism see F. W. Walbank, "Polybius and Rome's Eastern Policy" and "Polybius Between Greece and Rome," in *Selected Papers: Studies in Greek and Roman History and Historiography* (Cambridge: Cambridge University Press, 1985), 138–56 and 280–97.
3. Vergil, *Aeneid* 1.278–79.
4. Ibid., 4.270.
5. Augustus and Apollo: K. Galinsky, *Augustan Culture* (Princeton: Princeton University Press, 1996), 297–99. Horace: *Odes* 3.5.1–2. Vespasian: Suetonius, *Vespasian* 23.4. Claudius: "Seneca," *Apocolocyntosis.* Imperial cult between Greek "pull" and imperial "push": see for example T. Whitmarsh, "Thinking Local," in T. Whitmarsh (ed.), *Local Knowledge and Microidentities in the Imperial Greek World* (Cambridge: Cambridge University Press, 2010), 6–8, with references.

6. On resistance to Rome see A. Giovannini (ed.), *Opposition et résistances a l'empire d'Auguste à Trajan* (Vandoeuvres: Fondation Hardt, 1987); T. Whitmarsh, "Resistance Is Futile? Greek Literary Tactics in the Face of Rome," in P. Schubert (ed.), *Les Grecs héritiers des Romans* (Vandoeuvres: Fondation Hardt, 2013), 57–84. On Greek skepticism toward the imperial cult see G. W. Bowersock, "Greek Intellectuals and the Imperial Cult in the Second Century A.D.," in W. den Boer (ed.), *Le culte des souverains dans l'empire romain* (Vandoeuvres: Fondation Hardt, 1973), 179–212.

7. Plato: *Laws* 885b. Atheism and rejection of providence: Lucian, *Slander* 14. For Epicurean "atheism" see chapter 13.

8. On Dionysius and his *Roman Antiquities* see especially E. Gabba, *Dionysius and the History of Archaic Rome* (Berkeley: University of California Press, 1991), with 1–4 on his background in Halicarnassus; also, for an integrated account of Dionysius as an intellectual see N. Wiater, *The Ideology of Classicism: Language, History and Classicism in Dionysius of Halicarnassus* (Berlin: de Gruyter, 2011). For a readable account of Mithridates's life and campaigns see A. Mayor, *The Poison King: The Life and Legend of Mithradates, Rome's Deadliest Enemy* (Princeton, NJ: Princeton University Press, 2010).

9. Early Roman history as myth: T. P. Wiseman, *The Myths of Rome* (Exeter: University of Exeter Press, 2004). *Roman Antiquities* written for Greeks: 1.4.2; Romans were originally Greeks: 1.5.1–2. Dionysius and providence are discussed in the following paragraph.

10. Dionysius, *Roman Antiquities* 1.4.2–3.

11. The other candidate sometimes proposed (for example in Wiater, *The Ideology of Classicism*, 101–2) for association with Dionysius's list of malicious historians is Timagenes of Alexandria, but his professional career was spent largely at Rome, and (after falling out with Augustus) in Tuscany; he was never the courtier of a "barbarian" king. Life of Metrodorus: Strabo 13.1.55 and Plutarch, *Lucullus* 22.1–5 (testimonia 2 and 3 in F. Jacoby, *Die Fragmente der griechischen Historiker* [Leiden: Brill, 1923–] 2B 184). Carneades: Cicero, *On the Orator* 1.45 = testimonium 4a. Memory technique: Ibid., 2.360 = testimonium 5a (also 5b and 5c). There is some debate over whether there were two figures of this name or one: see Habinek's entry in I. Worthington (ed.), *Brill's New Jacoby* (Leiden: Brill, online version). On Timagenes see M. Sordi, "Timagene di Alessandria, uno storico ellenocentrico e filobarbaro," in *Aufstieg und Niedergang der römischen Welt* 2.30.1 (1982): 775–97. Oppositional writing at Mithridates's court: G. Bowersock, *Augustus and the Greek World* (Oxford: Oxford University Press, 1965), 108–9.

12. Nickname: Pliny, *Natural History* 34.16.34 = fragment 12. Ovid: Ex Ponto 4.14.37–40 = Jacoby testimonium 6b.

13. Counterfactual history: N. Ferguson (ed.), *Virtual History: Alternatives and Counterfactuals* (London: Penguin, 1997); for the Romans and steam power see N. Morley, "Trajan's Engines," *Greece and Rome* 47 (2000): 197–210. For more on anti-Roman histories of Alexander see T. Whitmarsh, *The Second Sophistic* (Oxford: Oxford University Press, 2005), 68–70.

14. *Alexander Romance* 1.29 (in the A and γ traditions; 1.26 in β).

15. Livy, *From the Foundation of Rome* 9.18–19; see R. Morello, "Livy's Alexander Digression (9.17–19): Counterfactuals and Apologetics," *Journal of Roman Studies* 92 (2002): 62–85, and S. Oakley, *A Commentary on Livy, Books VI–IX. Volume III: Book IX* (Oxford: Oxford University Press, 2005), 199–205, and appendix 5.

16. Plutarch, *On the Fortune and Virtue of Alexander* I–II; *On the Fortune of the Romans*. Philosopher in action: *On the Fortune and Virtue of Alexander* 327e–9d; quotation: 328e.

17. The Gauls and the Capitol: Plutarch, *On the Fortune of the Romans* 325b–d. Changing meaning of Fortune: 318a (the sentence is corrupt at the end, hence the ellipsis). Generally on the role of fortune in this text see S. Swain, "Plutarch's *De Fortuna Romanorum*," *Classical Quarterly* 39 (1989): 504–16.

18. Shooting star: *On the Fortune of the Romans* 326a; "much blood": 326c (alluding to Homer, *Odyssey* 18.149).

19. Lucian, *Zeus the Tragedian* 47–49.

14. Virtual Networks

1. On archaism and Atticism in later Greek culture see especially E. Bowie, "Greeks and Their Past in the Second Sophistic," *Past and Present* 46 (1970): 3–41, reprinted in M. I. Finley (ed.), *Studies in Ancient Society* (London: Routledge, 1974), 166–209; S. Swain, *Hellenism and Empire: Language, Classicism, and Power in the Greek World, AD 50–250* (Oxford: Oxford University Press, 1996); T. Whitmarsh, *Greek Literature and the Roman Empire: The Politics of Imitation* (Oxford: Oxford University Press, 2001), and *The Second Sophistic* (Oxford: Oxford University Press, 2005). The pomegranate example is from Phrynichus, *Selection* 223 (Whitmarsh, *The Second Sophistic*, 45). On oratory and impersonation see especially M. Gleason, *Making Men: Sophists and Self-Presentation in Ancient Rome* (Princeton: Princeton University Press, 1995). Marathon speeches: Polemo, *Declamations* 1–2.

2. Doxography: for revisionist accounts see especially the three volumes of J. Mansfeld and D. Runia, *Aëtiana: The Method and Intellectual Context of a Doxographer,* vol. 1, *The Sources* (Leiden: Brill, 1997); vol. 2, *The Compendium* (Leiden: Brill, 2009); and especially vol. 3, *Studies in the Doxographical Traditions of Greek Philosophy* (Leiden: Brill, 2010).

3. Plato, *Laws* 886a.

4. Philodemus, *On Piety* 19.519–33, with D. Obbink, *Philodemus on Piety* (Oxford: Oxford University Press, 1996), 142–43. On the Epicurean library in the Villa of the Papyri at Herculaneum, see M. Gigante, *Philodemus in Italy: The Books from Herculaneum,* trans. D. Obbink (Ann Arbor: University of Michigan Press, 1995), 1–13. For more on the reconstruction of *On Piety* see chapter 7.

5. See further above, p. 174.

6. I translate from column 16 of M. F. Smith, *Diogenes of Oenoanda: The Epicurean Inscription,* edited with introduction, translation, and notes (Naples: Bibliopolis, 1993). C. W. Chilton, *Diogenes of Oenoanda: The Fragments* (London and New York: Oxford University Press, 1971); many more fragments have since been published. On the inscription and what it tells us about philosophical and cultural life at the time see D. Clay, "A Lost Epicurean Community," *Greek, Roman and Byzantine Studies* 30 (1989): 313–35, reprinted in *Paradosis and Survival: Three Chapters in the History of Epicurean Philosophy* (Ann Arbor: University of Michigan Press, 1998), 232–56; P. Gordon, *Epicurus in Lycia: The Second-Century World of Diogenes of Oenoanda* (Ann Arbor: University of Michigan Press, 1996).

7. Agnosticism is atheism: see, for example, J. Bagnini, *Atheism: A Very Short Introduction* (Oxford: Oxford University Press, 2003), 22–25.

8. Cicero, *On the Nature of the Gods* 1.117–19; on its derivation from Clitomachus via Philo see M. Winiarczyk, "Der erste Atheistenkatalog des Kleitomachos," *Philologus* 120 (1976): 35–36; A. Dyck, *Cicero, De Natura Deorum Book I* (Cambridge: Cambridge University Press, 2003), 9, argues more neutrally for "academic material."

9. B. Anderson, *Imagined Communities: Reflections on the Origins and Spread of Nationalism* (London: Verso, 1991).

10. Aëtius, *Tenets (Placita)* 1.7.1–10; Sextus Empiricus, *Against the Mathematicians* book 9; see also Theophilus, *Against Autolycus* 3.7. On Aëtius see especially D. Runia, "Atheists in Aëtius: Text, Translation and Comments on *De Placitis* 1.7.1–10," in Mansfield and Runia, *Aëtiana Volume III*, 343–74.

11. Sextus Empiricus, *Against the Mathematicians* 9.54; for other references to atheists as groups see 9.14, 9.51.

15. Imagine

1. Age of ambition: P. Brown, *The Making of Late Antiquity* (Cambridge, MA: Harvard University Press, 1978). Tacitus: *Agricola* 30.

2. Plutarch, *Political Advice* 813e.

3. Integration: see for example C. Ando, *Imperial Ideology and Provincial Loyalty in the Roman Empire* (Berkeley: University of California Press, 2000). Regional dynamics: T. Whitmarsh (ed.), *Local Knowledge and Micro–Identities in the Imperial Greek World* (Cambridge: Cambridge University Press, 2010), with pp. 1–10 on "glocalization." Quotation: Minucius Felix, *Octavius* 6.1. Generally on the varieties of religion in the Roman Empire see M. Beard, J. North, and S. Price, *Religions of Rome*, 2 vols. (Cambridge: Cambridge University Press, 1998); J. B. Rives, *Religion in the Roman Empire* (Malden, MA: Blackwell, 2007); J. Rüpke, *From Jupiter to Christ: On the History of Religion in the Roman Imperial Period* (Oxford: Oxford University Press, 2011), especially 185–209. Networks: A. Collar, *Religious Networks in the Roman Empire* (Cambridge: Cambridge University Press, 2013).

4. Apuleius, *Apology* 56. Generally on Apuleius see S. Harrison, *Apuleius: A Latin Sophist* (Oxford: Oxford University Press, 2000).

5. Mezentius: Vergil, *Aeneid* 10.786–907. On Roman theomachies see P. Chaudhari, *The War with God: Theomachy in Roman Imperial Poetry* (New York: Oxford University Press, 2014).

6. Doxographic network: Aëtius, *Tenets* 1.7.1. Stereotypical accusations in Roman courts: C. Edwards, *The Politics of Immorality in Ancient Rome* (Cambridge: Cambridge University Press, 1993).

7. Aemilianus as Christian: J. Walsh, "On Christian Atheism," *Vigiliae Christianae* 45 (1991): 260; V. Hunink, "Apuleius, Pudentilla and Early Christianity," *Vigiliae Christianae* 54 (2000): 88–91.

8. Pliny, *Natural History* 2.5.

9. Lucian, *Demonax* 11, 32, 37, 27; see 5 for the "man of Sinope" (i.e., Diogenes the Cynic). For other sayings attributed to him see D. M. Searby, "Non–Lucian Sources for Demonax. With a New Collection of 'Fragments,'" *Symbolae Osloenses* 83 (2008): 120–47.

10. Lucian the atheist: *Suda,* under *Loukianos.* Lucian's European reception has been well studied: see, for example, C. Robinson, *Lucian and His Influence in Europe* (London: Duckworth, 1979); C. Lauvergnat-Gagnière, *Lucien de Samosate et le lucianisme en France au XVIe siècle: Athéisme et polémique* (Geneva: Droz, 1988); M. Baumbach, *Lukian in Deutschland: Eine forschungs- und rezeptionsgeschichtliche Analyse vom Humanismus bis zur Gegenwart* (Munich: Fink, 2002). More generally on Lucian: C. P. Jones, *Culture and Society in Lucian* (Cambridge, MA: Harvard University Press, 1986); R. B. Branham, *Unruly Eloquence: Lucian and the Comedy of Traditions* (Cambridge, MA: Harvard University Press, 1989).

11. Christians and the "impaled sophist": Lucian, *Peregrinus* 11–13.

12. Lucian's views on religion have been the subject of a number of discussions, none of them wholly satisfactory. The tendency has been to try to reconstruct a coherent religious attitude for the real Lucian behind the mask (a hopeless quest), rather than to explore his satirical strategies on their own terms. See M. Caster, *Lucien et la pensée religieuse de son temps* (Paris: Les Belles Lettres, 1937); O. Karavas, "ΝΗΦΕ ΚΑΙ ΜΕΜΝΗΣΟ ΑΠΙΣΤΕΙΝ (*Hermot.* 47): La religiosité de Lucien," in A. Bartley, *A Lucian for Our Times* (Newcastle: Cambridge Scholars Publishing, 2009), 137–44; M. Dickie, "Lucian's Gods: Lucian's Understanding of the Divine," in J. N. Bremmer and A. Erskine (eds.), *The Gods of Ancient Greece: Identities and Transformations* (Edinburgh: Edinburgh University Press, 2010), 348–61; F. Berdozzo, *Götter, Mythen, Philosophen: Lukian und die paganen Göttervorstellungen seiner Zeit* (Berlin: de Gruyter, 2011).

13. Lucian, *On Sacrifices* 1, 2.

14. Teapot: B. Russell, "Is there a god?," in J. G. Slater and P. Köllner (eds.), *The Collected Papers of Bertrand Russell. Volume 11: Last Philosophical Testament, 1943–68* (London: Routledge, 1997), 547–48.

15. Diogenes: Cicero, *Tusculan Disputations* 1.43. Charon: Lucian, *Charon* 11. On the *Dialogues of the Dead* see J. Relihan, "Vainglorious Menippus in Lucian's *Dialogues of the Dead,*" *Illinois Classical Studies* 12 (1987): 185–206. On the Cynics and their views of religion see chapter 11, pp. 159–161.

16. Lucian, *On Sacrifices* 15.

17. Lucian, *Timon* 1–4, 7.

18. Lucian, *Zeus Refuted* (quotation from 19): for the philosophical context of these arguments see P. Großlein, *Untersuchungen zum Juppiter confutatus Lukians* (Frankfurt am Main: Peter Lang, 1998).

19. Lucian, *Zeus the Tragedian* 35–53. Oenomaus of Gadara: J. Hammerstaedt, *Die Orakelkritik des Kynikers Oenomaus* (Frankfurt am Main: Athenäum, 1988); for the comment of Rabbi Abba ben Kahana see *Genesis Rabbah* 65:20, with C. Hezser, "Interfaces Between Rabbinic Literature and Graeco-Roman Philosophy," in P. Schäfer and C. Hezser (eds.), *The Talmud Yerushalmi and Graeco-Roman Culture* (Tübingen: Mohr Siebeck, 2000), 180. Another second-century critic of prophecy was Diogenianus the Epicurean (whose views are preserved by Eusebius, *Preparation for the Gospel* 4.3, 6.8): see J. Hammerstaedt, "Das Kriterium der Prolepsis beim Epikureer Diogenian," *Jahrbuch für Antike und Christentum* 36 (1993): 24–32.

20. Lucian, *Zeus the Tragedian* 18.

21. For orientation on Plutarch see D. Russell, *Plutarch* (London: Duckworth, 1971).

22. Theophrastus, *Characters* 16. Quotation: Plutarch, *On Superstition* 168d.

Jews keeping to the Sabbath while the city was captured: 169c; old women: 165f–166a (where there may well be a further reference to Judaism: modern texts of Plutarch read "baptisms" [*baptismous*], but this is an emendation by the eighteenth-century English editor Richard Bentley from the transmitted "keeping to the Sabbath" [*sabbatismous*]). There is a thoughtful discussion of *On Superstition* and its relation to Plutarch's thought at P. Van Nuffelen, *Rethinking the Gods: Philosophical Readings of Religion in the Post-Hellenistic Period* (Cambridge: Cambridge University Press, 2011), 65–71; see also H. Bowden, "Before Superstition and After: Theophrastus and Plutarch on *Deisidaimonia*," *Past and Present* 199 (2008): 56–71.

23. Atheism: Plutarch, *On Superstition* 170f.

24. Niobe: Plutarch, *On Superstition* 170b–c. Plutarch explicitly discusses the Epicureans alongside the *deisidaimones* at *It Is Not Possible to Live Pleasurably According to Epicurus* 1186b–c.

16. Christians, Heretics, and Other Atheists

1. For a sparkling account of the emergence of Christianity see D. MacCulloch, *A History of Christianity: The First Three Thousand Years* (London: Allen Lane, 2009). Conflicting accounts of Constantine's vision: Lactantius, *On the Deaths of the Persecuted* 44.5 and Eusebius, *Life of Constantine* 1.28–30. For a readable and authoritative account of Constantine's life and career see T. Barnes and R. Boxhall, *Constantine: Dynasty, Religion and Power in the Later Roman Empire* (Chichester: Wiley-Blackwell, 2014); see also N. Lenski, *The Cambridge Companion to the Age of Constantine* (Cambridge: Cambridge University Press, 2006), with Lenski's own chapter ("The Reign of Constantine," 59–90) on Constantine's reign. The Edict of Milan broadened an Edict of Tolerance that had already been issued by the eastern Augustus Galerius.

2. Third race: Clement, *Stromateis* 6.5.41 (Clement is quoting an earlier text). In general on the question of the existence of anti-Christian law see T. Barnes, "Legislation Against the Christians," *Journal of Roman Studies* 58 (1968): 32–50, concluding that such persecution as did occur was rooted in prejudice and not legislation. The so-called Decian persecution in 250 was in fact not targeted specifically at Christians: Decius's concern rather was to ensure that all citizens sacrificed for the health of the empire (J. B. Rives, "The Decree of Decius and the Religion of Empire," *The Journal of Roman Studies* 89 [1999]: 135–54). On the late-antique manufacture of martyr myth see L. Grig, *Making Martyrs in Late Antiquity* (London: Duckworth, 2004); and C. Moss, *Ancient Christian Martyrdom: Diverse Practices, Theologies, and Traditions* (New Haven: Yale University Press, 2012) and *The Myth of Persecution: How Early Christians Invented a Story of Martyrdom* (New York: HarperOne, 2013).

3. Indistinguishability of Christians and non-Christians (at least in North Africa): E. Rebillard, *Christians and Their Many Identities in Late Antiquity* (Ithaca, NY, and London: Cornell University Press, 2012), 67–68. That many attending Christian services also practiced other forms of worship is evident from the anxious instruction even of post-Constantinian church leaders like John Chrysostom and Augustine: see Rebillard, *Christians and Their Many Identities*, 74–75; and B. Sandwell, *Religious Identity in Late Antiquity: Greeks, Jews and Christians in Antioch* (Cambridge: Cambridge University Press, 2008), 82–90. Quotation: Edwards, "The Beginnings of Christianisation," 142. Generally on

the persistence of polytheist culture into the sixth century: G. Bowersock, *Hellenism in Late Antiquity* (Ann Arbor: University of Michigan Press, 1990); and A. Cameron, *The Last Pagans of Rome* (Oxford: Oxford University Press, 2011). R. Lane Fox, *Pagans and Christians in the Mediterranean World from the Second Century AD to the Conversion of Constantine* (Harmondsworth, UK: Viking, 1986) offers a rich storehouse of information on the relationship between Christian and polytheist cults; see also C. P. Jones, *Between Pagans and Christians* (Cambridge, MA: Harvard University Press, 2014).

4. Numbers of Christians: K. Hopkins, "Christian Number and Its Implications," *Journal of Early Christian Studies* 6.2 (1998): 185–226. Hopkins's figures for AD 200 have been thought by some too low: see, for example, Edwards, "The Beginnings of Christianisation," 138.

5. Emperor as chief priest: R. Gordon, "The Veil of Power: Emperors, Sacrificers and Benefactors," in M. Beard and J. North (eds.), *Pagan Priests: Religion and Power in the Ancient World* (London: Duckworth, 1990), 201–31.

6. *Codex Theodosianus* 16.1.2, 16.5.6; D. Hunt, "Christianising the Roman Empire: The Evidence of the Code," in J. Harries and I. Wood (eds.), *The Theodosian Code*, 2nd ed. (London: Duckworth, 2010), 147.

7. Heretics: 16.5 (Manichaeans are also mentioned here). Any crime: 16.5.40.1; Memory: 16.5.38. Apostates: 16.7. Jews: 16.8. "Pagans": 16.10. Public debate: 16.4.2. On the reuse of anti-polytheist discourse against "heretics" see R. Flower, *Emperors and Bishops in Late Roman Invective* (Cambridge: Cambridge University Press, 2013). Skepticism as regards implementation: A. Cameron, *The Last Pagans of Rome* (Oxford: Oxford University Press, 2011), 59–74.

8. Revised meaning of *atheos*: see G. W. H. Lampe (ed.), *A Patristic Greek Lexicon* (Oxford: Clarendon Press, 1961), 44. Lampe does cite a few instances of the "classical" meaning, but the vast majority are of the new kind. The earliest Christian instance comes in a widely cited phrase at Ephesians 2:12 (attacking "atheists in the cosmos"). "Polytheist atheists": for example "Sentences of Sextus" 599 ("A polytheist man is an atheist"), Eusebius, *Preparation for the Gospel* 7.19.8. Philo, *On the Special Laws* 1.345; *On the Decalogue* 91. War: *Questions on Exodus* 30 (the phrasing is taken from Demosthenes, *On the Crown* 262). Christian war on atheists: Eusebius, *In Praise of Constantine* 6.21; ps.-Chrysostom, *On John the Theologian* 614 (Migne). See also for example *Eusebius Life of Constantine* 3.3.1, *On the Praise of Constantine* 6.21, 7.6, 9.8. B. Shaw, *Sacred Violence: African Christians and Sectarian Hatred in the Age of Augustine* (Cambridge: Cambridge University Press, 2011); on the rhetoric of sacred violence in late-antique Christianity and early Islam, see also T. Sizgorich, *Violence and Belief in Late Antiquity: Militant Devotion in Christianity and Islam* (Philadelphia: Pennsylvania University Press, 2009).

9. Accusations of atheism against Christians: J. Walsh, "On Christian Atheism," *Vigiliae Christianae*, 45 (1991): 255–77; P. F. Beatrice, "L'accusation d'athéisme contre les chrétiens," in M. Narcy and É. Rebillard (eds.), *Hellénisme et christianisme* (Villeneuve d'Ascq: Presses Universitaires de Septentron, 2004), 133–52. Eusebius on Licinius: *Life of Constantine* 2.5.1, 2.5.4. "Away with the atheists": *Martyrdom of Polycarp* 9–10. Date of Polycarp's martyrdom: P. Hartog, *Polycarp and the New Testament* (Tübingen: Mohr Siebeck, 2002), 24–31. Many scholars date the text too to the second century, for no good reason that I know of. At Luke 23:18, the crowd cries out to Pilate to release Barabbas

but *aire* Jesus (compare Acts 21:36, used by the crowd of Paul); in John, when Pilate tells the Jews that Jesus is their king, they reply *aron, aron* (19:15). Intertextuality in the *Martyrdom of Polycarp:* C. Moss, "Nailing Down and Tying Up: Lessons in Intertextual Impossibility from the *Martyrdom of Polycarp,*" *Vigiliae Christianae* 67 (2013): 117–36 (emphasizing that the text encourages parallels with Socrates as well as Jesus). One explicit second-century association of Christians with atheism is Lucian, *Alexander or the False Prophet 25,* but there, crucially, the Christians are being lumped in with Epicureans, who were certainly thought of as (philosophical) atheists. For a third-century accusation against Christians as *atheoi* who "secede from ancestral customs" see Porphyry, *Against the Christians* fragment 1; the phrasing may however be paraphrased rather than verbatim.

10. Justin Martyr, *First Apology 5–6.* On such early imperial Christian appropriations (and condemnations) of Socrates see C. Taylor, "Socrates Under the Severans," in S. Swain, S. Harrison, and J. Elsner (eds.), *Severan Culture* (Cambridge: Cambridge University Press, 2007), 500–11. See also *First Apology 4,* where reference is made to the philosophers who "taught atheism" (*atheotēs*).

11. Christian reuse of philosophical atheism: D. Palmer "Atheism, Apologetic and Negative Theology in the Greek Apologists of the Second Century," *Vigiliae Christianae* 37 (1983): 234–59. Christian opposition to classical atheism: Theophilus, *Against Autolycus 3.7.* Clement: *Exhortation to the Greeks 2.20–21.* On the Christian reception of Euhemerism see R. P. C. Hanson, "Christian Attitudes to Pagan Religion," *Aufstieg und Niedergang der römischen Welt* 2.23.2 (1980): 934–38; M. Winiarczyk, *The Sacred History of Euhemerus of Messene* (Berlin: de Gruyter, 2013), 148–52.

Index

A Note About the Author

Tim Whitmarsh is the A. G. Leventis Professor of Greek Culture at the University of Cambridge. He has published widely on ancient literature, including *Beyond the Second Sophistic: Adventures in Greek Postclassicism* (University of California Press, 2013); *Narrative and Identity in the Ancient Greek Novel: Returning Romance* (Cambridge University Press, 2011); *Ancient Greek Literature* (Polity Press, 2004); and *Greek Literature and the Roman Empire: The Politics of Imitation* (Oxford University Press, 2001).

A Note on the Type

The text of this book was set in Sabon, a typeface designed by Jan Tschichold (1902–1974), the well-known German typographer. Designed in 1966 and based on the original designs by Claude Garamond (ca. 1480–1561), Sabon was named for the punch cutter Jacques Sabon, who brought Garamond's matrices to Frankfurt.

Typeset by Scribe, Philadelphia, Pennsylvania

Printed and bound by Berryville Graphics, Berryville, Virginia

Designed by M. Kristen Bearse